Zones of Anxiety

CONTEMPORARY APPROACHES
TO FILM AND TELEVISION SERIES

*A complete listing of the books in this series
can be found online at http://wsupress.wayne.edu*

General Editor

Barry Keith Grant
Brock University

Advisory Editors

Patricia B. Erens
Dominican University

Lucy Fischer
University of Pittsburgh

Peter Lehman
Arizona State University

Caren J. Deming
University of Arizona

Robert J. Burgoyne
Wayne State University

Tom Gunning
University of Chicago

Anna McCarthy
New York University

Peter X. Feng
University of Delaware

MOVEMENT, MUSIDORA,
AND THE
CRIME SERIALS OF LOUIS FEUILLADE

Zones of Anxiety

VICKI CALLAHAN

WAYNE STATE UNIVERSITY PRESS   DETROIT

© 2005 by Wayne State University Press,
Detroit, Michigan 48201. All rights are reserved.
No part of this book may be reproduced without formal permission.

09 08 07 06 05   5 4 3 2 1

Library of Congress Cataloging-in-Publication Data

Callahan, Vicki.
  Zones of anxiety : movement, Musidora, and the crime serials of Louis Feuillade / Vicki Callahan.
   p. cm. — (Contemporary approaches to film and television series)
  Includes bibliographical references.
  ISBN 0-8143-2855-5 (pbk : alk. paper)
  1. Feuillade, Louis, 1873–1925—Criticism and interpretation. I. Title. II. Series.

PN1998.3.F48C35 2005
843'.912—dc22   2004013600

∞The paper used in this publication meets the minimum requirements of the American National Standard for Information Sciences—Permanence of Paper for Printed Library Materials, ANSI Z39.48-1984.

For the beloved Finnegan

Contents

Acknowledgments ix

Introduction: Writing a Feminist Poetic History through the Cinema of Uncertainty 1

1. Louis Feuillade and the Cinema of Uncertainty: Scenes of Dislocation in Early Cinema/History 13

2. The *Fantômas* Series: Cinematic Vision and the Test of "Immediate Certainty" 45

3. "Qui? Quoi? Quand? Où?": Interrogating Woman in *Les vampires* and *Judex* 73

4. Stigma and Stigmata: The Cries and Cure of the Fantastic Narrative 117

Afterword: The Cinematic Legacy of Feuillade and Musidora and a Different Way of Knowing 145

Notes 153
Works Cited 171
Index 181

Acknowledgments

An evening's screening of Louis Feuillade's *Juve contre Fantômas* set in motion a rather remarkable sequence of events for me. The viewing produced an essay for a course on French cinema, and in turn an enthusiastic suggestion from the professor, Judith Mayne, that I pursue Feuillade's films as a dissertation topic. Due to this generous advice, the path to Feuillade and Musidora was opened to me, a path that brought me in contact with a series of wonderful scholars and archivists and even led to a number of long-lasting friendships.

The early stages of this project benefited enormously from members of my UCLA dissertation committee, Steve Mamber, Lucia Re, and Peter Wollen, and the suggestions of Noël Burch, Dudley Andrew, and Richard Abel. Richard Abel has been a particularly strong influence on this book in terms both of his own exemplary scholarship and his ongoing and generous commentary from the very beginning drafts of the research until now.

I am especially grateful to the Department of Film, Television, and Digital Media at UCLA for the Charles Boyer Research Fellowship and a travel grant, which provided essential support for extended research work. In the final stages, this research was supported in part by funds provided by the University of Wisconsin–Milwaukee. With regard to primary research material, I have benefited from the aid of numerous people. Kelley Conway deserves special thanks for introducing me to the French archives and for constantly helping with various archival "mysteries," or rather, procedures. Sylvia Walker supplied wonderful oversight to my translations in the project's early stages (with later aid on this task from both Kelley Conway and James Williams).

Tami Williams, Bernard Bastide, and Annette Förster provided not only helpful information on my research but also untold hours of wonderful conversations about French early cinema. Emmanuelle Toulet, Marianne Chanel, Jacques Champreux, Laurent Véray, and Tom Gunning have been extremely helpful in the Feuillade–Musidora quest. I would also like to express my deepest gratitude to the following individuals and institutions: Sarah Choyeau, Corinne Faugeron, and the Musée Gaumont; the Bibliothèque de l'Arsenal; the Vidéothèque de Paris, the Bibliothèque Nationale; the Bibliothèque du Film; Katherine Oakes and the British Film Institute; Monique Comminges and the Roger-Viollet Agency; Clemence Tallandier and Zeitgeist Films; Margareth Verbakel and Cordon Art B.V.

For screening many of the Feuillade serials and other early films, I would like to thank the following individuals and institutions: the Archives du Film, Bois d'Arcy (Michelle Aubert, Eric Le Roy, and Daniel Courbet); the Royal Film Archive of Belgium, Brussels (Marianne Thys); the Cinémathèque Française (Claudine Kaufmann); the National Film Archive, London (Bryony Dixon); and the UCLA Film Archive.

In addition, I want to acknowledge the efforts of several individuals, particularly in the latter stages of this project. Jennifer Bean, Sumiko Higashi, Judith Mayne, Kelley Conway, and James Williams all generously agreed to read and offer suggestions to the draft in its final stages. Patrick Gonder, a Ph.D. student at UW–Milwaukee, read and re-read the final drafts far too many times to mention. Skillful and serene copyediting was provided in the latter stages of this project by Kathleen Fields, Alison McKee, and Adela Garcia. I found all this commentary incredibly thoughtful, useful, and supportive, particularly given the diversity of perspectives involved. Also, Jane Hoehner deserves acknowledgement for her steadfast support and unbelievable patience as I worked on this book through a series of different jobs, computer crashes, and even one cross-country move.

Last, I need to give special thanks to three people who have been instrumental, each in different ways, to the completion of this book. Janet Bergstrom has been a wonderful teacher, mentor, and good friend as I worked through this seemingly endless task. She provided a number of key archival contacts that were essential to the completion of this project. James Williams, my former colleague at the University of Kent, has been an ongoing source of intellectual encouragement, scholarly projects, and general good cheer. John Callahan has truly seen this project from beginning to end. Certainly, he has seen and read more about Louis Feuillade and Musidora's films than he ever thought possible. It has been my family in its most extended sense—husband, relatives, friends, and animal companions (especially Finnegan)—that has kept me going throughout it all and for whom I am the most grateful. Given this stellar cast of scholars and friends, any errors or infelicities in the text that remain are, of course, my own.

Portions of chapters 3 and 4 were published as Vicki Callahan, "Zones of Anxiety: Movement, Musidora, and the Crime Serials of Louis Feuillade," in *Velvet Light Trap* 37 (spring 1996): 37–50. Copyright 1996 by the University of Texas Press.

Portions of the introduction and chapter 4 were published as Vicki Callahan, "Screening Musidora: Inscribing Indeterminacy in Film History," in *Camera Obscura* 48 (February 2002): 59–81. Copyright 2002, *Camera Obscura*. All rights reserved. Used by permission of the publisher.

Introduction
Writing a Feminist Poetic History through the Cinema of Uncertainty

> And let us imagine a real liberation of sexuality, that is to say, a transformation of each one's relationship to his or her body (and to the other body), an approximation to the vast, material, organic, sensuous universe that we are. This cannot be accomplished without political transformations that are equally radical. (Imagine!) Then "femininity" and "masculinity" would inscribe differently their effects of difference, their economy, their relationship to expenditure, to lack, to the gift. What today appears to be "feminine" or "masculine" would no longer amount to the same thing. No longer would the common logic of difference be organized with the opposition that remains dominant. Difference would be a bunch of differences.
>
> But we are still floundering—with few exceptions—in Ancient History.
>
> Hélène Cixous, "Sorties: Out and Out: Attacks/Ways Out/Forays"

What would it mean to write a feminist history of the cinema? A number of studies have influenced my thinking on this question since I first began working on the crime serials of Louis Feuillade: for example, Sumiko Higashi's *Cecil B. DeMille and American Culture,* Judith Mayne's *Directed by Dorothy Arzner,* Annette Kuhn's *Family Secrets: Acts of Memory and Imagination,* Lynne Kirby's *Parallel Tracks: The Railroad and Silent Cinema,* and Patricia White's *The unInvited: Classical Hollywood Cinema and Lesbian Representability.*[1] These works all present very different kinds of "history," but each challenges the boundaries of writing film histories, and all elegantly incorporate "textual analysis" with a specific engagement of spectatorship issues (though these are mapped out quite differently by each author).

The question of spectatorship, or rather the possibility of female spectatorship, has been central to feminist engagement with the cinema since Laura Mulvey's classic essay, "Visual Pleasure in Narrative Cinema." Mulvey's essay is primarily a critique of Hollywood film, but it also extends the debate on cinematic apparatus and codes of vision to questions of gender. If Mulvey's analysis of (mainstream) cinema as structurally phallocentric is correct, then why did feminists—and women, more generally—go to the cinema? Because experimental and non-narrative films could not guarantee an enlightened approach to the representation of women either, the question of an alternative film form became only one part of many feminists' critiques. "Visual Pleasure in Narrative Cinema" launched a torrent of responses; most endeavored to come to terms with women's place (or seeming theoretical absence) in front of the cinema screen.

In many ways, the methodological turn in film studies to history was an effort to answer the seeming paradox of female spectatorship raised by Mulvey's critique. Surely, women were at the cinema for some reason, perhaps not textually inscribed as willful and autonomous agents, but clearly they were physically and perhaps even subversively present in the audience. Heide Schlüpmann notes that the early years of cinema produced an alternative public space for women that countered traditional gender roles. Potential new identities for women emerged both through the kinds of stories addressed but perhaps most important through the very presence of the female star and the possibilities her performance represented, regardless of the plot's particulars.[2]

Shelley Stamp's examination of silent serials in *Movie Struck Girls: Women and Motion Picture Culture after the Nickelodeon* finds not only high numbers of women in the audience during the early cinema era but also the opportunity for agency for female fans of the cliff-hanger format. Utilizing both extratextual material on movie-star culture and the physical plights of the action-oriented serial queens, Stamp argues that these early films allowed women spectators a variety of highly pleasurable and nontraditional models of femininity.[3] However, as Stamp points out, all is not feminist utopia in these films, for to gain agency the heroine must face countless physical hazards as well as the more nebulous risks presented by "the inevitability of marriage."[4]

Silent cinema has become a central concern of feminist film history, possibly due to the seemingly simultaneous emergence of so many other key issues during this period—the "modern woman," consumerism, the rise of new technologies and the urban space, modernism's visual problematics, and the beginnings of psychoanalysis—that circulate around or intersect with questions of gender. Lauren Rabinovitz argues in *For the Love of Pleasure: Women, Movies, and Culture in Turn-of-the-Century Chicago* that the formal contradictions of early cinema, which framed and indeed regulated female spectators' agency, must be seen in light of these larger cultural upheavals, all of which function as ambivalent and disputed rather than as clearly hegemonic or liberatory practices. For Rabinovitz, early cinema is not a utopia or dystopia for feminists, but rather a contested area.[5]

While recent interrogations of female spectatorship have opened up many possibilities, the turn to history in pursuit of answers to this question presents a mixed blessing for feminist scholars. On one hand, the "archive" provides a real material base from which to begin an investigation. On the other hand, there are problems implicit in what "counts" as the archive, and a document's evidentiary "obviousness" can obscure our very presence in this process, that is, our own investment in the investigation. Moreover, the thrill of discovering various archival texts, of finding the "hidden" history, sometimes blinds us to the other text that sent us on this journey—the film itself. The examples of feminist film history previously noted have been ideal for my process of thinking about the creation of a countermodel in that each writer employs explicit attention to political and aesthetic issues. For me, this linkage of text, cultural analysis, and social change is the essence of feminist film history, no matter what framing device is employed (autobiography, cultural studies, reception studies, psychoanalysis, etc.).

My own intervention in this area of feminist film studies through this book is to try to sketch out a feminist *poetic* history. My hope is that the poetic might also address why women—as well as men—would sit in front of the cinema screen. Here, I am invoking a certain conventional usage of the term *poetic,* that is, a history with an attention to the formal properties of the cinema. I am also using the term in a manner consistent with the feminist theorist Hélène Cixous, whose writings, as will be obvious throughout this book, have been crucial to my thoughts on film history. Cixous has been a writer of some controversy within feminist theory; her work is often labeled as antimaterialist, utopian, and individualistic. In particular, her "division" between the political and the poetic provokes some critics to label her an essentialist.[6] But terms like *political* or *theoretical* are, for Cixous, fixed points of reference for a particular hegemonic discourse. The poetic is radical in that it recognizes or exposes the arbitrary and privileged nature of these fixed points, which masquerade as certainty. This "truth" is limiting; it prevents us from imagining an alternative or an "elsewhere," which if it exists at all must exist out there, outside ourselves, and ultimately outside our ability to change.[7] The poetic is a thing, or rather an event, in movement. Thus, for Cixous, any real change in dominant ideology/structures (and also ourselves) must be preceded by first a shift in point of view and then a thoroughgoing willingness to relinquish any attachment to immutable perspectives.[8]

The poetic constitutes materiality in its process of *transformation*. Perhaps no other term so clearly captures the essence of cinema, its ability to alter the truth from one frame to the next. The unique formal qualities of the cinema—often obscured, but most often highlighted in the silent cinema era—provide us with a model of historical rewriting. I propose a method of cinema history that is based fundamentally on the form of the cinema itself, which in turn opens up the kind of material applicable to our writing of history. Here, the importance of form is not a fixed product of technique; a 360-degree camera movement or a noncontinuity edit is not in itself a radical aesthetic (or nonpatriarchal). Rather, cinema as a process of knowing and, more important, not knowing is based on a thorough uncertainty, which is a function of film's potential unpredictability from frame to frame. It is this cinema of uncertainty as an alternative mode in cinema history that demonstrates the possibility for a poetic method of writing cinema history.[9]

The crime serials of Louis Feuillade, due to their rather unique configurations, are a particularly appropriate group of films for this effort. In this study, I will focus primarily on six serials Feuillade made between 1913 and 1920: *Fantômas* (1913–14), *Les vampires* (1915–16), *Judex* (1917), *La nouvelle mission de Judex* (1918), *Tih Minh* (1919), and *Barrabas* (1920).[10] Serialized films, especially in the crime or detective genres, were an important part of early cinema history. As I argue later when I examine the phenomenon of recursion, the format of the serial, with its repetitive structure, is a crucial factor in the mode of uncertainty. The first two titles, *Fantômas* and *Les vampires*, are technically series films since the link between episodes is tangential. The story line of a series film is not continuous in any meaningful sense, whereas its related format, the serial, often uses a cliff-hanger device to connect episodes and to entice the audience to return for an episode's "resolution."

Both *Fantômas* and *Les vampires* accentuate the mode of uncertainty built into their narrative structures by their exhibition context. Although both were the feature attractions on theater bills that mixed film screenings with live performance in the same evening, the appearance of these two series is best described as erratic. Like the main protagonists of these stories, Fantômas and Irma Vep, the series seem to appear at random intervals, making their *next* appearance a moment of great anticipation and suspense. In the later films *Judex, La nouvelle mission de Judex, Tih Minh,* and *Barrabas,* more appropriately labeled serials, a continuous (albeit excessive and repetitive) story line can be traced, and the episodes are clearly linked sequentially. These films, shown weekly, were accompanied by various forms of print serialization (newspaper and booklets), and unlike *Fantômas* and *Les vampires,* the order in which one watches these episodes matters. However, in all Feuillade's series and serials, the sheer volume of episodes contributes to a sense of chaos—the excess of plot produces disorientation. (*Fantômas* has a mere five episodes, but the rest of this group feature ten to twelve installments per serial.)

As a director, Louis Feuillade has had a rather mixed critical response throughout the years, but the recent miniboom in the literature on his films and various international retrospectives (combined with the DVD and video releases of *Fantômas, Les vampires,* and *Judex*) has raised the question of Feuillade's work yet again for film critics.[11] Most of this critique has been within traditional authorship studies, and while Richard Abel meticulously situates these films in terms of cultural context and issues of representation,[12] Feuillade still awaits a feminist critique. The pathway to my critique travels through an investigation of the star, Musidora—actress, writer, and filmmaker. Musidora is referenced numerous times throughout the Feuillade crime serials despite the fact that the actress is cast in only two of these films. Musidora functions as an ongoing figure of uncertainty, the untamed poetic body.[13]

For many feminists, the poetic body and the mode of "uncertainty" might not seem to be ideal platforms for a model of film history, that is, a work driven largely by archival research, practical realities, and political change. If we think of Trinh T. Minh-Ha's description of the "poetic" we can see how instability might inform and illuminate our understanding of subjectivity and, in turn, situate a spectatorship that begins to acknowledge social and cultural differences.

> In poetical language, there is no "I" that just stands for *my*self. The "I" is there; it has to be there, but it is there as the site where all other "I"s can enter and cut across one another. This is an example of the very strength and vitality of poetical language and of how it can radically

contribute to the questioning of the relationship of subjects to power, language and meaning in theory. Theory as practiced by many is often caught in a "safe place" to theorize about others.[14]

In the poetic we do not have what Susan Bordo has derided in contemporary feminist theory as the "dream of being everywhere,"[15] which obscures difference. Rather, we have what Trinh refers to as an "empty" subject position, one without a "single process of centering."[16] This position liberates us to imagine ourselves in very particular material and temporal positions. While this idea may sound incredibly naive and utopian, surely the cinema allows us to do this on a daily basis. It is this very mobility that makes Musidora such a powerful image, one we both desire and fear. In this sense, the poetic body offers a place to view the historical blind spots of film studies and feminist studies—race, class, and sexuality—and perhaps most important, a place to write new histories.

Writing a poetic history is, for me, consistent with a number of other feminist historical projects. Both the Women Film Pioneers project and the Women Make Cinema book series are efforts to destabilize past narratives in film history and to search out areas typically written out of past accounts of the cinema.[17] Alison McMahan's book on Alice Guy Blaché (part of the Women Make Cinema series) is an explicit rewriting of film history, this time carefully inserting the contributions overlooked or denied the first woman filmmaker.[18] The Women Film Pioneers project, a collective effort of numerous film scholars, extends the discussion of "authorship" and "agency" during the early cinema years even further, asking historians to reconsider what counts as a site of creativity and significance in this era. The project, which has been instrumental in restorations, exhibitions, and research on early cinema, looks at the largely neglected or even unknown work of women who worked as screenwriters, stars, producers, and directors in international film. At stake in these efforts is not only a recovery of lost data, events, films, and artists but also the reinscription of women into the cinema space.

But the search for "agency" in feminist studies is, as noted earlier, a tricky one, and it often presumes that this term designates clearly defined terrain. In part, the rejection of psychoanalysis and its notion of the unconscious produced some understandings of agency, which defines any action as "willful" and "good" if consistent with the feminist (nonpatriarchal) project. The difficulties are in knowing what might in fact be willful (even leaving aside the unconscious, there are certain empirical limits to choice) and, more troubling, what in fact might be good. Both of these terms are historically specific and matters of some dispute. Judith Mayne argues that given that "dominant ideology is neither a person nor a one dimensional set of concepts, it is virtually impossible to say with certainty that a particular effect is complicit or resistant to the force of the institution."[19]

The problem comes from assuming that we can locate who and what is oppressive *and* that we will respond to it as such. Spectatorship models organized solely around socially based and consciously chosen identification, no matter how historically complex, limit the possibilities for the spectator's response due to the models' inherent instrumentality in presuming that we would not act against our own interests. Such models also assume that identity is coherent and discrete, a supposition that speaks to the larger, dubious prospect that dominant (white, middle-class, heterosexual) ideology is a fixed point of reference, or rather the paradigm for all identity (even if via negation). Perhaps more to the point, as Teresa de Lauretis notes in *The Practice of Love: Lesbian Sexuality and Perverse Desire*, so long as the discussion remains at the level of direct identification—of one's particular recognition of a "likeness"—and absent the complexities of female desire, the possibilities for sexuality, especially lesbian desire, will be unexamined if not erased. In this context, the paradigm of heterosexuality as fixed and essential proscribes all other possibilities as aberrant, predevelopmental (the pre-Oedipal mother-daughter relation), or the asexualized terrain of "woman-identification."[20] De Lauretis asks us to rethink not only the category of heterosexuality but also the very way in which that paradigm is put in place, that is, not as a structure, but as an unstable, ongoing process. Rather than a fixed Oedipal model, de Lauretis posits "a relatively open-ended process of sexual structuring, overdetermined by vicissitudes and contingencies in the subject's internal and external worlds."[21]

How can cinematic form draw our attention to this instability, to the ongoing intersection of the "subject's internal and external worlds?" As de Lauretis argues, any feminist critique is faced with the contradiction of being "at the same time inside and outside the ideology of gender, and conscious of being so, conscious of that twofold pull, of the division, that doubled vision."[22] But the poetic or the cinema of uncertainty creates a kind of passage between these worlds, or perhaps more to the point, a gap where we might see the singularity, intersection, and mutability of the structures.

The Feuillade-Musidora "collaborations" are particularly instructive about the location and utility of uncertainty in the cinematic form. Their films both together and apart function as a kind of test for Thierry Kuntzel's remarks about the cinematic machine: "The most astonishing characteristic of this apparatus resides in its movement . . . in projection, everything happens as if it were inscribed and then erased on the screen without stop."[23] Throughout the Feuillade crime serials, the recording function of photography is called into question by a variety of cinematic devices, such as the dissolve, the "shock cut," and recursive narrative and visual patterns. Perhaps most significant, these devices are used in a highly realistic aesthetic so that a disjunctive or dislocating cut that "demonstrates" the impossible across frames—a body flying out the window only to land unharmed on the street—is made doubly unnerving by the seeming facticity of what we are viewing. David Bordwell's careful discussion of Feuillade's mise-en-scène sets out a strong argument for Feuillade's deep space aesthetic as an alternative style to classical *découpage,* but here I would like to extend the possibility of alterity in Feuillade to our very mode of knowledge.[24]

Although apparatus theory is one influence on my readings of Feuillade's crime films, my use of this methodology understands the machinery as having a specific temporality, or rather, having a tie to a particular moment and to the technology of the period in which it was developed. The difference of early cinema was not a transcendent one, but rather a product of its times. Film form cannot be seen in isolation; it must be seen as part of a larger historical text. The very things that undermined vision and knowledge in the nineteenth and early twentieth centuries—a variety of technologies and discourses, including photography and cinema—contributed as well to counterforces that repressed this radical movement. Thus parallel to and intersecting with the cinema of uncertainty is a response to this new way of seeing and thinking about the world, a tension that is there from the beginning of cinema.[25] To put it another way, the cinema provides us with multiple possibilities and histories, which are not simply subversive or oppressive depending on the era.

One of the key elements, though, in denying cinema's disruptive potential does lie with linear, and then in its more structured form, classical narrative. While the "cinema of attractions" theoretically precedes this linear storytelling model and precludes the politics of patriarchal

An illustration of recursion is found in M. C. Escher's *Day and Night*. © 2001 Cordon Art B.V. —Baarn—Holland. All rights reserved.

cinema, as it is driven more by exhibitionism than by voyeurism, "showing" rather than "telling," several feminist scholars have pointed to the role of narrative in controlling woman's agency in cinema from its beginnings.[26] But the key is to examine the diversity and complexity of narrative forms, which existed in early cinema and indeed exist today. Tom Gunning's essay "Non-Continuity, Continuity, Discontinuity in Early Cinema" certainly points us to these narrative possibilities, and my project on Feuillade can be seen as an effort to map one discontinuous narrative form that countered the Griffith-Hollywood classical paradigm of linearity, coherence, and certitude. Alongside its radical vision, the cinema of uncertainty provides a narrative to match, and this narrative form can be found even *after* the classical continuity system was codified, that is, after the "cinema of attractions" is less distinct or "goes underground" into avant-garde cinema or appears as disruptive moments in classical film (around 1908).[27] The films of D. W. Griffith often operated by uniting disparate space-time coordinates in a relentless trajectory aimed at one place and one truth. The narratives found in Feuillade's serials functioned quite differently and induced dislocation and uncertainty through a method based on nonlinearity, randomness, and, perhaps most important, recursion.

My use of the term *recursion* in this context is borrowed from mathematics, although my interest in the concept is not so much one of computation as it is of logic. The term is used to highlight not content but function. Recursion patterns are a form of repetition that enables us to isolate the similar workings of different numbers and formulas without necessarily performing all the calculations (which could be quite burdensome). In essence, the function is repeated, despite seemingly different or unrelated forms. The similarity is in the process, regardless of the content. Consequently, the repetition is paradoxically revealed, as Douglas Hofstadter notes, in increasingly "*simpler versions of itself*"[28] in the most complex circumstances (since we are seeing the distilled or abstracted form). This process of abstraction or simplification leads us to a radical shift in perspective in that complex and dissimilar items are now demonstrated to share similar qualities, or more radically a "non-dualistic or non-differentiated relationship."[29] Hence, we begin to see the significance of seriality in Feuillade noted earlier. A chase sequence or a fall sequence must repeat itself in different forms throughout the crime series: a detective or journalist may chase the criminal; the criminal may chase the representative of law/stability; criminal gangs may chase each other or may shift sides and then even join the law and return to crime again. The key is not the pursuit and solution of a particular crime but the chase *function* (the simpler version of itself).[30]

The procession of recursion drifts from narrative to visual expression (a type of recursive moment in itself). For example, the black bodysuit serves as the marker of criminality in the *Fantômas* series (and in *Les vampires*, with an important difference), but it rarely serves as a reliable marker, for there are ongoing problems of identity at all levels—the criminal, the detective, the ordinary citizen.

The disturbance posed by these recursion patterns and others is such that by the next film series, *Les vampires*, the threat of the shifting, unstable subject must be displaced onto the literal "figure" of the woman—it is now Musidora in the bodysuit. As noted previously, the recursion process is one of simplification. To put it bluntly, the displacement of the disturbance becomes Musidora = uncertainty. This is why Musidora becomes so essential to the history of our understanding of Feuillade's films, to the history of cinema itself, and why everyone remembers her almost exclusively in the bodysuit. Musidora represents an effort to place or to fix this instability, but this instability is at the heart of cinema, at the center or noncenter, as the case may be, of ourselves.

The woman star is a particularly apt place to engage this instability, given the attention to surface and theatricality, as Schlüpmann notes. The star roles extend our understanding of performance to the performative, to the nonessential aspect of any term or category. Jennifer Bean argues that silent-era stars, especially those women featured in death-defying stunts and serialized adventures, are important not so much for their discovery of the "true" modern woman but for their destabilization of the "classical humanist subject regulated by reason and self-will, in favor of a modern subject premised on corporeal spontaneity and flexibility. Early women stars reflect a personhood construed as both non-knowledgeable and unknowable."[31] The action star was a walking epistemological trauma consistent with whole series of alterations regarding human sense and sensation, and their stunts seemed to belie limits of what we thought the body could endure and what we could envision. Jonathan Crary sees the various theories of perception that developed in the nineteenth century as questioning the reliability of vision, and in turn, all established truths: "what was at stake and seemed so threatening was not just a new form of epistemological skepticism about the unreliability of the senses but a positive reorganization of perception and its objects. The issue was not just how does one know what is real, but that new forms of the real were being fabricated and a new truth about the capacities of the human subject was being articulated in these terms."[32] Musidora's star persona resonates with the "unknowable"; her presence in the bodysuit represents a thoroughgoing displacement of certitude—a displacement of an effort at displacement. Through this recursive process, even our time function appears not as linear time but as nested or clustered time, and while we still have a sense of history, our sense of chronology must be reconsidered. Musidora formally represents, then, the time image of cinema. For Deleuze, the time image is a kind of "aberrant movement"[33]—the aberration being affected by the dropping out of linear, continuous time, or to be precise, the elimination of a human-constructed time as particular and arranged units. This is Deleuze's point in saying that time is "shattered from the inside" whereby "perception and actions ceased to be linked together, and spaces are now neither co-coordinated nor filled."[34] This does not mean that actions are disconnected from materiality (note critics' emphasis on the "realism" in Feuillade) as much as they are freed from a singular bound narrative (discrete time or being), and multiple narratives might unfold (duration or becoming). The time image thereby reveals "the dissipation of centers and the false continuity of the images themselves."[35] For Deleuze, "the direct-time image is the phantom which has always haunted the cinema, but it took modern cinema to give a body to this phantom."[36] I argue that the body of the phantom appears or is seen even earlier—in Musidora's bodysuit. The phantom circulates throughout the serials, reappears in Musidora's own films, and is explicitly invoked by later French filmmakers. This book traces the "dissipation of centers" or the "empty" subject of the cinema screen, a process of reversal and abstraction that produces the "phantom," Musidora, and defies all patriarchal logic.

1 | Louis Feuillade and the Cinema of Uncertainty
Scenes of Dislocation in Early Cinema/History

> All ways of differently thinking the history of power, property, masculine domination, the formation of the State, and the ideological equipment have some effect. But the change that is in process concerns more than just the question of "origin." There is phallocentrism. History has never produced or recorded anything else—which does not mean that this form is destinal or natural. Phallocentrism is the enemy. Of everyone. Men's loss in phallocentrism is different from but as serious as women's. And it is time to change. To invent the other history.
>
> Hélène Cixous, "Sorties: Out and Out: Attacks/Ways Out/Forays."

> It is we, with our language, who make the law. Who draw the borders and produce the exclusion. Who grant admittance. Who are the customs officers of communication: we admit or we reject . . . ordinary human beings do not like mystery since you cannot put a bridle on it, and therefore in general they exclude, they repress it, they eliminate it—and it is settled. But if on the contrary one remains open and susceptible to all the phenomena of overflowing, beginning with natural phenomena, one discovers the immense landscape of *trans*, of the passage. Which does not mean that everything will be adrift: our thinking, our choices, etc. But it means that the factor of instability, the factor of uncertainty, or what Derrida calls the undecidable, is indissociable from human life.
>
> Hélène Cixous, *Rootprints*

> The earth seen from the point of view of the moon is revived; it is unknown, to be rediscovered.
>
> Hélène Cixous, *Rootprints*

EARLY CINEMA/FRENCH SILENT CINEMA

This book is an effort to situate the crime serials of Louis Feuillade within early film history from an explicitly feminist perspective. To a certain extent, I will argue that a series of six films made by Feuillade between the years 1913 and 1920 can be read as one text. These films—*Fantômas, Les vampires, Judex, La nouvelle mission de Judex, Tih Minh, Barrabas*—share not only a consistency of narrative structure and visual style but also a progressive revelation of the threat posed by the figure of the criminal in the films. This threat—a "dislocation"[1] of both cinematic and ideological subjectivity—plays out under a variety of guises throughout the serials, with each variation unveiling another layer of social, cultural, and aesthetic disturbance. Part of this work will involve a mapping out of these layers of dislocation, with a second objective of then reading this map through the lens of feminist theory and history—a process that involves another sort of dislocation, this time of the historiographic variety.

Research on early cinema history has undergone tremendous growth and innovation in the last two decades. Of particular interest to this study are the efforts by a number of authors to define early cinema as an autonomous entity in itself, something more than the first flickerings of classical narrative film.[2] The separate works of Noël Burch and Tom Gunning have been especially influential in sketching the parameters of this alternative cinematic form and moving early film history out of excessively teleological or biographical accounts (e.g., the great [male] pioneers of cinema: Edison, Porter, Griffith).[3]

Previous histories of early cinema emphasized an understanding of the era as "primitive" steps leading inevitably *toward* the classical, continuity style that came to define the Hollywood studio system.[4] Although he retains the term primitive, Noël Burch's analysis of early cinema presents a markedly different perspective. To be precise, Burch describes the first part of the silent era as a "primitive mode of representation."[5] His designation serves to demarcate both an ideologically and formally distinct, although not entirely separate, entity from the classical model, which he has labeled the "Institutional Mode of Production."[6]

In fact, Burch's link between the primitive and classical modes makes for some of his most provocative remarks concerning the cinema. The primitive mode's unique characteristics—autarchy, or self-sufficiency of the tableau-style image; horizontal and frontal camera placement; the long take; and a decentered or multicentered placement of figures and action—function to place the film spectator in a position of externality to the image.[7] Moreover, this externality is heightened by the exhibition practices of the era, which placed films at fairgrounds and nickelodeons—crowded and disruptive environments.[8] One product of these formal qualities and contextual settings was that early cinema developed as an art form that was essentially more presentational than representational, one that was "closer to the plebian circus and the aristocratic ballet than to the theatre of the middle classes."[9] All these factors contributed to the construction of a viewer who had a strong sense of separation, a distance from the image, or as Burch puts it, "an awareness that one was sitting in a theatre watching pictures unfold on a screen in front of one."[10]

Alongside this externality, functioning as a type of contrapuntal force, early cinema had another project, which consisted of centering the spectator/subject within a particular type of vision.[11] Burch's point is that the roots of classical cinema can be found during the primitive era. However, the essential "difference" of early cinema is its ability, through these distancing formal devices (frontality, nonlinearity, etc.), to foreground what the classical cinema will later disguise: the spectator's linkage to a ubiquitous camera's vision, a vision that is typically voyeuristic and male.[12]

While Tom Gunning's work builds on several aspects of Burch's description of early cinema—similar formal properties, a fundamentally presentational mode, and the spectator's "externality" to the image—Gunning deviates from Burch on several key points. For Gunning, early cinema presents a much more discrete and autonomous entity than Burch's "primitive mode." Unlike classical film, the pre-1906 era of filmmaking, which Gunning has labeled the "cinema of attractions," is best characterized by the attention to spectacle rather than narrative.[13] Although not completely devoid of the narrative patterns found in classical cinema, early cinema (pre-1906) is driven more by the desire to *show* rather than to *tell* something.[14] With its emphasis on the ability of the cinematic image to render events visible,[15] the "novelty" of the new art form "lay in the lifelike illusion of motion the apparatus produced; storytelling was secondary."[16] Moreover, the cinema of attractions offers a different spectator position than later, narrative dominated filmmaking, with its emphasis on direct address, shock, and surprise.[17]

Although several narrative forms exist in early cinema, the lack of narrative dominance and especially the lack of narrative absorption for the spectator produce a style of cinema closer to later avant-garde filmmaking practices,[18] and perhaps more significant, construct a spectator position quite different from the one outlined by Burch. Since the paradigm at work in "attractions" is centered more on display than on the construction of a diegetically enclosed universe of the later classical model, the pleasure for the early cinema spectator is less one of voyeurism than exhibitionism.[19] In this crucial turn, Gunning maps out for us an alternative path that cinema could have taken, a particularly important option especially if one sees voyeurism as the origins of women's objectification in the cinema. The degree of alterity, and indeed, the spectatorial position interpellated (masculine or feminine, controlling or liberatory), is a matter of some debate among feminists, but clearly the codes of early cinema put questions of spectatorship in the foreground.[20]

Both the "primitive mode" and the "cinema of attractions" function as a type of counterhistory of early film, a history that occasionally veers, despite Burch's and Gunning's separate disclaimers,[21] toward utopian and dualistic paradigms. The populism characteristic of the primitive mode in Burch's analysis (for it is the emergence of bourgeois narratives that end the primitive era) and the capacity of the "cinema of attractions" to distance the spectator, or to defamiliarize everyday objects in Gunning's account, serve to divide cinema history into two parts (an early and a classical era) and, then, to valorize the first part of that history.

To be sure, Gunning's and Burch's projects were essential to moving early film beyond historical interpretations that portrayed the era as an incompletely formed version of classical film. However, Burch's impetus toward a materialist reading of early cinema as a "working class" or "popular" cinema at times counters other work on exhibition and reception contexts in France during this era. French cinema, from the early traveling street fairs (*fêtes foraines*) to the grand movie palaces (Gaumont Palace opened in 1911), was marked by a mixed clientele with respect to class, sex, and even age (children were important to audience demographics as well).[22] The mass-based art form was forced to address competing interests and expectations, often within the same film.

Gunning's work underscores the variety of narratives available and the complex process of negotiation between the "attractions" and "classical" eras with considerable detail and nuance, and there is certainly nothing inevitable about the trajectory of the cinema's development, in contrast to Burch's account, where the institutional mode lurks at the fringes of the primitive. Gunning's writings complicate the division between these two periods by analyzing the appearance of spectacle *and* narrative elements in both eras. Gunning also outlines a "transition" period from 1908 to 1913, which further removes his analysis from any simple binary model.[23]

Nonetheless, the problems in the early-classical division become apparent with filmmakers like Feuillade and with those films that do not fit neatly into either category or may be included in the "transitional" terrain. Perhaps as Gunning pointed toward the "cinema of attractions" as a unique group of films "possessing a style and logic of their own,"[24] we now need to consider an alternative category for yet another "style" and "logic" in cinema history.

Feuillade

Feuillade's crime serials, with a rather mixed set of characteristics, seem to defy any clear placement of the filmmaker within the previous models of early film. Burch, for example, places Feuillade's films (at least the early serials) in the primitive mode of representation due to their tableau framing and editing style, frontal camera, and multiple and noncentered placement of action in the frame.[25] A close examination of the Feuillade serials' narrative structure would seem to put these films within the framework of the "cinema of attractions" and "primitive mode." Both Burch and Gunning outline a discontinuous, nonlinear style of filmmaking for the primitive era (which ends, like the cinema of attractions, around 1906–8) that Feuillade's serials, despite their later turn to melodrama, seem to retain.[26]

Conversely, the basic chase structure and melodramatic story lines (the fallen woman, the woman in peril, the family crisis) of the serial format suggest the beginnings of classical, linear filmmaking. As Richard Abel points out, Feuillade's films represented mainstream French narrative filmmaking during the 1910s and early 1920s.[27] Indeed, these films were attached to story lines and characters that were renowned and in massive distribution (through a variety of popular press formats). However, Feuillade's working methods on the set belied the notion at times of proximity between the films and literary tie-ins. According to Francis Lacassin, the performers arrived for the week's work with only minimal instructions, which allowed for an ongoing modification of scenarios and improvisation.[28] This does not mean that the printed and visual matter were dissimilar as much as that the cinema version could be seen as a kind of distillation, or again, abstraction, of elements.

Stylistically, while there are numerous examples of tableau framing and the use of deep space in Feuillade's crime films, Abel points out that even in the first films of the *Fantômas* series (1913) there is nonetheless careful use of a continuity editing style[29]—one of the defining features of classical, narrative film. But, while Abel appears to agree with the general framework and periodization of the "cinema of attractions," he also focuses an important part of his history of French film on its distinct features during its transition to narrative cinema.[30] In *The Ciné Goes to Town,* Abel states that "the historical specificity of early French cinema created a partially overlapping, yet distinctly alternative model of film representation and narration to that which ultimately would become dominant in the American cinema."[31]

Feuillade's crime serials present one example of this alternative model in cinema history. These films suggest that Feuillade should be seen as more than a "transitional" figure in French film in that they (at least within the six serials that will be examined here) represent not simply an amalgam but rather a consistent and distinct visual and narrative style. Both Ben Brewster and David Bordwell see Feuillade's work as part of a specific tradition in cinema history, mainly European based, built on "staging in depth."[32] Here the action is organized not across edits but within the space of the frame.[33] In Feuillade's films, our attention is often guided, Bordwell notes, by character movement and skillful staging that works to conceal and reveal information during the course of a shot—a particularly appropriate strategy for films concerned with conveying mystery and intrigue.[34] For Bordwell, Feuillade represents, along with several other filmmakers, another way to tell complex stories clearly.[35]

While I agree that the "staging in depth" model accurately describes Feuillade's visual style and outlines a distinct path beyond the usual "attractions" and "classical" paradigms in film history, there is still more to be said about what is at stake in these films. If we think about all the models set forth so far, whether primitive, attractions, classical, institutional, or the staging in depth variants (i.e., whether showing or telling), all presume we are working with *declarative* utterances. I contend, however, that in the work of Feuillade, and perhaps other filmmakers, another type of statement is made, one that is more *subjunctive,* or rather is motivated by an exploration of the *possible* rather than what *is.*[36]

Possibility is then best approached by the poetic, by a movement that reveals becoming rather than being. And here is where uncertainty resides, in this refusal to be one fixed entity (no matter how many we might invoke). This kind of movement toward uncertainty is embedded in the cinema and is indicative of a mode that always circulates but is rarely in the foreground of film history (either aesthetically or critically). The mode is unusual when we think of its heritage, since it seems to borrow from many different literary, theatrical, and popular culture forms. In terms of literary models, the cinema of uncertainty is closest to the mode of the fantastic as outlined by the critics Irène Bessière and Rosemary Jackson.[37]

It should be emphasized here that the fantastic as utilized by Feuillade is simply one aspect of the alterity pointed out in Richard Abel's work. I am not claiming that the mode of the fantastic can explain the difference of early French cinema (or French cinema in total), for clearly this history contains far too many heterogeneous elements to generalize. Nor do I believe the fantastic is sufficient in itself to explain the strange workings of Feuillade's serials of uncertainty. For that we will need to look at a range of influences, especially the role of melodrama. All the same, the fantastic does serve as the center of energy behind this mode, especially due to the form's special relationship to knowledge. Furthermore, an examination of the fantastic can open up a discussion of a key literary tradition little examined with respect to cinema history—the influence of the short story, the serialized novel, and the popular press on cinematic style.

FANTASTIC

The fantastic is quite often discussed as a genre, but the "genre" of the fantastic by itself is inadequate to describe the Feuillade serials. These films represent—as do other French films of the era—a mélange of several genres: the detective story, the horror tale, the melodrama, the Grand Guignol, and even a subgenre of the news item or documentary, the *faits divers*. I am using the term *mode* to discuss a variety of issues—formal, historical, cultural, epistemological—that extend beyond the limits of most genre studies.

The fantastic is defined by its lack of rigid location or placement; it is, in fact, a mode characterized by *movement* and *dislocation*. As Rosemary Jackson notes in *Fantasy: The Literature of Subversion*, the salient quality of the fantastic is its alterity, that is to say, its relationship of inversion to realist texts.

> The fantastic is predicated on the category of the "real," and it introduces areas which can be conceptualized only by negative terms according to the categories of nineteenth century realism: thus, the impossible, the un-real, the nameless, formless, shapeless, un-known, in-visible.

What can be termed a "bourgeois" category of the real is under attack. It is this *negative relationality* which constitutes the meaning of the modern fantastic.[38]

This "negative relationality" and what Jackson has labeled its attendant "flux and instability"[39] may help to explain the efforts to classify Feuillade's work as "transitional." It may also account for critical commentaries on Feuillade that designate his work as exemplary of "fantastic realism" or that note the peculiar mixture of the real, ordinary, and everyday alongside the fantastic in his films.[40] The filmmaker Georges Franju expresses his sense of the mode with particular reference to the silent-era director: "The fantastic in Feuillade possesses an obvious relationship with my own conception [of the fantastic], since my idea is resolutely realist and tends to show—through and even beyond the fantastic, what is a means, a tool, and not a goal—what there is of poetry, tenderness, violence, and drama in the most intimate and familiar reality."[41]

The description of Feuillade's work by the use of contradictory, ambivalent, or dualistic language (the real/fantastic, everyday/marvelous, tender/violent) speaks to the difficulty in locating his films within a particular genre, style, ideological, or, indeed, metaphysical frame of reference.

Many discussions of the fantastic begin with Tzvetan Todorov's analysis of the genre.[42] For Todorov, the fantastic is situated in a space between the real and the illusory or imaginary, or as he describes the particular literary categories in question, the fantastic is that period of "hesitation" between the genres of the "marvelous" and the "uncanny."[43] Todorov's account is particularly useful in examining Feuillade and the cinema's use of the fantastic due to his focus on uncertainty in the genre's definition and its central characteristics of relationality and movement. All the same, Todorov's work, while important to outlining the narrative structure and thematic consistencies of the genre, does not address the relationship of the fantastic to historical and cultural institutions.[44]

Moreover, Todorov's concentration solely on the formal properties of the fantastic sets aside not only the politics of dislocation at the social or cultural level but also does not engage with such politics with regard to issues of the self.[45] This is particularly unusual given that two chapters of Todorov's study (chapters 7 and 8) look specifically at "themes" of "the self" and "the other." Todorov's account is again strictly formal, and no effort is made to draw out the implications of these chapters into a larger political and, especially, gendered context.[46] The absence of gender is especially notable given that Todorov defines *l'étrange* (translated by Richard Howard in an English edition as "the uncanny") as bounded both by rationality/reality and by *das Unheimliche*, which as we will see is a definition of uncertainty by Freud based on gendered subjectivity (both Freud's and his patients). Todorov creates some ambiguity or confusion of the term *l'étrange* by not developing the relationship between what he describes as a primal fear and the limits of reason. Todorov gestures toward a link between subject constitution and knowledge processes, but he does not explore the implications the connection raises.[47]

As Rosemary Jackson argues, the politics of the subject—and its cultural construction—could be abstracted from Todorov's discussion of the genre, but only through the addition of a psychoanalytic frame of reference.[48] In order to facilitate this political reading, or perhaps to reincorporate repressed elements within Todorov's text, Jackson makes two moves. First, she renames Todorov's categories—the fantastic is no longer that moment of hesitation between the "marvelous" and the "uncanny" but between the "marvelous" and the "mimetic." Although her argument is that these labels situate the fantastic within two recognized modes in literature (the "uncanny" not being a literary mode),[49] the corollary is the centrality of the "real" (and its status) to the discussion.

The movement of the uncanny out of the terms of opposition enables Jackson to make her second move: to foreground the importance of the uncanny (and essays on the uncanny by Freud and Hélène Cixous)[50] to the basic structure of the fantastic—in effect, making the fantastic and the uncanny equivalents. If that is the case, the uncanny is then situated at the point of hesitation, at the focal point of uncertainty. But the epistemological status of the uncanny is a disputed terrain within psychoanalytic readings, as we will see shortly.

The politicization of the fantastic also returns us to certain historiographic issues surrounding film studies and Feuillade's work. Although I will make the claim for alterity in the crime serials of Feuillade, I will also argue, following Irène Bessière's argument on fantastic narratives, that these films illuminate both "primitive" and "classical" texts. For Bessière, the fantastic narrative is not a moment of hesitation between the marvelous and the uncanny (as in Todorov) but a place of convergence, a site of "contamination" between the realist novel and the fairy tale[51] (a reconfiguration of the oppositional categories similar to Jackson's). Cinema finds a similar site of contamination somewhere between realism and melodrama.

For Bessière, the alternative order the fantastic introduces does not present a utopian world or a subversive moment but rather functions in support of dominant institutions. As she notes, the fantastic does not "describe the illegal to challenge the norm, but to confirm it. . . . Narration always double, the fantastic installs the strange in order to better establish censorship."[52]

Looking at the short story roots of the fantastic, the double movement of subversion and censorship twists around the question of gender. In one of the earliest noted examples of the genre, Jacques Cazotte's *Le diable amoureux* (1772),[53] Alvare, a Spanish cavalier, enters a magic circle and invokes Beelzebub. Then there appears a dog, which is quickly transformed into a young page boy (named Biondetta) and once again transformed into a woman (Fiorentina)—or has "she" simply been misidentified?[54] He begins an affair with the woman, but the gender "confusion" is sustained as he continues to call Fiorentina *Biondetta*. Alvare breaks from this relationship by deciding "to open my heart to my mother and again put myself under her protection."[55] However, his conduct with Biondetta causes his mother's death, but he quickly realizes *this was only a dream*. At last, he is safe with his mother from these dreams and desires, but most significant, he realizes from his mother's wisdom that the whole affair is but a "derangement of my intellects."[56] His words thus link the male universe, rationality, and male heterosexuality—and the mother's central role in establishing these arenas. The story concludes with the mother underlining the "lesson" of Alvare's gender-bending dream: he must resolve to fight off temptation.[57] But what is this temptation? His lover is labeled as a woman, but it is not clear if this is but a displacement of his anxiety surrounding his "derangement."

Displacement or not, the representation of woman as an unknowable and shifting identity, in perpetual metamorphosis, is repeated in numerous fantastic tales. *La morte amoureuse* (The Beautiful Vampire), by Théophile Gautier, describes the beautiful courtesan Clarimonde as an angel, demon, or both.[58] When the priest Romuald is called to her deathbed (it is perhaps a dream) he allows her to drink the blood from a cut finger. She "recovers" only to alternate with her corpselike state. The priest, in turn, falls under Clarimonde's spell; he notes her "chameleon"-like quality: to possess her was to possess twenty women.[59] Romuald concludes ironically (and ambivalently, for we do not know if it was merely a dream or a recollection) that the vampire made him happy, but he warns that to look on a woman for "one minute may make you lose eternity."[60] Here, eternity is not so much infinity (or infinite possibility) as much as eternal grace—*a fixed state of being forever*. This state can be destabilized or threatened with only "one minute," which given the rhetorical opposition in place (one minute versus eternity) seems like a temporal flash and underlines the randomness and chaos that we are faced with in our lives (and in our identities).

The female vampire figure, both literally and figuratively, has played an important role in cinema. In the silent era especially, there is "the vampire" as sexual predator in *A Fool There Was* (Frank Powell, 1915). Here the woman, the home-breaker or "vampire," destroys a successful businessman. His destitution is chronicled not only by his family's shattered lives but also by his *physical* deterioration (graying hair, weakness, slowness). His very life is being "drained" from him by "the vamp." The actress, Theda Bara, who played the vamp, states in an interview that the term *vampire* often stands in for "*feministe*."[61] As Sumiko Higashi notes, the liberated woman of the era was also linked to consumerist excess.[62] Thus in *A Fool There Was*, "the vampire" drained the man not only physically but financially. This is a theme we will see again in *The Cheat* (Cecil B. DeMille, 1915), when a wife's (Fanny Ward) excessive spending habits force her to borrow money from Tori (Sessue Hayakawa), a Japanese businessman, which leads to a sequence of tragic events. Here, the wife's (and modern woman's) excess is displaced onto the Asian merchant, a move consistent with the orientalist discourse of the period whereby the "East" represented exoticism, leisure, and consumption.[63]

But there is another variant of the vampire tale also worth noting. To return to the short story format, J. C. Le Fanu's "Carmilla" is yet another account of the female vampire. However, Carmilla's victims are young women. That Carmilla's attacks are, like all good vampire assaults, highly eroticized now reframes the anxiety to one concerning lesbian desire. The female narrator notes that:

> My strange and beautiful companion would take my hand and hold it with a fond passion, renewed again and again; blushing softly, gazing in my face with languid and burning eyes, and breathing so fast that her dress rose and fell with the tumultuous respiration. It was like the ardour

of a lover; it embarrassed me; it was hateful and yet overpowering; and with gloating eyes she drew me to her, and her hot lips traveled along my cheek in kisses; and she would whisper, almost in sobs, "You are mine, you *shall* be mine, and you and I are one for ever." Then she has thrown herself back in her chair, with her small hands over her eyes, leaving me trembling.[64]

But lest one worry that the narrator's "trembling" was of "suspect" status—that is to say, a reciprocal passion—any fear of homosexuality is displaced onto other possibilities for Carmilla's "aberrant" behavior:

Was she, notwithstanding her mother's volunteered denial, subject to brief visitations of insanity; or was there here a disguise and a romance? I had read in old story books of such things. What if a boyish lover had found his way into the house, and sought to prosecute his suit in masquerade, with the assistance of a clever old adventuress?[65]

However, none of these "reassuring" alternatives ring true, and Carmilla will have to be destroyed. Once again, the monster confuses the gender paradigms, a characteristic of the "unnatural" and inexplicable criminality, which we will also find in the crime series of Feuillade.

Melodrama

As we saw in the case of *A Fool There Was* and *The Cheat*, the image of horror (as seen in "the vamp," destitution, and dissipation) overlaps with issues surrounding the well-being of the family—the terrain of melodrama. As Peter Brooks points out, melodrama as a form emerged as a product of post-revolutionary France. Here the past markers of knowledge had been overthrown (e.g., the Catholic Church and the monarchy), and melodrama stepped into this epistemological void to bring clarity out of chaos.[66] As a consequence, melodrama drives toward what Brooks calls the "moral occult," or rather, the location of higher "spiritual" truths in a "post-sacred" universe.[67]

With melodrama, we would seem to be far from the cinema of uncertainty and the fantastic, but, in fact, the proximity between the fantastic and melodrama is quite close, or more accurately, the two modes intersect. Both the fantastic and melodrama concern an epistemological crisis, with the fantastic lingering within the moment of doubt, and melodrama tirelessly assuring us that truth is "out there" somewhere. In some sense, one could argue the two modes or genres are reverse images of each other, and we will see some instances of this as we work through the Feuillade serials. In any event, the problem in both cases centers on *legibility*, on the reliability of all signs (visual and linguistic).[68] The territory of legibility, and particularly what Martin Jay has called "Cartesian perspectivalism" or a faith in the truthfulness of human vision, was severely in crisis by the nineteenth century.[69] Photography and other optical devices did little to affirm or deny vision's trustworthiness since these technologies were often used to relay the infidelity and illusory nature of the image and in turn destabilized our privileged sense of sight.[70] Donald Lowe argues that by the early twentieth century, a shift in the very sense of perception, from singular and objective to multiperspectival, took place.[71]

Perhaps most interesting, the "voice" of truth in melodrama is the individual, and although characters may have little depth, the pronouncements emanating from the "I" are frequent and crucial; as Brooks notes, "the statement 'I am the man . . .' returns again and again. Both heroines and villains announce their moral identity."[72] The reassertion of the "I" can be seen as indicative of the threat noted above to "Cartesian perspectivalism" since the objective world that one can know through sight is not unrelated to the integrity of the self. Thus a crisis in either field, vision or subjectivity, implies a crisis in the other. Let us remember also that the notion of identity is precisely the area under question in the fantastic. But while melodrama presents one "logical" option to the fantastic's crisis of knowledge, even within melodrama categories are not fixed. As Daniel Gerould points out:

> Contingency rules; things can and will be otherwise. The individual can make of himself what he will. Naively optimistic, unscarred by any tragic awareness of man's limitations, the melodramatist nurtures a faith in human equality, the power of innocence, the triumph of justice (often outside social institutions and their imperfect structures).
>
> Heroes and heroines of melodrama make their own destiny and forge their own morality. Good and evil are diametrically opposed in melodrama, but far from immutable; the absolutes are only provisional.[73]

A perfect format for a culture in upheaval or transition, melodrama provides clarity, but perhaps one of only a fleeting or illusory nature. Thus melodrama and the fantastic share a number of affinities, and the oscillation between the two is expected. Such alternation is typical of the Feuillade serials, as they shift back and forth between these generic or rather modal alternatives.

Feuillade serials belong, as do many cinematic melodramas, within a particular turn-of-the-century theatrical tradition, which featured not only these moral debates but action, spectacle, and adventure. Ben Singer's excellent study of melodrama in early cinema cites the crucial role of sensationalism in the genre, with this quality being indicative of a cultural obsession with the "shocking" and the "grotesque" associated with the urban space.[74] The catastrophic event, carefully detailed in the popular press and later integrated into melodramatic formats, highlighted the perceived violence, randomness, and irrationality of modernity. As Singer notes, the city dweller, while perhaps perversely riveted by these brutal tales, was also nostalgic, no doubt, for a life before such daily and seemingly ubiquitous traumas.[75]

Sensational violence mixed with heavy doses of sentimentality and nostalgia are key components of Feuillade's serials. Maureen Turim situates Feuillade's crime serials in line with the French stage tradition of melodrama, which featured a variety of subgenres in the crime, bandit, suspense, or mystery formats. Like their French stage precursors, Feuillade's serials seemed to defy their middle-class settings with a disturbing undertone of antibourgeois sentiment.[76]

Early crime films, like Feuillade's, are also consistent with another popular stage tradition in France, the Grand Guignol, a rogue variant on the melodramatic form highly influenced by the *faits divers*, or tabloid crime stories of the era.[77] As purveyor of cruel and shocking stories determined to offend all those of good taste through a brutal invocation of violence, the Grand Guignol was an enormous success, especially with society women, according to Mel Gordon.[78] As Tom Gunning notes, the Grand Guignol refined melodrama's interest in sensation to its most material and physical form, so that visceral rather than visual knowledge is key.[79] Such materiality left little room for the higher truths found in melodrama, and while we still recognize good and evil in these plays, an explicit reversal of their fortunes took place such that typically "vice is rewarded and virtue suffers horribly."[80] With the inversion of melodrama's moral structures by the Grand Guignol, we are left with an unstable and senseless universe.[81] These recursive twists through truth and uncertainty, stasis and shock, domesticity and violence are typical of the Feuillade serials and demonstrate how much both these forms the fantastic and melodrama speak to each other as

Louis Feuillade, photo courtesy of the Musée Gaumont.

genres. As we will see, shock for Feuillade is a particularly important formal strategy, incorporated in narrative and visual style but always leading us back to the universe of the uncertain.

FEUILLADE AND THE CRITICS

The uncertainty found at the level of form is, in turn, replicated in the critical language surrounding Feuillade. Francis Lacassin, an important and prolific historian and critic of Feuillade,[82] points to an ongoing contradiction within the filmmaker's own life and work. While Feuillade's films were praised by the surrealists and often labeled subversive or disruptive by the Paris police (he had numerous battles with the censors over the *Fantômas* and *Les vampires* series), Feuillade was himself the product of a conservative upbringing (including both seminary and military training).[83] Such political contradictions appear also in the critical and popular discourse surrounding Feuillade. There is a highly repetitive and sometimes vehement debate on the aesthetic merits of Feuillade's films, which begins almost at the start of his career and continues until the mid to late 1960s.[84] Typically, the attacks (and praise) were directed toward questions of film genre and narrative, with some French film critics considering Feuillade an *archaic* filmmaker, one whose films—particularly the serials—were detrimental to the development of French cinema. *Hebdo-Film* noted as early as *1916* that "the obsession with the crime film has been fatal to M. Feuillade. He has sacrificed everything to Fantômas, Skeletons, Ghosts, Vampires who bore us today. He tries desperately to exploit an exhausted mine, the products of which could not be sold anymore."[85]

The serial form was frequently under attack, but it was the melodramatic aspects within Feuillade's work that were particularly singled out—from critics as diverse as Louis Delluc to even Lacassin.[86] Lacassin notes with respect to the *Judex* sequel:

> Wisdom had ordered, however, not to venture beyond the first triumph which had exhausted the subject and the emotional capacity of the crowd. The vision of *La Nouvelle Mission de Judex* is rendered tiresome due to the absence of subject and the emptiness of action that a formidable length aggravates. This second serial carries to their height the moral preoccupations that were already weighing down the plot of the first film.[87]

Delluc was less kind; he labels *La nouvelle mission de Judex* an example of the *"abominations feuilletonnesques"* and adds, with some exasperation and exaggeration, "The second *Judex* is inferior to all the French productions of the period."[88]

For the critic Ado Kyrou, it is precisely the questions of genre and "aesthetic" values that point to the true issues at stake in Feuillade (and French cinema):

> After the war of 1914–1918, two very distinctly defined tendencies enjoyed the favors of the public and the critics. On the one hand, the *ciné-romans,* melodramas, burlesques, the films directly derived from Méliès, and on the other hand, the intellectual, literary films, the "scientific films." The majority of the public followed the first, the majority

of the critics the second. This proves best the superiority of the public over the critics.[89]

This distinction, which for Kyrou can be traced throughout French cinema, is thus between a reactionary art form for bourgeois intellectuals ("art cinema") and a subversive cinema that engenders a more populist following.[90]

In contrast to Kyrou, André Thirifays argues that while Feuillade's serials, and their literary ancestors, the *feuilleton*, might be charming in their simplicity, they are nevertheless neither "fantastic" nor "poetic," merely "dull, foolish, and cynical" (*"plates, sottes, et cyniques"*).[91] Although Thirifays's critique attributes both the attraction and the banality of Feuillade's serials to early cinema's naïveté (he is writing in the 1960s), it is important to reiterate here that the same commentaries were directed toward his films while they were still in production. Nonetheless, the issue of class circulates throughout these critiques, as seen in this article from 1916 attacking Feuillade's continued interest in the subgenre of crime film called the *policier apache*: "But that a man of talent, an artist, as the director of most of the great films which have been the success and glory of Gaumont, starts again to deal with this unhealthy genre, obsolete and condemned by all people of taste, this remains for me a real problem."[92]

The politics of Feuillade's films, which make them such a site of debate within French cinema history (demonstrated in the language of subversive/conservative cinema and populist audiences/"all people of taste"), are often disguised by formal discussions of aesthetics, genre, narrative repetition, and melodramatic excess. But these formal elements are key to the fantastic and invariably extend the question of politics beyond narrowly framed class issues to a politics of the subject and the conditions of its construction. The movement between realism and melodrama, the fairy tale and the *faits divers*, and even the "primitive" and the "classical" produces an ideological and cinematic mode of dislocation. Each serial produces its own variant of a disturbance—from the social to the psychic—but one with quite consistent features.

Feuillade, Gender, and Anxiety

A crucial part of reading the threads of consistency can be tied to questions of sexual difference. Feminist film studies spent the last few years in a fervent debate over the utility, or lack thereof, of psychoanalysis to questions of gender and sexuality. This troubled history produced a concerted effort among many feminists (especially younger scholars) to distance themselves from psychoanalysis. In part, this act of separation can be traced to real issues regarding the accessibility of academic language, especially within feminist film theory. Moreover, as noted in the introduction to this book, the possibility of female spectatorship seemed to be excluded by feminist theories utilizing psychoanalysis, and as a consequence, a rather wholesale rejection and erasure of Mulvey, and indeed, film theory itself, appeared underway in the name of female agency and visibility. A certain "amnesia" with regard to the insights of prior feminist work did have a few countervailing forces, but the question of psychoanalysis for feminist film studies, and especially for feminist film history, has been, unfortunately, largely ignored.[93]

Psychoanalysis, however, is crucial to this history of Feuillade and Musidora. First, psychoanalysis provides, as we know, a superb description of the norm of heterosexuality, which serves as the foundation of patriarchal culture. Moreover, it documents the "failures" of this norm, and the "failure rate"—especially as Freud himself notes with regard to female sexuality—is so high that one must be suspicious of the "norm" itself.[94]

Second, the very method Freud utilizes of "reading" and "reorganizing" a patient's narratives, ironically, undermines the more "scientific" or "objective" purposes the analysis might hope to achieve. Perhaps more troubling from the perspective of the analyst, the "detached observer" is also called into question so that the reading provided by the "expert" may in fact be read and reorganized as well. This particular strategy has been especially central to French feminists, including Hélène Cixous, Sarah Kofman, and Luce Irigaray.[95] Both this description of the "norm" (and its "failures") and the strategy of reading "against the grain" are essential to writing this poetic history.

The dilemma for feminists is that the description of the psychoanalytic discourse, which must include the institution's own participation in dominant ideology, always risks a recitation that *legitimates* and closes off further analysis. Since our expression of the patriarchal norm is invariably bound by patriarchal language, how does any discussion escape the language, the norm, the "master plot" of our oppression?[96] This master plot of heteronormativity read through the Oedipal, that is, male trajectory of sexual identity is what de Lauretis calls Freud's "passionate fiction."[97] To interrogate Freud's theory as a "passionate fiction" tells us as much about the storyteller, his context, and our own relationship to the narrative of heterosexuality (for example, as mastery, reappropriation, or disdain) as it does about the viability of that narrative. Here the poetic turn is quite useful, for we can explore the categories employed by psychoanalysis, such as "anxiety," while in movement between those "internal and external worlds" de Lauretis points us toward. Our engagement with the uncertain resists any singular perspective as irrevocably true. Any suspension of singularity may place us within the terrain of contradiction, but this may be precisely the area we need to explore. The application of psychoanalysis must be mindful of a tension or oscillation between the map outlined by the analyst and our reading of this map. We also need to think of a reading bound not by subjectivity as much as by "empty" subject perspective; that is, multiple readings are dependent not on multiple persons but rather positions, which any *one* person might achieve.

ZONES OF ANXIETY

A well-known film poster displays an image of a masked but rather elegantly dressed man standing over the rooftops of Paris. This image, an advertisement for Louis Feuillade's serial *Fantômas* (1913–14), has the distinction of being the first film poster censored in Paris. The poster was seen as a direct affront to public order, partly, no doubt, for its attractive and indeed glamorous display of a popular fictional criminal. However, it is important to note the character's specific placement in the city space; he is, in fact, standing in a quite menacing fashion directly over the Palais de Justice.[98]

French popular culture and literary tradition had long maintained a certain fascination and sympathy for the crime figure, but this preoccupation had become intolerable in an era that featured highly publicized accounts of anarchist gangs and urban criminal activity.[99] In some sense, the "popularity" or prominence of the crime figure should also be linked to a general sense of social instability at the turn of the twentieth century.[100] Crime and the disorder it represents thus stand in for a range of cultural, perceptual, and philosophical shifts—particularly around issues of class and gender.[101] In an effort to investigate the heart of this disturbance, the figure of the criminal as presented in six of Feuillade's films (*Fantômas, Les vampires, Judex, La nouvelle mission de Judex, Tih Minh,* and *Barrabas*) will be situated within an analysis of the "uncanny" with particular reference to Freud's article "*Das*

Unheimliche" (The Uncanny) and Hélène Cixous's response, "Fiction and Its Phantoms: A Reading of Freud's *Das Unheimliche*."[102]

For the modern viewer, the crime serials of Louis Feuillade may present a particularly uncanny cinematic experience. My use here of the term *uncanny* is two tiered; at one level I am appropriating Freud's definition of the uncanny as "something familiar and old-established in the mind and which has become alienated from it only through the process of repression."[103] Moreover, Freud states that it is the repetition and recurrence of that which "ought to have remained hidden but has come to light"[104] that makes the "something familiar" now truly "uncanny" and, thus, frightening.[105] But the utility of Freud's definition of the "uncanny" as a device of historical placement for the Feuillade serials is perhaps extended by a second level of understanding of the term: Hélène Cixous's reconfiguration of the uncanny in her examination of Freud's essay. Cixous argues that Freud's exposition of castration anxiety (and its attendant repression) as the analytical terminus of the uncanny is itself a form of repression.

What has been repressed by Freud, according to Cixous, is perhaps the key component of the uncanny—uncertainty.[106] Freud's declaration that it is the fear of castration and not intellectual uncertainty that defined the uncanny—and the very language of his declaration ("this short summary leaves no doubt"; "there is no question therefore"; "the fear of castration itself contains no other significance and no deeper secret than a justifiable dread of this rational kind")[107]—functions to highlight the act of repression *within* Freud's own text. As Cixous notes, "The fear of castration comes to the rescue of the fear of castration."[108] Most important for my reading of Feuillade's serials is Cixous's understanding of the uncanny's instability and uncertainty not only as some particular anxiety beyond castration but as a function of the uncanny's status as a "relational signifier."[109] That is to say, the uncanny is not a thing but a relationship, movement, or passage between the familiar and the unfamiliar.

Samuel Weber's discussion of Freud's essay points toward the larger concern of knowledge and vision since the uncanny ultimately can be seen, in his terms, to "dislocate" the ruling perceptual model of Western thought, and here dislocation leads to an infinite movement:

> For what the child "discovers"—that is interprets—as "castration" is neither nothing nor simply something, at least in the sense in which the child expects and desires it to be: what is 'discovered,' is the absence of

the maternal phallus, a kind of negative perception, whose object or referent—perception—is ultimately nothing but a difference, although no simple one, since it does not refer to anything, least of all to itself, but instead *refers itself indefinitely*.[110]

In this scenario not only is the *status* of evidence upset—verification of castration rests on an absence—but the very *act* of perception must be called into question in that the subject "will never again be able to believe its eyes, since what they have seen is neither simply visible nor wholly invisible."[111] Furthermore, this perceptual crisis has important implications for subjectivity as well, as the construction of identity is founded on the "vision" of difference, on evidence that as Weber notes is "almost nothing, but not quite."[112] Thus, accompanying the crisis of perception is a crisis of subjectivity.[113]

A fundamental disturbance circulates around the figure of woman, but this disruption, if we follow Weber's reading of the uncanny, moves beyond a metaphor for male anxiety and represents a "dislocation" of epistemological and ontological categories. Hence, the necessity in cinema, according to Mary Ann Doane, is to bring the femme fatale, the site of the "epistemological trauma," under control—either through punishment or death.[114]

Given the contradictory forces (of stasis and motion, of the seen and unseen) that serve as the driving mechanisms of the cinema,[115] it might be argued that the woman's body is the ideal stand-in for the cinema as a machine of the uncanny, as the problem located somewhere between the "neither simply visible nor wholly invisible." The effort in film to master the female body (and in turn the cinema) is, in effect, a restaging of the twin crises of vision and subjectivity. For Weber the contradictory double movement of anxiety and its denial seen in the uncanny is relentless:

> But the uncanny is not merely identical with this indecidability: it involves and implies a second moment or movement, namely the defense against the crisis of perception and phenomenality, a defense which is ambivalent and which expresses itself in the compulsive curiosity, the *Wissgier,* the craving to penetrate the flimsy appearances to the essence beneath—and below!—the desire to uncover the facade and to discover what lurks behind, "the thing on the doorstep" or "the haunter of the dark" (to cite the titles of two of Lovecraft's stories): or apparently far less menacingly, a simple woman, Clara.[116]

The instability of early cinema, or moreover the cinema itself, must be examined with the mechanisms of defense that simultaneously accompany this sense of dislocation; that is to say, the unstable subject of cinema is always paired with a "coherent" (even if illusory) subject. To put this another way, early cinema does not represent a moment *before* social and sexual identity but rather reenacts the *founding* moment of this identity.[117] The threat then posed by cinema—and logically played out on the figure of castration, woman—is not simply subject instability or mobility but rather the knowledge that *any fixed* subject position is based on an illusion. This shifts the framework of cinematic dislocation from the realm of a specifically *male* crisis—the slippage of the categories of masculinity and femininity—to a more profound disturbance, one that speaks to an epistemological and cultural upheaval. Such disturbance produces a double movement of denial (or as in Bessière's fantastic, censorship): "This desire to penetrate, and ultimately to conserve the integrity of perception: perceiver and perceived, the wholeness of the body, the power of vision—all this implies a *denial* (*Verneinung* is the Freudian term) of that almost-nothing which can hardly be seen, a denial that in turn involves a certain structure of narrative, in which this denial repeats and articulates itself."[118]

My analysis of Feuillade's crime serials maps out a series of movements, or rather repetitive, redundant, and recursive structures, that serve as an index of the uncanny circulating around the era's historical conditions and within cinematic form itself. The serials' resistance to static or immobile location—the categories of "primitive," "classical," or "transitional" all appear as inadequate labels for these films—is suggestive of their uncanny status, and thus my mapping of the disturbance within the films must be fluid or mobile. The continuous alternations between the familiar and unfamiliar are presented in what I will call shifting zones of anxiety. The salient quality of these zones is this movement—an ongoing process of instability and dislocation. But whether the zone of anxiety is located at the level of visual style, narrative, or the figure of the star, the movement in Feuillade's serials ultimately turns us back toward, and foregrounds, the uncanny or uncertainty at the heart of the cinema.

To begin a discussion of the uncanny in Feuillade's films, let us make a heuristic move forward in time to the 1928 documentary *La zone*, by the French filmmaker Georges Lacombe. *La zone* is a portrait of *chiffonniers* (rag-pickers), whose lives are both structured and supported by the refuse of modern urban life. As Walter Benjamin has noted, these trash collectors were figures of sympathy and fascination in late-nineteenth-century Paris.[119] That Lacombe featured this group in a film of the late 1920s speaks to the longevity of the *chiffonnier* as both social reality and cultural icon of marginality. I cite Lacombe's documentary film here, in a discussion concerning the crime serials of Louis Feuillade, because the representation of space in *La zone* is useful in visualizing a certain trajectory of anxiety in Feuillade's films.

Lacombe opens the film with a definition of "the zone."[120] He provides a map for us with an area marked off by shading—this is the space inhabited by the poorer classes. Their lot is epitomized by the rag-picker—a hard worker who scratches out a bare living by collecting the refuse of the modern urban environment. The *chiffonnier* combs the city by day for bits of cloth, paper, and glass that he/she can recycle for the funds that will support his/her existence on the literal margins of the urban space. Lacombe's film is essentially sympathetic to the plight of these workers, but it is crucial to see in his map an explicit and physical marking of class differences across the Paris landscape.

This image of "the zone" is an appropriate one, for the late nineteenth and early twentieth centuries in particular saw these suburban regions as marginal, perilous, and essentially crime ridden. However, as the urban areas and technologies developed, the space of the inner city itself became increasingly suspect. The advances of modern life were not without its trade-offs. As Eugen Weber notes, "in 1900, the first Paris Metro line opened and proved phenomenally successful, despite somber warnings against the dangers of electrocution, asphyxiation, and pickpockets, which made it known at first as the 'Necropolitain.'"[121]

The seeming ubiquity of danger and lawlessness, and the ensuing Parisian dwellers' preparedness for this state of affairs, was mocked in a fictionalized short placed alongside more standard "documentary" items (parades, fashion items, political dignitaries) in a Gaumont newsreel of 1911. The sequence entitled "*La loi du progrès: Passage à tabac*" features a robber waiting to ambush a man walking down the street. As the thief jumps out from his hiding place to attack the pedestrian, the victim suddenly pulls a gun. After startling the robber out of his plan, the man proceeds to show the robber that his defense was really a cigarette holder disguised as a gun (seen in close-up). Enjoying this joke on his own gullibility, the thief then shows (again highlighted in close-up) his similar "weapon"—a smaller version of the gun/cigarette holder. The fake gun is presented as a popular device that the knowledgeable Parisian carries with him on the street, useful for either protection or assault. The sequence is interesting not just for its preoccupation with street crime and for the blurring of boundaries between criminal and citizen (the two men utilize the same strategies and in fact finish by sharing the joke until the would-be robber is chased off by a policeman) but also for the crisis of knowledge it foregrounds (and is foregrounded through the technique of the close-up). The city dweller is unable to discriminate between lethal and harmless objects. This is perhaps the most frightening aspect of the modern urban space—the unpredictability of crime, danger, and disorder.[122]

With respect to the Feuillade films, there is an effort both to document and to delineate the criminal figure. Much like the Lacombe film, difference (and by extension in Feuillade, disorder) is seen as confined to the margins of the city. However, as the serials chronologically progress, there is a sense of a shrinking zone of comfort. My "mapping" of anxiety in these films is influenced by José Monleón's excellent book *A Specter Is Haunting Europe*, which traces from gothic literature to the *roman populaire* and stories of the fantastic a movement of disturbance and criminality from the social periphery to the individual.[123] A similar process appears at work in the Feuillade serials, and I am particularly interested in the implications of this trajectory with regard to issues of class, gender, ethnicity, and sexuality.

In *Fantômas*, and to a certain extent, *Les vampires*, crime-filled or hazardous areas are generally in the outlying or unknown areas of Paris: on commuter trains, the suburbs, in deserted villas, or in the still unfamiliar Paris Metro (e.g., in one sequence of *Juve contre Fantômas*, Fandor—Juve's journalist partner—tracks the criminal Joséphine, an ally of Fantômas—through the Paris Metro). Beginning with *Les vampires*, an even more disturbing tendency can be seen. The space of the seemingly known and familiar is now equally dangerous. Bodies begin to fall out of closets in quite respectable neighborhoods of the city, and a severed head turns up in the aristocratic country lodgings of the hero's old family friend.

Again, like "*La loi du progrès*," ordinary objects within the home may carry multiple, illusory, and sometimes deadly functions. An otherwise unexceptional fountain pen, as in *Les vampires*, may contain poisonous ink. Or, an innocent straw basket is used to transport the kidnapped, the anaesthetized, or the murdered (*Les vampires, Judex*).

Every object presents the possibility of a new or ambivalent meaning and use. The danger, unpredictability, and strangeness of the heretofore familiar is once again evocative of Freud's essay on the uncanny. Freud's discussion begins with a linguistic turn, outlining at one level the relationship between *unheimlich,* or uncanny, and its lexical root:

> The German word "*unheimlich*" is obviously the opposite of "heimlich" ["homely"], "*heimisch*" ["native"]—the opposite of what is familiar; and we are tempted to conclude that what is "uncanny" is frightening precisely because it is *not* known and familiar. Naturally not everything that is not new and unfamiliar is frightening, however; the relation is not capable of inversion. We can only say that what is novel can easily become frightening and uncanny; some new things are frightening but not by any means all. Something has to be added to what is novel and unfamiliar in order to make it uncanny.[124]

In an effort to illuminate this "something," or essential quality, of the uncanny, Freud then enters into a rather lengthy series of definitions of both *unheimlich* and *heimlich*. The definitions end as the two terms begin to intersect, most significant, around the issue of vision. At one point, Freud cites a definition of *heimlich* as "what is concealed and kept out of sight" and then compares a definition of its "contrary": '*Unheimlich*' is the name for everything that ought to have remained . . . secret and hidden but has come to light."[125]

Feuillade's serials feature a preoccupation with questions concerning vision, foregrounding the cinema's endemic ambivalence regarding knowledge and sight, a phenomenon consistent with the era's own crisis in perception. Thus, the crime films function as a type of metacommentary on the relationships among modernity, cinema, and the uncanny. But perhaps the crucial issue to highlight at this point in the outline of the serials' trajectory is Freud's central argument that "the uncanny is that class of the frightening which leads us back to what is known of old and long familiar."[126] More specifically, the source of anxiety is defined with respect to the question of sexual difference; that is to say, terror can be linked to the primally familiar—the female body.[127]

As the area of comfort contracts for the city dweller in the world of the Feuillade serial, there is a concerted effort to contain incoherence and disorder and, in turn, to define more clearly the supposed source of disturbance, criminality. In this new definition, the criminal is female. To be sure, in *Fantômas* (the first series), the title character is male, but it is important to remember that Fantômas's "defining" marks are his disguises; that is to say, he is rarely recognizable. These films are followed by *Les vampires* and *Judex*, where the center of unlawfulness is both female and easily identifiable (even in her assorted "disguises").

Musidora

The femme fatale in *Les vampires* and *Judex* is portrayed by the actress Musidora. Famous for her black *maillot de soie* (silk bodysuit), Musidora is a true icon of the French cinema. Despite her appearance in only two of these serials, there are few accounts of Feuillade that neglect to mention her participation in his films.[128] But Musidora must be seen as more than a fascinating star persona of the silent era. In fact, she plays a pivotal role in understanding the fundamental structure supporting each of the six serials.

To examine Musidora's function in these serials it is necessary to return to Freud's essay on the uncanny and to Hélène Cixous's reading of his text. Freud centers his analysis of the uncanny on a discussion of the short story by E. T. A. Hoffmann, "The Sandman," which traces a young student's descent into madness. Freud's account, as Cixous points out, is effectively a rewriting of the text as a type of case study of the student, Nathaniel.[129]

At the center of Nathaniel's crisis lies the problem of recognition; he cannot be certain if the eyeglass merchant, Coppola, is really Coppelius, the assassin of his father; and perhaps more disconcerting, he cannot be certain if the woman he loves is, in fact, a woman or an automaton. Nathaniel faces this confusion at different points in the story with two separate women: Olympia and Clara. The shifting points of view in narration throughout the text leave as uncertain both the "real" identity of numerous characters and Nathaniel's mental state. Although Nathaniel has been driven to madness and suicide by the end of the story, the "explanation" for the events is by no means clear; that is to say, it is not certain if the center of the disturbance is Coppelius, Olympia, Nathaniel, or Clara.

But in effect, Cixous argues, Freud's account is an effort to explain, to define, and ultimately, to contain the source of this disturbance and uncertainty. Her reading of Freud's essay is as an examination of what has been left out of Hoffmann's text and, furthermore, of the insights of such elisions on the uncanny.[130] The reconstruction of

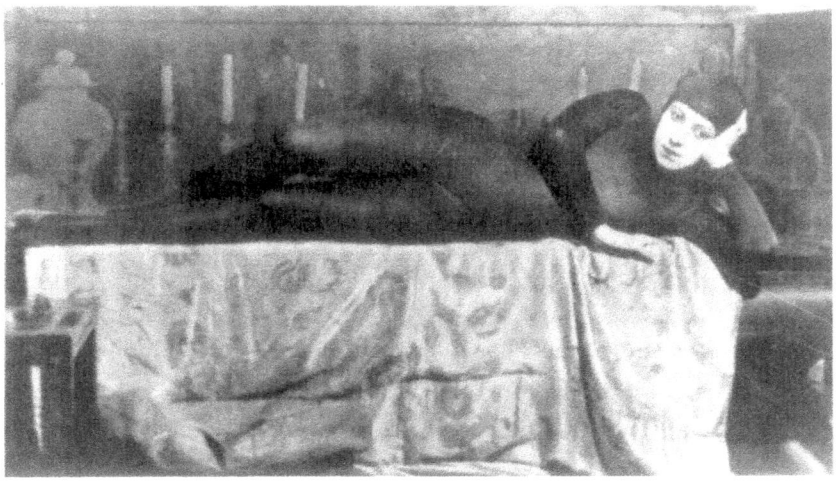

The infamous *maillot de soie*. Publicity photo of Musidora in *Les vampires*. © Roger-Viollet.

the story as *Nathaniel's* case history serves to eliminate not only a number of important characters and multiple points of view, but moreover, it alters the narrative structure and textual ambivalence of the work.

> The two versions of the Sand-Man have to be read in order to notice what has been slipped into one version from the other. As a condensed narrative, Freud's story is singularly altered in the direction of a linear, logical account of Nathaniel and strongly articulated as a kind of 'case history,' going from childhood remembrances to the delirium and the ultimate tragic end. All through the story, Freud intrudes in various ways: in one instance to bring the fantastic back to the rational (the *Unheimliche* to the *Heimliche*); in another instance, he intrudes to establish explicit liaisons which are not conveyed as such in the text.[131]

In Freud's reading, Coppola and Coppelius are one and the same, both standing in for Nathaniel's childhood fear of "the Sand-Man"—a figure that poses the threat of castration.[132]

In a later essay by Freud, "The Passing of the Oedipus Complex," the force and possibility of castration is rendered by a particular event—the sight of the female body. Although at first the (male) child is reluctant to engage the idea, "the child whose own penis is such a proud possession obtains a sight of the genital parts of a little girl; he must then become convinced of the absence of a penis in a creature so like himself. With this, however, the loss of his own penis becomes imaginable, and the threat of castration achieves its delayed effect."[133] In the case of "The Sand-Man," the figure that would appear to function as the center of castration anxiety, that is, woman—either the doll Olympia or Clara, Nathaniel's beloved—is relegated somehow to the margins of the text. Cixous argues that in Freud's essay, Olympia has become no more than an extension of Nathaniel's Oedipal struggles.

> It follows that if in the ordering of this new text, a dismembered, tightened-up, and reassembled Olympia takes on a new importance, she is at once, retrieved by the interpretation: "she can be nothing else than a personification of Nathaniel's feminine attitude toward his father in his infancy," says Freud. To be sure! Homosexuality returns in reality under this charming figure. But Olympia is more than just a detached complex of Nathaniel.[134]

For Cixous, Olympia's story not only indicates Nathaniel's resistance to castration but, more important, is evidence of an analogous resistance at the heart of Freud's own reading.[135] It is this resistance that silences Olympia, presenting her as merely a sign of castration with, as Cixous restates Freud's text, "'No meaning' other than the fear (resistance) of castration."[136] To put this another way, Cixous's reading exposes Freud's "passionate fiction"[137] that the Oedipal scenario is the only narrative possible, a story line that effectively erases women (as subjects) and proscribes desire within a limited heteronormative paradigm.

At first glance, Musidora's characters (Irma Vep in *Les vampires* and Diana Monti in *Judex*) appear as little more than the cliché of the femme fatale—a threatening woman who destroys men and must be punished by the end of the film, preferably by death. The black bodysuit that situates Musidora as object of desire (as evidenced from numerous commentaries on the star) also returns us to the site of the female body as difference, that is, as sign of castration. The dramatic long shots of Musidora in her bodysuit, in tandem with the use of close-ups of her eyes, situate the star as a type of fetish object for the serials. However, beyond the fetish, the same bodysuit produces a parallel effect. Musidora's costume is almost identical to one worn by the master criminal, Fantômas. The suit functions both to reveal *and* to conceal difference and thereby reaffirm the notion that this is "a creature so like himself."[138]

In effect, the problem that circulates around Musidora is one addressed in "The Sand-Man"—that of recognition. This issue of recognition repeatedly returns the investigation of woman and the uncanny to questions of visibility. Furthermore, the attention to problems of vision throughout the serials links together a series of investigations on the limits of knowledge. Thus it is possible to see the fetishistic use of the female body, the examination of a variety of physical evidence (as seen, for example, in the use of technology and gadgetry as the "explanation" of mysterious events), and the interest in hypnotic powers (often explained by the mesmerism of an individual's eyes) as similar lines of inquiry. But if this is a crisis of knowledge, is woman merely a metaphor for the dilemma? Must we yet again move Olympia and Musidora to the margins of the text?

Musidora's centrality to these films is due not only to her placement at the literal center of the films (she's the one unambiguous force of evil across two of Feuillade's most popular serials) but also to the relentless efforts, through a multiplicity of strategies, to contain her threat. The use of the close-up, the framing of her face and body, and of course, her *maillot de soie* can all be seen as attempts to see, to define, and ultimately to deny what Weber has termed the "almost nothing, but not quite"[139] of castration. Moreover, the repetitiveness of the narratives in question (*Les vampires* and *Judex*) indicates a pattern that continually points to and punishes the crimes of femininity.

Beyond the thematic considerations of the disclosure and punishment of the femme fatale, the circularity of the fantastic narratives in Feuillade indicate that the anxiety at work can be found at the most basic structural level of the films. The movement of the narrative restages the movement of cinematic vision and the slippage between the visible and the invisible, a circular movement, but one with ellipsis and ultimately without closure.

Even in death the woman may escape. Both of the two serials that feature Musidora end with her death. But in each instance, there is something that eludes the control of male authority. Beyond her star persona and thematic control of the films, the image of Musidora represents another layer of resistance to social and cultural order. The very structure of the fetish guarantees this resistance. As Linda Williams notes in her discussion of early cinema, "the very nature of the fetish disavowal also assures that the woman is defined entirely in terms that will perpetuate the nagging fear of the lack she represents."[140]

Ultimately, then, Musidora's defeat is never quite complete or satisfying. In *Les vampires*, Irma (Musidora) is killed by the nervous bride of the journalist/detective, Philippe Guérande, who has pursued her relentlessly throughout the series. The bride's act is more a response of terror than competence and anger. In *Judex*, the evil Diana proves even more elusive: she dies from her own action as the result of an escape attempt.

In the next two serials, *La nouvelle mission de Judex* and *Tih Minh*, the zones of anxiety and female criminality shift ground, once again disturbing the efforts to "survey" or contain the threat. Now her actions are frequently the products of hysterical illness or hypnotic trances. On one level, this places the nature of the woman criminal within the realm of a scientific or medical discourse; her actions, unlike Irma's and Diana's, are explainable. Nonetheless, there is something about the nature of the "illness" that leaves the woman inaccessible and unknowable (either through a loss of memory, as in *La nouvelle mission de Judex*, or a loss of memory and speech, as in *Tih Minh*). Moreover, as we will see when we look at these later films more closely, Musidora "returns" to the scene of the crime (although not literally on-screen) in a number of extratextual and filmic references.

In the last serial, *Barrabas*, the zones of anxiety shrink once again. The lead male character, Jacques Varèse (Fernand Hermann), must deal with the trauma of criminal markings as literally inscribed on his body (an outlaw gang has tattooed its insignia on his arm, an act that sets in motion a series of questions about the character's "true identity," his past, and his family's history). This trauma, as we will see in the next chapter, is actually a repetition of a mystery seen in *Fantômas contre Fantômas*. Here, the criminal, Fantômas, is supposedly identifiable by a wound on his arm. When the inspector Juve awakes the next day in his cell (he has been arrested on suspicion that he may, in fact, be Fantômas), an identical mark is found on the detective's arm. The distinction between the two narratives is that the mark in *Fantômas* becomes one of numerous trails (this one, as so many others, is false) to the identity and capture of the criminal, Fantômas; in *Barrabas* the mark serves as the major drive of the narrative.

Beginning with *Judex*, we can trace another slight shift in the Feuillade's crime films. Although still within the realm of the fantastic, these films are much more inflected with traces of melodramatic narrative and performance style. The sense of dislocation moves from the space of the female body to those areas somewhat less tangible—the female psyche and the world of the family (this is particularly true in the last three serials, *La nouvelle mission de Judex, Tih Minh,* and *Barrabas*). Nonetheless, the physical markings of crime on Varèse's body return us ultimately to the uncanny and multileveled anxiety that this phenomenon entails. But always at the center of anxiety is the figure of woman, making this Musidora's as much as Feuillade's story.

2 | The *Fantômas* Series
Cinematic Vision and the Test of "Immediate Certainty"

> "I" is, therefore, not a unified subject, a fixed identity, or that solid mass covered with layers of superficialities one has gradually to peel off before one can see its true face. "I" is, itself, *infinite layers*. Its complexity can hardly be conveyed through such typographic conventions as I, i, or I/i. Thus, I/i am compelled by the will to say/unsay, to resort to the entire gamut of personal pronouns to stay near this fleeing *and* static essence of Not-I. Whether I accept it or not, the natures of *I, i, you, s/he, We, we, they,* and *wo/man* constantly overlap. They all display a necessary ambivalence, for the line dividing *I* and *Not-I*, *us* and *them*, or *him* and *her* is not (and cannot) always (be) as clear as we would like it to be. Despite our desperate, eternal attempt to separate, contain, and mend, categories always leak.
>
> Trinh T. Minh-Ha, *Woman Native Other*

Zone 1: The Urban *Unheimliche*

The opening moments of the first episode in the *Fantômas* film series (1913–14) feature a prescient bit of dialogue when the startled crime victim, Princess Danidoff (Jane Faber), inquires of the well-dressed thief suddenly before her: "Who are you?" This question is, in effect, the distillation of the epic battle that is to be played out in the series and throughout the crime films of Feuillade. The thief's answer is equally telling: he hands her a blank card (shown in close up) that reveals his name only after the outlaw has made his hasty and courteous exit (he kisses her hand before running out the door). The conflict presented to us is over the boundaries of certainty and uncertainty, the terrain of the fantastic, but more important over the *agent* of those distinctions—the self. The link between certainty and self—and the contradiction therein—is acutely drawn for us in Nietzsche's "Beyond Good and Evil," an important philosophical text for turn-of-the-century culture:

> There are still harmless self-observers who believe that there are "immediate certainties" for example, "I think," or as the superstition of Schopenauer put it, "I will"; as though knowledge here got hold of its object purely and nakedly as "the thing in itself," without any falsification on the part of either the subject or the object. But that "immediate certainty," as well as "absolute knowledge" and the "thing in itself," invoke a *contradictio in adjecto*. . . .
>
> In place of the "immediate certainty" in which the people may believe in the case at hand, the philosopher thus finds a series of metaphysical questions presented to him, truly searching questions on the intellect; to wit: "From where do I get the concept of thinking? Why do I believe in cause and effect? What gives me the right to speak of an ego, and even of an ego as cause, and finally of an ego as the cause of thought?" Whoever ventures to answer these metaphysical questions at once by an appeal to a sort of *intuitive* perception, like the person who says, "I think, and know that this at least, is true, actual, and certain"—will encounter a smile and two question marks from a philosopher nowadays. "Sir," the philosopher will perhaps give him to understand, "it is improbable that you are not mistaken; but why insist on the truth?"[1]

The crime and detective genres, in both their literary and cinematic incarnations, relentlessly pursued questions of certainty and the link between knowledge and identity. As several scholars have noted, a fascination with the crime figure and his or her pursuer was central to early French cinema beginning with Victorin Jasset's films *Exploits de Nick Carter* (1908), which were based on a popular weekly series of short (around thirty pages) and inexpensive novels tracing the exploits of an American detective.[2]

Although Feuillade dabbled in the detective genre with a four-film series shaped around a modern sleuth named Jean Dervieux (René Navarre), his most noteworthy exploration of crime reverses perspective by foregrounding the exploits of the lawbreaker Fantômas—a move that as Francis Lacassin notes is more consistent with the heroes of French adventure literature, from Rocambole to Arsène Lupin.[3] Moreover, Feuillade's series of five films[4] featuring Fantômas, as Richard Abel notes, are part of a larger trend in French cinema starting around 1911–12 (beginning with the criminal series *Zigomar*) whereby the male hero shifts from an agent of the law to the "master criminal of the modern city."[5]

This new character of crime, Fantômas, is played by the *same* actor, Réne Navarre, who performed as Dervieux. This reversal of actor-character is not unique to Navarre in Feuillade's ongoing troupe of performers, but it does initiate a whole series of reversals in Feuillade's crime films that we can follow at the levels of style, narrative, and performance. The drive of each reversal is to put into question the veracity of all that is "immediately certain" before us.

The assault on certainty is made explicit by an immediate attention to the questions and problems of disguise. In episode 1 of *Fantômas*, the introductory "prologue" presents: "Mr. Navarre in the role of Fantômas." The actor Navarre is first shown "as himself" and then transformed through a series of overlapping dissolves to the multiple disguises the criminal will utilize in the episode: a bearded thief clad in evening dress, a hotel bellhop, and a dark-haired, mustachioed fellow (who we will learn later goes by the name of Gurn). Three of the episodes open with a similar introductory sequence, although there are variants with respect to the specific "characters" presented (which vary by episode).[6] This presentational strategy has an important variant in episode 2, *Juve contre Fantômas*, when the disguises of the detective, Juve (Bréon), are equally put on display.

This opening sequence (and the two others similarly structured) operates on a variety of levels. On one level, the episode's first four shots serve an important explanatory function. That is to say, as the adventures of the criminal, Fantômas, and the detective, Juve, unfold through a dizzying number of disguises, crimes, and pursuits, the opening provides the viewer with some preliminary visual clues of the many-layered mystery (or mysteries) to follow.

It should be noted here that the *Fantômas* films were accompanied—as were most series or serial films—by a variety of written material, both inside and outside of the cinema setting. The basic text of the series film might be drawn from a novel, adapted from a *feuilleton* (a novel serialized in a newspaper), or developed specifically as a joint undertaking by a newspaper and a film production house (the *ciné-roman*—this will be the format for Feuillade's later serials beginning with *Judex* in 1916, typically with Feuillade receiving a coauthor credit on the publication).

In addition, information on these films was available at the cinema itself. Viewers at screenings during this period were generally given program notes. An evening's program would consist of a number of different films (travel films, comedies, short dramas), and several of these might have a brief synopsis (a paragraph). If the film was to be the evening's main film, the program highlight, there might be a rather lengthy summary of the film's story line. An examination of the programs from the period demonstrates that this practice was common for all genres of films and was not limited to the crime or mystery formats.

According to *Le Courrier Cinématographique*, Gaumont released a forty-page publicity booklet with the first film in the series, *Fantômas*, which included a detailed synopsis of the action and numerous photos of the lead actors and actresses in the production. *Le Courrier Cinématographique* was primarily an industry journal, and the Gaumont brochures are discussed in the issue as a marketing tool for distribution rather than a theater supplement for the audience. These booklets do contain a good deal of additional narrative information, including details of character motivations, for example, and may have been intended for audience use. While there is some evidence to suggest that these booklets were available at the films, it is unclear if this information was in wide distribution. The length and high quality of the material involved suggest that the booklets were narrowly circulated or, perhaps, sold separately. Several of the original theater programs from the *Fantômas* series (much smaller and less glossy than the aforementioned brochures) do not provide even minimal plot summaries, despite their often convoluted plots, while other films on the program are summarized—often including a particular film's resolution. Only one of the extant programs, from episode 5, *Le faux magistrat* (Tivoli-Cinéma program), currently found at the Bibliothèque de l'Arsenal, contained a synopsis of the story. While it is possible that the audience already knew some elements of the story from the novels, notoriety, or even separately distributed programs, it also seems likely that to a certain extent the narrative line as a coherent, re-constructible entity is unimportant, as we shall see.[7]

The literary inspiration for Feuillade's films was Marcel Allain and Pierre Souvestre's villainous Fantômas, who was featured in a series of crime novels. The series, which began publication in 1911, consisted of a staggering thirty-two volumes produced over a mind-boggling thirty-two months.[8] Like the Nick Carter novels, they were inexpensive, approximately the cost of a newspaper for a week's time, but with regard to volume, the *Fantômas* books were an even better entertainment value, as each edition was four hundred or more pages.[9]

But there were important changes from the novels to the film beyond what one might expect given the sheer volume of written material for *Fantômas*. As the historian Robin Walz notes, the novels favored dialogue over descriptive text,[10] while the films work quite differently with their realist mise-en-scène, long takes, location shooting, and minimal dialogue intertitles. Moreover, as Lacassin points out, Feuillade alone selected what material to utilize from the novels and proceeded to streamline the narratives in a consistent and significant fashion:

> Feuillade pruned the digressions, suppressed the repetitions to the benefit of terror, conserved the scenes in the sewers and the pursuits on the roofs to the detriment of the trips to London and to the South of Africa, and among the murders and injuries, he showed the most spectacular. From each of these volumes of four hundred pages, he conserved the essential, distilling thus a precise and subtle essence, taken from the strange, the gloomy, and the cruel.[11]

In short, Feuillade saved the good parts—the most disturbing and the most *sensational*. Sensationalism, as we know, was an important part of turn-of-the-century urban culture due to the dramatic alterations in daily life presented by the emergence of new technologies, industrialization, and shifts in social boundaries (especially the rise of the working class and new definitions of gender). As noted earlier, the "shocks" attendant to modern life had their cultural corollaries: the public's fascination with sensationalism through the *faits divers,* or tabloid tales of crime; the Grand Guignol's frightening and bloodthirsty plays; and bizarrely, the popular tours of the Paris morgue.[12]

The publicity materials and programs that accompanied the *Fantômas* series played into this preoccupation by the explicit and repeated use of the term *sensational*. The opening two-page advertisement by Gaumont in *Le Courrier Cinématographique* (April 1913), featuring a full-page color image of the masked bandit in evening dress, announces the film's appearance with the claim: "the most sensational film of the year defies the competition and the last minute imitations." Another two-page foldout in the same journal shows us Fantômas again, with the first image repeated and accompanied by two other images of the criminal in disguise. In this instance, the only text is the film's appearance date and the repeated tagline "the most sensational film." There is no mention of the director or the performers in this part of the journal, although a later section featuring a part of the film scenario does mention three of the principal actors (René Navarre, Jane Faber, and Renée Carl).[13]

The seeming void in the place of individuality (here with respect to the artists involved) is found in another Gaumont publicity insert, despite a turn to an emphasis on written material in the advertisement. The text is somewhat telling both for that sense of shock and terror that it plays on (over the front page image of a door read the words: "If you fear violent emotions, don't open this door"[14]) and for its absence of character specificity even in its promotion of a "marker" of identity. The following occurs alone on one page as a dialogue exchange:

FANTÔMAS!
WHAT DID YOU SAY?
I SAY . . . FANTÔMAS!
WHAT DOES THAT SIGNIFY?
NOTHING AND EVERYTHING?
NEVERTHELESS, WHAT IS IT?
NO ONE, BUT HOWEVER, SOMEONE.
FINALLY, WHAT DOES HE DO, THIS SOMEONE?
he FRIGHTENS (il fait PEUR)[15]

However, perhaps most important, the process of distillation or abstraction toward these sensational elements also has an interesting byproduct—a diminution, and indeed almost absence, of character. The development, or rather lack therein, of character is significant, as it is the transition from pure spectacle and action to a highly individualized and psychologically complex agent of action that is seen as central to the move from the "cinema of attractions" to the "cinema of narrative integration." As Tom Gunning argues, the Jasset crime series were crucial for an increased attention to characterization. While the *Nick Carter* and *Zigomar* films, like the *Fantômas* series, highlighted the question of disguise for both the criminal and the detective (disguise being an essential component of the modern criminologist's tools), the question of unstable identity is less in play. As Gunning points out, character is established in the Jasset films by the stark contrast between good and evil.[16] For the *Fantômas* series, it is precisely *those boundaries* that are put into question. The mutability of Fantômas is, in fact, his true crime, and this is the illegality that Juve has been put on the path to regulate.

But the criminal's malleable identity is revealed at the end of episode 1 to be uncontrollable, as Fantômas magically appears before Juve in his office only to taunt him and then to disappear in an equally mysterious manner (represented through the use of superimposition again). The title card informs us: "Henceforth, Juve will have only one obsession, to capture Fantômas." With the opening of episode 2, the drive of his obsession becomes clear, as the danger and contagion of indeterminacy spreads. For now, Juve's identity has been destabilized as well, and as noted before, the detective appears in the prologue in a series of disguises. Moreover, the narrative develops the confusion and mutability of roles. In episode 4, *Fantômas contre Fantômas,* both the public and the police suspect that Juve's "true" identity is one and the same as the master criminal. And while wrongly imprisoned, Juve, develops a wound on the arm that only the *real* Fantômas could have incurred outside the jail (the sign is later explained as a cut placed on Juve after being drugged). However, in perhaps the strangest and most disturbing variant along these lines, Juve takes on the role of Fantômas (episode 5, *Le faux magistrat*) after freeing the outlaw from a Belgian prison (and substituting himself in the cell) with the hopes of recapturing Fantômas in Paris (where he can be executed).

The Limits of the Photographic Image

Given the problems of character void and identity mutability, the opening prologues in the *Fantômas* series provide an essential clarification function with respect to spectator orientation. For Tom Gunning, the *Fantômas* film prologues are primarily driven by this motivation and help to situate both the audience (with respect to the characters) and the characters (with respect to the law). Gunning argues that the *Fantômas* novels maintain a sense of character ambiguity much more rigorously, and the film's opening sequences draw our attention to the ongoing visual transformation of characters (as in an illusionist show) rather than to the mutability of identity.[17]

But the very way Feuillade chooses to represent character disguise and shifts of identity perhaps illuminates the question of character definition and ambiguity. The strategy of disguise is recurrent in the crime serial format in general, and two examples are particularly informative for the way they represent alterations in appearance. The first example is drawn from the serials of Victorin Jasset. In both Jasset's *Zigomar* (1911) and *Nick Carter* series (1908–10)—and there is even a *Zigomar contre Nick Carter* film (1912)—the detective and the criminal make frequent use of disguise. Gunning notes (as he also does with Feuillade) that Jasset's representation of a character's change (through disguise) is essentially a development of the "trick film" and of *extra*-cinematic forms (the vaudeville quick-change artist and the magician). Jasset's scenes of disguise are often shot against a black background and with the use of the stop-motion device and spliced film, creating the effect, as Gunning calls it, of the magician's "presto" change. A new character or identity abruptly and instantly appears before us with the stop motion eliding the change of costume.[18]

Like the Jasset films, a second example, the German film *Wo ist Coletti?* (*Where is Coletti?*) by Max Mack (1913), shares a preoccupation with the act of disguise. Both filmmakers, Mack and Jasset, will sometimes use screen time to demonstrate to the viewer the very process of disguise (i.e., the act of putting on a disguise). But in the case of Mack's film, this process takes on an almost ritualistic quality, given the repetitiveness of the act of make-up (and also "revealment"—the removal of the disguise is yet another essential part of the film) and the care given to the event of disguise (that is, as we seemingly watch the make-up routine in "real time").

In contrast, how has Feuillade chosen to represent the transition from one character to another in the *Fantômas* series and its opening sequences? Examining these first series of shots again, we notice that the shots are linked by the device of the dissolve. As the rest of an episode and series unfolds, we note that Feuillade rarely spends screen time on the transition process. Each new character is presented as an identity *already* transformed (but in a manner quite distinct from the "presto" change). This strategy is also employed with some frequency in the Jasset films,[19] but it is raised to a high art in Feuillade. We often see Loupart, Chaleck, Tom Bob, the banker Nanteuil, or "the man in black" (Fantômas in a bodysuit and hood) in the middle of their criminal activity, without the preliminary act of disguise, or for that matter, any introduction beyond the opening sequence (this presentation style of new or disguised characters introduced *in medias res* is also found, sometimes maddeningly so, in *Les vampires*). Feuillade's later serial, *Judex,* does feature a key disguise/transformation scene, but this is part of the series' turn to a more melodramatic form. The question of identity is now linked with the duality and clarity, rather than the multiplicity and disorder, of identity. The dissolves, then, move us from one identity to another, helping to anchor us to the definition of the characters to follow but at the same time demonstrating, through the very movement of the dissolve, the unsteadiness, or *unheimlich* dimension of that anchor.

The joyous "man in black" at the end of *Juve contre Fantômas,* episode 2 of *Fantômas.* Louis Feuillade. © Production Gaumont, 1913.

Moreover, Feuillade's use of the dissolve here could be read as a type of commentary on the photographic and cinematic process. The individual shots—against a white background, with a minimal amount of movement (only a slight shifting of the eyes and a change in the position of the arms)—call to mind the genre of the portrait photo, and the important subgenre of the period, the crime portrait. The crime photo portrait was an important component for the emerging field of "scientific" police work. The criminologist Alphonse Bertillon developed a system of identification in the late nineteenth century that combined both a verbal description (*le portrait parlé*) and a sectional photography of body parts (close-ups of the numerous shapes and peculiarities that might be seen in the human ear, for example).[20]

Tom Gunning argues that this new system of identification was an effort to control the body through an archive of written and visual information. This record makes disguise or disfiguration by the criminal largely ineffective since the "file" of data would be so unique and complete that only full-body alteration could escape the catalog.[21] However, beyond such police efficacy, Gunning points out a larger issue at stake through a quotation from the criminologist Gallus Muller that the drive of the system was "to fix the human personality, to give each human being an identity, and individuality, certain, durable, invariable, always recognizable, and always capable of being proven."[22] It is interesting that this system of control emerges not only within the context of an era driven by the shift to an urban mass culture and demarcated by shifts in class and gender boundaries but also within a period that saw increasing efforts to fix identity via the creation of the unique individual—both socially and cinematically.

Robert Nye points to an analogous development in the cultural representation of the criminal during the Belle Epoque. Crime was seen not as the product of class but rather the outgrowth of a larger cultural "pathology" of "*dégénérescence.*"[23] That is to say, the turn toward medical, or even vaguely social, illness was a movement toward individual rather than political solutions.

Despite an increase in working class and immigrant numbers and the attendant social inequities between classes, crime was often not portrayed as the product of any such distinction but rather the result of dangerous individuals or groups, like the notorious *apaches* (criminal gangs).[24] This denial of class or political issues was made possible, paradoxically, by the emergence of elements within the workers movements that rejected many of the old categories of cultural identity based on the nation, military, capital, and religion. The breakdown of clear social markers of identity enabled those in authority or under threat to label all disruptions as anarchism.[25] Anarchist rhetoric and violent action provided further excuse to term any dissent as criminal. As Eugen Weber notes, the issue of labeling such acts was complicated, in turn, by many crime gangs' explicit invocation of revolutionary goals, such as the redistribution of property. Even the infamous Bonnot gang of thieves claimed an anarchist agenda.[26]

Within this cauldron of confusion, the photographic image proved of limited value. To return briefly to the German film *Wo ist Coletti?* the unreliability of the photograph is key to the narrative's drive. In the film, the "famous" detective Coletti makes a public wager of 100,000 marks that even with his photographic likeness spread on posters throughout Berlin, no one could track him down within the time limit of forty-eight hours. Then, disguising his own barber as himself, he sends the city of Berlin on a frantic chase after the wrong man. It is a false image, then, that sets the chase in motion. However, it is another image—this time a printed one—that ends this part of the pursuit. The barber reveals his "true" identity by presenting the crowd, which has trapped him, with a business card. After this preliminary data is offered, the barber then unmasks (and thereby restarts the chase). The ruse of the photograph and the disguised barber is then replayed for us later in the film as part of a newsreel. The audience within the film—armed with the knowledge of cinematic documentation (and particularly its detailing of the process of disguise)—roars with laughter at the gullible Berliners taken in by the photo image. Mack's invocation of the "documentary moment" within the setting of the film comedy holds out a fervent hope in the "truth" of the cinematic image—and its separation from the photographic image. However, this hope in the cinema is tenuous, for sitting at the back of the theater is once again Coletti in disguise, this time as a woman.

It is this separation—and this tension—between the cinema and the photograph that Feuillade's work examines. To return to the dissolves yet again, the movement of the dissolve is the linking of two autonomous images. It is not, for example, a dissolve that speeds up an action in process (like the make-up ritual). Even the representational skills of photography could not give us such an insight. A photograph would either have to show the transformation of character as overlapping and therefore blurred images (rather than brought to resolution in the cinematic image), or the process would have to be shown in separate sequences.

The evidentiary limits of the photographic image—and indeed of the entire Bertillon procedure—are examined quite explicitly in the third episode of the *Fantômas* series, *Le mort qui tue*. Here, despite the painstaking detail of the criminalist's procedures—one sequence takes the viewer carefully through the measurement and marking processes (of fingerprints and body parts) of a suspected murderer, Jacques Dollon—the real culprit (who is, of course, Fantômas) escapes detection.

The sequence in the designated "anthropometric" division of the police department begins in a medium long shot with four representatives of the police and Dollon. As Dollon sits at the back center of the frame, he is surrounded by the various police officials, each with a clearly specialized task: one officer in uniform serves as guard; another man, more formally dressed, appears to oversee and scrutinize the procedures; and two men are in charge of the measurements (one to take the data physically and one to record the results). At one point, they move to the foreground of the frame and begin a lengthy series of shots on fingerprinting. The process is shown at first in medium long shot, but there is then a cut to an insert of the individual prints being made. The length of time and the use of the close-up designate the care, but ultimately the futility, of the process. Moreover, the very success of an ensuing crime is built on a manipulation of the criminalist's methodology and, in turn, scientific ideology (i.e., the detective's faith in the infallibility of the procedure itself). By stealing the skin from the hand of a murdered Jacques Dollon and then leaving these prints at the scene of a robbery, Fantômas demonstrates the poverty of the still image—particularly its inability to *identify* with certainty these carefully extracted marks or traces of the body. The police photograph the signs of the criminal act (a thumbprint on a woman's neck) and then discover an impossible match with a dead man (Dollon). The photographic image is in itself, then, incomplete.

The ambivalence toward the reliability of the photographic and cinematic image is seen also in another Feuillade film, *L'erreur tragique* (1913), released just a few months before the *Fantômas* series began. In this film, a husband (René Navarre) becomes convinced of his wife's (Suzanne Grandais) infidelity after seeing her walking with another man in the background of a fictional film (a revelatory byproduct of location shooting). The husband buys the film and studies each frame under a microscope to validate his suspicions. However, written material—much as in *Wo ist Coletti?*—changes his reading of the photo image: a letter from the wife's brother raises the possibility that the liaison was familial. On meeting the brother, the husband refers to the original piece of evidence—the filmstrip—to exonerate his wife. The photo/cinema strip matches, and the husband must now rescue his wife from a carriage "accident" that he has initiated. The husband and brother arrive late on the rescue scene, but the wife is merely wounded. The film closes with an embrace of all the family members at home.

As Richard Abel notes, *L'erreur tragique* can be read as a response by Gaumont (and Feuillade) to censorship restraints of the time. The film takes to task the "bad readers" (and censors) among the cinema audience who misread the innocent and wholesome image before them.[27] But how, precisely, does this misreading occur? The husband assumes a particular interpretation of the image by looking at a frame *in isolation*. Written material produces another innocent narrative, which both alters how we see the surrounding frames and demands that we extend the *duration* of the filmstrip to a more complete understanding of the possibilities therein. *L'erreur tragique* can then be read as a critique of the photographic image (and its potential falsity and illusion), the misguided attention of the cinema spectator, but perhaps most important, the revelation of other narratives *over time*.

Thus both *L'erreur tragique* and the openings in *Fantômas* point us toward the problem of uncertainty and the essential quality of the cinema as movement. What is placed in the foreground particularly through the vehicle of the dissolve is the space between photographic images, and what emerges is film movement as signifying the relationship between the frames. This relationship engenders the uncertain (or Cixous's *Unheimliche*), and the space, or gap, like the dissolve, always blends over into the next frame, image, or action, thereby repeating the process of stability/instability and certainty/uncertainty.

Time and the Cinematic Apparatus

The "photographic" poses in the *Fantômas* openings suggest a similar process noted by Thierry Kuntzel in an experimental animated film whereby the individually formed and discrete image explicitly highlights the erasure of movement (or the "illusion" of movement) between the similarly discrete photographic images experienced in cinema.[28] Kuntzel's argument echoes the critique of the "cinematographical mechanism of thought" that the nineteenth-century philosopher Henri Bergson describes in *Creative Evolution*. The critique was a refutation of the logic, "the mechanistic illusion" that Bergson believed the cinema replicated. Bergson argues that "cinematographical" reasoning incorrectly attempts to segment reality into instants, but the recombined whole of reality—"becoming"—is more than the sum of these instants.[29]

Bergson notes that what escapes the process of segmentation and the ensuing re-combination as rational order is movement. His language maps out a terrain similar to the uncanny:

> Install yourself within change, and you will grasp at once both change itself and the successive states in which *it might* at any instant be immobilized. But with these successive states, perceived from without as real and no longer as potential immobilities, you will never reconstitute movement. Call them *qualities, forms, positions,* or *intentions,* as the case may be, multiply the number of them as you will, let the interval

between two consecutive states be infinitely small: before the intervening movement you will always experience the disappointment of the child who tries by clapping his hands together to crush the smoke. The movement slips through the interval, because every attempt to reconstitute change out of states implies the absurd proposition, that movement is made of immobilities.[30]

Bergson's critique was part of a larger turn-of-the-century discourse surrounding questions of time and, specifically, the changing parameters of time. There were considerable debates and concerns regarding the definitions of time within a variety of contexts: public versus private time, the quandary of understanding time as either flow/duration or as discrete, segmented units. These debates were fueled in part by changes in technology and especially new developments in communication and transport that altered our perceptions of time and space. The railroad, automobile, telephone, telegraph, phonograph, and radio in effect "reduced" distances by their ability to move us quickly (whether physically or virtually) and seemingly effortlessly through space.[31] These inventions were often great equalizers or destabilizers, depending on your perspective, as now both lower and upper classes could transverse distances with minimal expense, and as Eugen Weber notes, public transportation systems ensured that differing classes utilizing these services would rub elbows at some point during their day.[32]

The segmentation of time was tied to efforts to "rationalize" the technology through its measurement and standardization. The proliferation of watches, clocks, and uniform time zones provided the mechanisms to control the new machinery, a strategy in turn applied to the workforce itself (through the methods of Taylor and Gilbreth).[33] On the other hand, there was also the understanding that these efforts to compartmentalize, segment, and even speed up our activities over time were producing a disoriented and sometimes even disturbed populace (and there were a variety of psychological studies that attempted to deal with modern nervousness).[34]

Perhaps more unsettling is the re-conceptualization of time that comes from philosophy and science. In 1905 we have Einstein's article in *Annalen der Physik* in which he destroys the obvious "truth" of absolute space and time and proposes instead the relative and constructed nature of our fundamental categories.[35] Crucial for our context, Einstein came to these ideas in the absence of experimental results, since he deemed physical data as *unreliable* and rather formed his theory on the basis of *intuitive* knowledge and logic.[36]

Within this cultural preoccupation and uncertainty regarding time, the technology of cinema emerges. The ambivalences of the era with respect to private/public, rational/irrational, or discrete/absolute times are woven right into the fabric of cinema itself, and it is this tension that is revealed in the opening *Fantômas* sequence.[37] Furthermore, these ambivalences, these tensions, are critical to the understanding of the organization of time and movement and the spatial representation of their instability throughout the Feuillade crime serials.

NARRATIVE STRUCTURE

If we look at the narrative structure in Feuillade's crime serials, it is possible to note an important variation from the typical sequential development of time in a serialized crime drama. Usually, the crime film follows an extended chase structure; that is, X pursues Y. The pattern can be extended in a number of ways: (1) X can chase Y until completion of the act, but then Y escapes and the chase begins again; (2) X's pursuit of Y can be complicated by the issue of disguise, so that the chase frequently dead-ends and must be restarted with the trail of the new identity (Y2); this leads to (3) X changes identity (through disguise) to become X2 pursuing Y2. Despite a number of variable detours along the way, we still have an essentially linear trajectory at work (and this is the basic structure of the Jasset films).

Feuillade's films, however, break with this pattern. It is true that we may have X's pursuit of Y, but often, the situation reverses, and Y now pursues X (that is, Fantômas pursues Juve or Fandor). In the Bercy shoot-out from *Juve contre Fantômas,* Juve and Fandor are lured separately by the possibility of finding Fantômas in hiding. At first, Juve and Fandor mistake each other for the criminal. They no sooner realize their error than they are suddenly surrounded by the criminal's cohorts—the gang seems to appear magically from behind storage barrels and commence firing on the duo. Juve and Fandor improbably flee the scene by jumping in one of the barrels and rolling it into the river, where they float away from the gunplay. Thus, it is not just the reversibility of events but the speed and unpredictability of the action that produces a disturbing effect.

If you consider that many episodes of Feuillade's serials have, generally speaking, a rather tenuous linkage of essentially autonomous sequences, and that in some instances the reversal may occur within the sequences themselves, then the potentiality for nonlinearity and, more specifically, chaos becomes clear. If one factors in the problem of disguise, and the knowledge that Feuillade will typically throw another character, Z, into the chase unit (as he does in *Fantômas contre Fantômas,* where at one point there are actually three men dressed and running about as the "man in black"), then the chaos escalates exponentially.

The tri-leveled chase, with several exchanges of allegiances and reversals of the directionality of the pursuit, is a key component of *Les vampires* (as we will see later). The third variable in the chase structure is not as prominent in the later serials—*Judex, La nouvelle mission de Judex, Tih Minh,* and *Barrabas*—but these serials do feature the other noted components: shifting allegiances and two-way pursuits. Although these last four serials may be seen as a turn toward a more traditional melodramatic narrative, the unfolding of these narratives is in no sense straightforward. There is still a system in place of autonomous, highly repetitive episodes, which are then overlaid with a more linear familial crisis. Although there are variations between the six serials, the essential narrative form is similar.

My use of the term *nonlinearity* may appear misleading. Due to the basic chase structure and seemingly Manichean framing of the series, there appears to be a particular narrative trajectory that can be mapped out over the films (i.e., the pursuit and punishment of evil). However, there are several points to be made regarding that particular narrative structure. First, while the pursuit of Fantômas by Juve/Fandor, or for that matter, Juve/Fandor by Fantômas, is an ongoing saga, it can never be completed. Although Fantômas is trapped on numerous occasions, the seizure of the criminal is not a device of closure but rather an opportunity to repeat the narrative, for the capture is almost always immediately followed by an escape.[38] Moreover, the very implausibility of these escapes (through the aid of prosthetic body parts, mobile walls, and assorted traps) and the complete lack of narrative preparation or privileged information on the part of the viewer make the notion of closure, in the sense of resolution, impossible.

The repetitive patterns bear some resemblance to the serial structure that Umberto Eco outlines in Eugène Sue's novel *Les mystères de Paris.* Rather than a "constant curve" of narrative where a variety of information is drawn closer and closer together until climax and resolution, *Les mystères'* (and *Fantômas's*) structure is a "sinusoidal," one of "tension, resolution, renewed tension, further resolution, and so on."[39] Also in this structure, a number of minor narratives weave in, out, and around a broad moral schema and larger narrative event, which itself has a circuitous trajectory[40] (e.g., in *Les mystères de Paris*, Rodolphe's vengeance of injustice and the construction of Rodolphe's ideal family, with his long-lost daughter Fleur-de-Marie and honorable new wife, Clémence).

However, while the structure of repetition and multiple story lines link *Les mystères de Paris* and *Fantômas* in the serial form, there are important differences. Perhaps most important, *Fantômas* does not have a unifying narrative event (e.g., Rodolphe's discovery that the abandoned street urchin Fleur-de-Marie is really his daughter, whom he believed dead); rather, the unifying material of the *Fantômas* series is largely abstract. In part the lack of unity takes us back to the question of character. For example, Sue's novel foregrounds and coheres around family relationships. To a certain extent we see an attention to family in the *Fantômas* novels by Allain and Souvestre, where the outlaw's daughter has an ongoing and important role in the narrative (but we find out, of course, that *Fantômas* may not be her true father and that he may have a long-lost son). But such familial ties are almost completely lacking in the film series. As Richard Abel notes with regard to *Les vampires*, the main villain (Irma Vep) seems to exist in the absence of any personal history, much like Fantômas.[41] The one consistent relationship throughout several of the episodes in the series is between Fantômas and Lady Beltham, but even that "attraction" is hard to comprehend. In *Juve contre Fantômas*, Lady Beltham begs Fantômas/Chaleck/Gurn to turn away from the life of crime and start over in some new place with her. Fantômas agrees but says he just wants to kill Juve first (a less-than-romantic response). By the next episode (*Le mort qui tue*), all such pretense has been dropped as Fantômas enlists Beltham's help in an extortion plot with the compelling information that he could easily have her killed if she refused to aid him. Thus, neither romance nor family provides cohesion to our narrative.

All the same, it might be argued that *Fantômas* coheres around an overarching moral schema: good pursues evil. But to go back to the series' repeated strategy of the introductory dissolves, it is not clear that we can identify good or evil solely through narrative events. Moreover, unlike the classic detective story or Sue's *Les mystères*, there is no unfolding of truth in *Fantômas*. The narratives are, in fact, singularly uninformative from the perspective of inductive or deductive reasoning. Events are not explained so much as revealed or simply presented to us as *faits accomplis*—although the manner of presentation and overall realist mise-en-scène (location shooting, detailed internal sets that are shot with an extreme depth of field) produce a certain logical effect. Indeed, the very genre of the detective story leads the viewer to anticipate that the story will have a certain coherence and order. But the solution of a crime or mystery in *Fantômas* is foremost a ruse, or rather a displacement, for an overall schema that circulates around problems of recognition and of knowledge. In this sense, it is the uncanny that provides the primary narrative drive.

The first episode in the series, simply titled *Fantômas* (May 1913), demonstrates several of these narrative traits. The episode is divided into three parts and separately labeled. After our introductory prologue of Navarre/Fantômas in character/disguise, the "story" begins. In the first section, "Le vol du Royal-Palace Hôtel," Princess Danidoff is robbed of a large sum of money, and the thief, as noted earlier, leaves his blank calling card (which later reveals that he is Fantômas). A bellboy is summoned by the cries of Princess Danidoff. Fantômas, seemingly trapped, overpowers the hotel employee and for good measure borrows his clothes as a disguise. Juve and Fandor, the detective and journalist on the trail of the criminal, are introduced examining the disposed disguise in their office.

The speed, unpredictability, and imminent reversibility of these events are underlined in the scenarios for the films. The scripts use the phrase "*au moment où*" ("just as" or literally, "at the moment when") repeatedly as a way not only to introduce an escape but often in conjunction with a narrative development, or more specifically, an abrupt shift in the anticipated direction of events. For example, the scenario for the opening episode reads as follows:

> She [the Princess] finds herself, just as ("*au moment où*") she is ready to go to bed, face to face with a man in evening dress, courteous but implacable, who threatens her, not verbally, but by the look in his eyes, to hand over the sum of money that she had just withdrawn ("*vient de retirer*").
>
> The princess must submit herself to him. Just as ("*au moment où*") the thief is going to leave, she runs to the phone in order to sound the alarm. Fantômas pushes her away and locks her up.[42]

At this point in the film and scenario, Princess Danidoff's role in the episode is complete, and she disappears until the third installation of the series (*Le mort qui tue*).

The scene now shifts to a drawing room (the second part of the episode is entitled "La disparition de Lord Beltham"), where a man and woman are in conversation. The couple leaves and Inspector Juve enters the room, noting a hat left on the table. When the woman reenters, Juve questions Lady Beltham about the disappearance of her husband. As part of the inquiry, she produces an address book, which Juve examines, and then he departs. The sequence is presented almost completely in long shot (with extreme depth of field). However, there are two important close-ups, cut-ins of clues leading to the missing Lord Beltham. But the close-ups do not fit the category of evidence as much as form a chain of signs. In the first close-up, the hat on the table has the initial G, which Juve links to the name "Gurn" in Lady Beltham's book (the second close-up). Gurn's apartment, in turn, produces the corpse of Lord Beltham. The trail reverses, and when Juve returns to Lady Beltham's, he finds and arrests her lover Gurn, who is, actually, Fantômas. Thus, while there is a relation among the elements involved, the logic that links them is incomplete and often tenuous—the scenario notes that Juve returns to Lady Beltham's home as the result of intuition.[43] With the arrest of Fantômas, the third part of the episode, "Autour de l'échafaud," begins. There is no further information on the circumstances surrounding the death of Lord Beltham (and Lady Beltham's role in the murder, for example), nor is there an account of Gurn's/Fantômas's trial. The story is centered on Lady Beltham's efforts to free her lover. In the only elaborate escape plot featured in the series (the rest are usually the product of some trick), Lady Beltham bribes several policemen in order to communicate with Fantômas in jail and, then, to arrange a meeting outside the prison for the couple.

The meeting is part of a larger effort to spring the criminal. There is, fortuitously, a stage play featuring the exploits of Fantômas, and Lady Beltham arranges a swap of the lead actor and the prisoner. It is again a photographic image that aids in the deception, for the actor uses a newspaper photo as a model for his costume and make-up. The police are easily confused by the disguise and return the "wrong" Fantômas (the actor, drugged) to jail. Among the authorities, only Juve recognizes the error, and he "unmasks" the actor, pulling off the disguise and declaring, "This man is not Fantômas!"

The episode then closes with a type of epilogue as the phantom presence torments Inspector Juve as he sits in his office. Fantômas offers himself for arrest, but as Juve rushes toward him, the ghost disappears. The episode ends, then, not with a cliff-hanger—as the Fantômas novels and serial films do[44]—but with an escape, which is precisely how the film opened (following the prologue). This structure is in place for all but one of the five episodes, episode 2, where we still have an escape, but with a cliff-hanger that carries over to the opening of episode 3 (the safety of Juve and Fandor is left in doubt after a building they are searching explodes).

The repetitive micronarratives featured in each of the episodes, with varying degrees of linkage between events, are then part of a larger structure of repetition and reversal, forming a type of recursive pattern founded on the question of uncertainty. While each of the episodes are based on the novels of Allain and Souvestre, and thus it might be argued that the notion of clarity and coherence comes from extratextual sources, it should be remembered that each of the novels feature four hundred pages of similarly repetitive and essentially unreconstructible narrative(s). Again, the element most likely retained by a reader of the novels (and films) is the notion of Fantômas as *"insaisissable"* (elusive) in an essentially nonterminable event. This sense of narrative circularity and infinitude is consistent with the mobility of the *Unheimliche*. As Cixous notes:

> "The prefix *Un* is the token of repression," says Freud. Let us add this: any analysis of the *Unheimliche* is in itself an *Un*, a mark of repression and the dangerous vibration of the *Heimliche*. *Unheimliche* is only the other side of the repetition of the *Heimliche* and this repetition is two faced: that which emerges and/is that which is repelled. The same is true for the text which pushes forth and repels until it reaches an arbitrary end. (The *Unheimliche* has no end, but it is necessary for the text to stop somewhere.) And this "conclusion" returns and passes as a recurrence and as a reserve.[45]

The emphasis in the serials is not on the end point, the seizure of Fantômas, but on the identification and tracking of the criminal. The focus of attention is not on a sequential revealing of information, and in this sense it is very different from the structure of the "fantastic" that Todorov describes with regard to literature. According to Todorov, the fantastic narrative must be read from beginning to end, and once read through—and the particular problem resolved (the event was the result of a dream or has a supernatural explanation)—uncertainty (and thus, the fantastic) is defeated.[46] But Feuillade's narratives remain fixed at the level of uncertainty, and repeated screenings do not "explain" previously unforeseen actions (or even narrative details). Nor is order of particular importance. To a certain extent, blocks from various episodes could be interchanged with little shift in continuity and coherence. This will be particularly true in Feuillade's next film series, *Les vampires*, where narrative "comprehension" would be affected little by massive reordering of episodes.

Without a solution, an endpoint, the episodes of *Fantômas* circulate endlessly; the focus is on movement, action, and a process of investigation. Hence, there is need for the narratives to examine each space closely. However, these explorations often serve multiple functions. For example, the city space, as noted earlier in the discussion of the zones of anxiety, is under suspicion, and there is an ongoing effort to survey and patrol the urban area right from the beginning of Feuillade's crime series. The lengthy shots through the Paris street scene and across the city's rooftops—used in both *Fantômas* and *Les vampires*—are part of this surveillance. At one level, these shots are tracking narrative action, but more broadly they can be seen as part of an investigatory gaze (the long take, the use of camera movement to follow an action) used to map urban instability. In *Le mort qui tue* (episode 3) this activity is foregrounded and doubled for us. The journalist, Fandor (Georges Melchior), is seen climbing over the rooftops in an effort to solve the Dollon mystery. Juve, now in disguise as a *clochard*, watches Fandor's actions from a nearby studio apartment. Throughout the sequence, we are presented with both Fandor's and the cinema's investigatory gaze (in the second instance, as seen through Juve's binocular vision). The repetitive use of the street/rooftop sequence in *Fantômas* and *Les vampires* performs a separate but equally important narrative function. Often unmotivated—it is not particularly clear in *Le mort qui tue* why Fandor is walking around on the roof—these sequences provide a pause and a link between bursts of activity. In some sense, it is possible to see these sorts of sequences as a physical marking out, or a sort of a bridge, between events in an episode.

Nonetheless, these bridges always return us to our starting point—the search for Fantômas and certainty about who may, in fact, be Fantômas. Each episode contains a narrative strand that develops the problem of misrecognition. There is an ongoing failure of friends, lovers, coworkers, and mortal enemies to recognize one another on the basis of physical data. As we recall, episode 4, *Fantômas contre Fantômas*, features an almost bewildering exchange of identities between the criminals and the law. At one point, the *apaches*, hoping to finally get their cut of some stolen loot, capture Juve in belief that he is Fantômas. Both Juve and Fantômas play on this misdirection. Fantômas, disguised as an American detective, Tom Bob, directs the police to the gang's hideout (conniving to keep the spoils himself). Meanwhile Juve, seeing the cops arrive, pronounces "Je suis Fantômas" and directs the gang into capture, telling them the police are merely other criminals in disguise.

In the *Fantômas* novel *Les amours d'un prince*, Juve tracks the character Jacques Bernard throughout a sequence, believing him to be Fantômas. However, Bernard, in reality, is Juve's partner, Fandor, and it is only in hearing Fandor's voice that this particular mystery is solved.[47] A variant of this is replayed in *Le mort qui tue* when Fandor, believing that Juve died in the blast at the end of episode 2, runs into a tramp in the street who seems familiar but is recognized only after hearing his voice (it is, of course, Juve). The crisis of knowledge in the novel, and Feuillade's crime films, is then particularly related to visual evidence—how to see, to locate, to represent the criminal figure.

Juve's relentless pursuit of the criminal moves through different parts of the cityscape and is curiously paralleled by a similar tracking of a seemingly ancillary character, Joséphine, by Fandor in *Juve contre Fantômas*. The *Fantômas* series contains only two women characters of any note: Joséphine and the recurring character of Lady Beltham (Princess Danidoff has a minor role, mainly as a robbery victim). And it is not without interest that they both share in the exploits of Fantômas, although both have very different criminal profiles.

Ann-Louise Shapiro has noted in her article "Love Stories: Female Crimes of Passion in Fin-de-Siècle Paris" that there was a real disparity at this time between the steady or even declining rate of actual crimes committed by women and the vastly expanded discussion of this phenomenon within the culture.[48] In no small part, Shapiro argues, this emphasis on the female criminal was linked to an emerging feminist movement and the phenomenon of the "new woman."[49]

A number of historians have pointed out that the late nineteenth century through World War I was a particularly critical moment in the development of French women's rights. Several legal decisions provided significant changes in women's status; 1884 saw a law reestablishing women's right to divorce and in 1907 married working women won the right to the full control of their own wages.[50] There was also an active suffrage movement and a vibrant feminist press (more than thirty publications were in existence between 1900 and 1914), and several international congresses organized around the topic of women's rights convened in Paris during this period (particularly heavily attended were the congresses held in 1900, 1907, and 1908).[51]

Running parallel to these political activities was a growing discussion in popular journals concerning the social threat posed by the *nouvelle femme*. The term was "invented" purportedly by the turn-of-the-century feminist press, and the discourse around the new woman became one of intense negotiation in a variety of national contexts as it migrated into mainstream usage, with multiple connotations vacillating between a figure of idealized morality and an "unattractive" and "unsexed" creature.[52] Debora L. Silverman notes that in France, the term *new woman* was used primarily to describe women who sought change within the domestic and professional arenas, that is, those women who rejected the traditional world of marriage and the family for a career. Like her sometimes distinct feminist counterpart, the new woman was essentially drawn from the middle class, but despite this background both groups of women posed a direct threat to bourgeois stability.[53] A parallel problem occurs with the middle-class female consumer. Vital to a new economic force and appealed to as purveyors of modern taste and beauty, the woman shopper was also seen as a disruptive force in that consumerism could dangerously lead to pleasure-seeking individuals distracted from the duties of the home.[54] Seemingly driven by self-gratification rather than disinterested selection, the woman consumer was frequently portrayed, Lisa Tiersten notes, as irrational, mercenary, and aligned with corruption. And of course, with this trajectory, it is but a short step from female consumer to prostitute.[55]

The modern woman, the career woman, the female shopper, and the working-class woman are all objects of interest but also distrust during the era. Working-class women were especially held in suspicion, with the domestic servant being particularly singled out as someone unreliable at best and more likely, criminal.[56] Thus, conflicts of gender and class work to escalate middle- and upper-class fears.

To return to Shapiro's discussion of the *femme criminelle* for a moment, a variant of the crime story began to emerge during this era as a response to the myriad levels of social disturbance—that is, the crime of passion. While Shapiro examines the complex ways these stories negotiate the crisis surrounding social and sexual instability, of particular interest to an examination of the crime serials of Feuillade is the notion Shapiro poses that a crime of passion became a mechanism to defuse the very issue of female criminality. That is to say, the woman criminal becomes "understandable," or more likely, "tolerable," once placed within the context of heterosexual romance and love. As Shapiro notes: "In establishing legitimacy of certain kinds of crimes of passion, underlining the powerlessness of deceived wives and abandoned mistresses, they promoted, above all, the restoration of the traditional family."[57] Shapiro points out that this idea, the "legitimacy of *certain kinds* of crimes of passion," is critical; that is, what is important are the "facts" behind a woman's crime. While a criminal act performed during a moment of uncontrollable emotions did have a type of romantic cachet, there was a sense of a distinction between appropriate and inappropriate passionate impulses. The woman's crime, according to the popular discourse of the era, should be contained by a desire to protect her family or social status, two arenas generally established by her relationship to a man. As Shapiro notes, during this period the belief was "the relationship was her life."[58] The crime of passion functions, then, as a type of legitimation of the traditional, bourgeois family structure.[59]

In addition, the woman criminal's particular emotional response came under scrutiny. There were, in effect, "normal" and "abnormal" labels attached to the affective impulses of the *femme criminelle:* the first emphasized despair, powerlessness, and general anguish, and the second, a more "vicious" and uncontrollable "fury."[60] *Fantômas*'s Lady Beltham—and her melodramatic performance style—fits easily into the first category. Her passivity, typified by slow movements or stasis that at times appears to border on paralysis, is broken only by large gestures signifying her angst over her affair/crimes with Fantômas. She is drawn again and again to the irresistible power of her lover. At one point in *Le mort qui tue,* Nanteuil/Fantômas tells her, "You know that your life is in my power and it is in your interest to submit yourself to my will."[61] In *Juve contre Fantômas* she flees to the sanctuary of a convent in order to escape Gurn's/Fantômas's control. The respite from evil is only temporary, however, and he wins her back simply by *telling* her who he is; as previously noted, she doesn't appear to recognize him in disguise. As the scenario notes, "She went to the rendezvous and again fell under the influence of a man from whom she wanted to flee."[62]

Her associations and activities with Fantômas are horrible but on

Lady Beltham (Renée Carl) can't say no to the *insaisissable* but irresistible Fantômas/Tom Bob (René Navarre) in *Fantômas contre Fantômas*, episode 4 of *Fantômas*. Louis Feuillade. © Production Gaumont, 1914.

some level understandable. At least she has the good sense and upbringing to feel and to demonstrate remorse over her actions. She is appalled by the sheer joy of Fantômas as he hears the scaffold being prepared for the unlucky actor, Valgrand. Beltham is hardly innocent in this instance, as she has seduced and drugged Valgrand in order to replace Gurn/Fantômas at his execution. Moreover, let us not forget that we are first introduced to Lady Beltham through the disappearance of her husband, who we later learn has been murdered (undoubtedly by her lover Gurn/Fantômas).[63] Lady Beltham does her best to stay away from Fantômas, but she is lured back time and again by love or explicit threat (and the distinction between the two is often unclear).

In contrast, neither Joséphine's (in *Fantômas*) nor Irma Vep's (later, in *Les vampires*) behavior can be defined as normal. Although it is not possible to label Joséphine as a whirlwind of anger and fury, there is something highly disturbing about her manner. In the scenario and film credits for *Juve contre Fantômas,* we see that Joséphine is known as *la pierreuse* (the streetwalker). Perhaps most troubling is that not only is there an absence of excessive emotion registered on the woman's face and body but Joséphine is able to move from "working girl" status to a persona of respectability with seeming ease. This confusion no doubt is enhanced by the increased affordability of goods with the rise of department stores and the appearance of the unchaperoned woman shopper throughout Paris.[64] Now, like Fantômas, the woman can hide the signs of her criminality. As Joséphine appears from a house Fandor has been staking out, the publicity booklet for the film states: "It was really Joséphine, but she was no longer the streetwalker; elegantly dressed, she was presenting, from the tip of her boots to the feather of her hat, the appearance of a respectable *petite bourgeois* woman."[65]

Her crime is then twofold. First, her actions, unlike Lady Beltham's, cannot be contained by the label of "a crime of passion," but they are villainous acts that escape the bounded explanations of female desire. Furthermore, her proximity to Fantômas, notwithstanding her literal textual isolation, with respect to issues of morality, mobility, and misrecognition, puts in danger the very notion of the woman criminal, or indeed, the woman as site of difference. If we remember Shapiro's point that the interest in female criminality far outweighed actual rates of women's criminal activity, then it is possible to see the effort to define clearly one category of criminals (i.e., woman) as part of a larger strategy to contain a crisis of social and sexual identity. The ongoing problems of recognition that circulate in Feuillade's texts suggest that it was not only the bourgeois family and heterosexual romance that were threatened but our very ability to make categorical judgments or definitional statements—at either the level of the psyche or the material world.

In contrast, Joséphine (Yvette Andreyor) appears in only one episode of the series, and although linked to Fantômas's criminal gang, she rarely appears onscreen with her colleagues. When she and Fantômas do occupy the same cinematic space, they quickly part company. In one instance, she meets Loupart/Fantômas on the street, but only to exchange a note and they then move off screen in separate directions. A robbery sequence of the Fantômas gang works in much the same fashion. Joséphine has enticed the wine merchant, M. Martialle, to travel with her by train, but this romantic escapade is really an ambush by Loupart and his cohorts. Again, as Loupart/Fantômas and

For Joséphine (Yvette Andreyor), there are "only parties and pleasures." *Juve contre Fantômas,* episode 2 of *Fantômas.* Louis Feuillade. © Production Gaumont, 1913.

the gang enter the train compartment for the crime, Joséphine exits—it is almost as if the screen cannot contain the presence of both these figures at the same time.

Although Joséphine's minimal screen time and physical separation from the central figure of the series seem to place her in a secondary position, Joséphine's very absence, movements, and exits haunt the text. One note seems to point to her romantic attachment to Fantômas ("dearest Loupart" the letter they exchange begins), but her actions throughout the film appear to point in another direction. As I trace her actions throughout the film, she enjoys her role in setting up a robbery, she celebrates a night on the town despite her date's drunken stupor, and finally, and most important, she reveals the location of Fantômas to Inspector Juve without much high-pressured persuasion. According to the publicity booklet accompanying the scenario, Joséphine tires of Fantômas and takes up with a rich American boxer who supports her in style: "There are only parties and pleasure."[66] In other words, Joséphine is a cold-hearted and calculated criminal—a double, if you will, of Fantômas. No wonder she is eased to the margins of the narrative. But the surface-level textual minimalization of Joséphine must be read in light of Fandor's tracking of her through the urban space. Her very mobility in the city is disturbing, particularly in contrast to the "respectable" Lady Beltham's stasis; Joséphine travels through the streets, into the metro, onto a commuter train, and out into the evening (she turns Fantômas over to Juve and Fandor at a nightclub, The Crocodile). The threat Joséphine poses to Fantômas and the definition (i.e., location) of the criminal activity and identity are such that the very place of the uncanny must shift ground in the next series, *Les vampires*. The uncanny alters its locus from the urban space and the enigmatic, elusive criminal to the domestic space and the criminal now figured in the body of the woman. Joséphine becomes the agent of this transition.

3 | "Qui? Quoi? Quand? Où?"
Interrogating Woman in *Les vampires* and *Judex*

> Again, the beautiful Olympia is effaced by what she represents, for Freud has no eyes for her. This woman appears obscene because she emerges there where one did not expect her to appear, and she thus causes Freud to take a detour. And what if the doll became a woman? What if she *were* alive? What if, in looking at her, we animated her?
>
>   Hélène Cixous, "Fiction and Its Phantoms"

Zone 2: Dislocating the Familiar

The recursive patterns of repetition and reversal are accelerated in Feuillade's next film series, *Les vampires* (1915–16), where the blocks of activities and number of characters significantly multiply in a seemingly random fashion. Over ten episodes, *Les vampires* follows the exploits of Philippe Guérande (Edouard Mathé), a young newspaper reporter, as he tracks the formidable criminal gang known as "the Vampires."[1] Philippe's ostensive role is to record the activities of the gang for the mass press, but his true function throughout the series is rather one of a private detective, aided in tracking the outlaws by Mazamette (Marcel Levesque), a former clerk for the journalist (and reformed Vampire). The police play more of a background role in this series; on occasion they follow up on Philippe's tips or complete an arrest. However, the real status of legal authority is demonstrated in the opening episode, when Philippe's pursuit of the gang is initiated by the decapitation of the police inspector. The journalist's "chase" continues for ten episodes as an endless parade of criminal figures and gangs wreck havoc on Paris and its outlying suburbs.

The tri-level chase structure seen one time in *Fantômas* (episode 4, *Fantômas contre Fantômas*) is a recurrent aspect of the narrative form in *Les vampires*. Episode 6, *Les yeux qui fascinent*, even contains a quad-level chase structure (three separate and competitive sets of criminal gangs and their pursuers, Philippe and Mazamette). In this instance, you have a narrative action within an episode that has four levels of repetition (with each chase almost functioning as a self-contained unit).

With each narrative repetition, you have a form of narrative movement; without some change in the story the narrative must come to an end. To put this another way, there is a displacement of anxiety from one object to another each time the narrative is repeated. If you examine the variations in the repetitions from *Fantômas* to *Les vampires*, it is possible to see that the shift in the object of anxiety becomes a type of literal *dis*-placement. The site of anxiety is now located in a physical place; that is, a particular referent is now fixed for the disturbance. Rather than the amorphous danger of indefinable criminality in the city space as seen in *Fantômas*, we will now have an ongoing movement toward a clearly demarcated threat, or rather, a highly particularized space identified as perilous. And this process of movement can be traced to an ever-intersecting crisis in personal and public space. As Annette Michelson has noted, the sense of a spatial "dis-location" in *Les vampires* is tied recurrently to issues of personal identity:

> Haussmann's pre-1914 Paris, the city of massive stone structures, of quiet avenues and squares, is suddenly revealed as everywhere dangerous, the scene and subject of secret designs. The trap door, secret compartment, false tunnel, false bottom, false ceiling, form an architectural complex with an architectural structure of middle-class culture. The perpetually recurring ritual of identification and self-justification is the presentation of the visiting card; it is, as well, the signal, the formal prelude to the fateful encounter, the swindle, hold-up, abduction or murder.[2]

Although these same issues are central to the structure of the narrative in *Fantômas*, I argue that it is the escalation and accumulation of these mininarratives in *Les vampires* that provoke the shift in the frightening object as the series unfolds. In other words, the crisis is such that a new object must be both recognizable and *recognizably different*. And the spatial location of the danger, suggested in the second episode of the series, *La bague qui tue* (The Ring which Kills), takes on an explicit placement in the following episode, *Le cryptogramme rouge* (The Red Cryptogram). But there are two levels of space that must be considered here in this discussion. First, there exists the substitution at the level of literal and metaphorical placement of the story: from the space of the city and the figure of the criminal (in *Fantômas*) to the space of the home and the body of the woman (in *Les vampires* and, later, *Judex*). The threat that circulates at the margins of the text in *Fantômas*—that is, the potential terror *embodied* in female criminality—will become explicit in these next two serials.

Second, there is particular narrative representation of space that mimics the series' temporal structure by its elliptical, catastrophic, and chaotic form. The uncanny of the cinematic apparatus is represented at the level of both narrative order and narrative space. These are characteristic structures of the mode of uncertainty.

In contrast, "classical" film narrative effaces manifestations of spatial discontinuity or the *Unheimliche,* and thus the movement between spaces in "classical" cinema is continuous and seemingly effortless.[3] For example, D. W. Griffith's film *The Lonely Villa* (1909) uses the match cut as a mechanism of effacement. In this film, a woman and her two daughters face onrushing robbers after the husband is sent away from the home by a false note. After a telephone warning, the husband returns to the home and saves the family from the robbers just before the completion of the break-in. In this case the match cut is used repeatedly, exactly at the point between interior and exterior spaces so that a seamless and continuous flow of movement between inside/outside spaces can occur.[4]

Ironically, this smooth transition occurs precisely at the site of the most extreme disjunction between spaces, both in terms of the narrative space (inside and outside the home) and the physical space of the film itself (the literal cuts within the film material). Here the device of the match cut (the cut and the linkages within an action) serves to smooth over the essential gaps in space and time necessary to shoot the film (that is to say, to set up the camera in two different spaces).

Feuillade's transitions between spaces are an inversion of this "classical" cinema form. The interstitial spaces between the frames, between the narrative sequences, are, rendered as present, made "visible" and even at times physically represented. In *Les vampires,* the viewer is presented not just with omniscient but also often impossible vision. For example, in episode 4, *Le spectre,* Juan-José Moréno (Fernand Hermann), a freelance criminal, has stored the body of a dead man—a corpse he found while casually walking along some railroad tracks—in his room's rather large safe. He needs the man's body to perfect a disguise that he will utilize in a bank fraud plot (a plot that, in fact, the Vampire gang has initiated separately from Moréno's involvement). The back wall of his safe, however, is not secure; a member of the Vampire gang, Irma Vep (Musidora), has the adjoining apartment and is able to access Moréno's safe. The demonstration of this scam within a scam—the Vampires are attempting to rob a fellow criminal, and Moréno is trying to reap the rewards of the Vampire's own plot against the bank—proceeds with a rather noteworthy representation of space. At one point in the story, Irma's door to the safe is opened and the body falls out into her room. The outer wall separating the viewer has been removed so that we have the ability to see both rooms simultaneously (an event that allows us to be in two separate spaces at once). Although the movement of the object surveyed is continuous, that is, we see the body move as it falls from Moréno's to Irma's apartment all in one take, the logic of our movement in space as viewers is somewhat disorienting in its simultaneity and ubiquity. This strategy, not an unusual one for early cinema, could be seen as an example of Feuillade's stylistic ties to the "attractions" or "primitive" era. Setting aside for a moment whether these serials represent a prior or distinct coterminous form to the classical model, a key point to note here is that the subject positioning constructed by continuity cinema is one of unity, a singular position that coheres as we move through time and space, while our early cinema/uncertainty variant asks a viewer to split across spaces simultaneously. However, alongside the dispersion of the viewer's/subject's position the overall representation of space in Feuillade, especially in *Fantômas* and *Les vampires* appears realistic and documentary-like through its use of deep space, static camera, minimal cut-ins, and few "trick" effects. Some critics have seen Feuillade's overall staging as consistent with an alternative French or European style (compared to the classical/American cinema).[5] But this alternative style also produces an alterity of vision. Ben Brewster notes that Feuillade's cut-ins create a fixity of viewpoint both through their minimal camera set-ups and cut-ins, which rarely change angle but travel along the same line of sight. The cut-ins are usually driven by what Brewster labels an "epistemophilia" and evidentiary presentation of clues.[6]

But precisely what is the status of the vision and knowledge incurred via the presentation of data? Repeatedly, the "documentation" is invoked to underline the *improbability* of what we are seeing. *Fantômas* shows us a glove made of human skin being easily removed from the master criminal's hand (*Le mort qui tue*), which serves as our "explanation" for a dead man's fingerprints at a robbery.

While these are sensational and crowd pleasing Grand Guignol–type flourishes in *Fantômas*, *Les vampires* revels in the spectacular display of a cinema of the impossible: a simple handshake turns diabolical as a poisoned tack in a glove produces temporary paralysis; a contorted cryptogram is quickly and inexplicably decoded; field-size cannons are wheeled about apartment rooms and fired out the windows with pinpoint accuracy on nightclubs and even a *moving* steamship (this last event saves Irma Vep from a police-imposed exile).

The improbability continues with a repetitive formula organized around a catastrophic fall that seems to be invoked at least once during each of the ten episodes of the series. Episode 6, *Les yeux qui fascinent*, demonstrates the basic blueprint for the plunge (with some minor variations) when Irma is kidnapped by Moréno. He takes her immobile body—he had the foresight to hypnotize the troublesome Vep—to the window and abruptly hurls it out of the upper-story hotel. We are trapped momentarily in the inside space until an abrupt cut frees us to look on the other/outside. The body, well in the process of falling, is awaited on the sidewalk below by Moréno's cohorts, who are "armed" with a blanket.

They catch the plummeting body shortly after we arrive on the scene, and the overall effect is a strange mix of shock, terror, and comedy. The comedy, of course, is not only the defeat of logic with this ultimately "harmless" fall—the delay in the cut, which functions as a type of narrative ellipsis, forces us to fill in the detail of the story, the crash to earth of the body, and then at the last minute, removes this imagined image from us—but also our repeated assumption, as viewers, that the "rational" world will stabilize Feuillade's films.

A variant of this comedic/horrific turn will be found in Feuillade's later serial, *Tih Minh*, when bandits throw the heroine, Tih Minh (Mary Harald), over a wall, which she somehow manages to latch onto in her fall. We are then given an extreme long shot to provide us with a sense of the distance Tih Minh will plunge, and then a cut-in to a medium shot shows Tih Minh clinging to the wall (shot from the back of the wall). Next, there is a brief cut to Jacques d'Athys (René Cresté), and as the hero begins to move over the wall to rescue her, a title card interrupts the action: "Someone arrived who wasn't expected" (*arrivait quelqu'un qu'on n'attendait pas*). In long shot we return to the base of the wall, where Delorès (Georgette Faraboni) is wandering down the street (in a semi-hypnotic trance), then a cut back to Jacques's rescue efforts, and with his movement over the wall, a cut to a long shot of an object falling with Delorès in the frame waiting below, fortuitously gazing upward (she is, after all, according to an earlier title an "extraordinary clairvoyant"). The fall/rescue is then completed in long shot by Delorès's agile reception of Tih Minh's body. These shock cuts produce a frightening movement of the body through space and are frequently, although not exclusively, visited upon the female body. The overlap of visual style and narrative form underline the larger narrative structures (i.e., the zones of anxiety). *Les vampires'* young journalist, Philippe, must endure a tumble out of an upper-story window, a fall down a flight of stairs, and several kidnappings, but it is clear that the favored site of physical movement, in its most terrifying iterations, during this series and the next three which follow it (*Judex, La nouvelle mission de Judex,* and *Tih Minh*), is generally speaking the woman's body. At one point (episode 10, *Les noces sanglantes,*), Irma Vep escapes from the police by rolling a rope around her waist and then literally unraveling the bundle of rope (and herself) down the side of a tall building. These extravagant movements enable us to move the literal site of narrative, close off a particular narrative action, and initiate the next narrative strand. This is increasingly true as the serials progress from *Les vampires,* and, as we will see in *Tih Minh,* the sole narrative drive appears at times to be the ongoing exchange of the lead woman's body, Tih Minh, between the criminals and her family.

It is in this context that I want to examine one of the film posters used to advertise Feuillade's *Les vampires*. The caption beneath the image asked "*Qui? Quoi? Quand? Où?*" but the information produced by these questions of "who, what, when, where" are framed by, or perhaps more accurately here, *frames* the female body. The original poster features a caricature of the film's female villain, Irma Vep, in triplicate (i.e., there are three panels with the same image and series of questions repeated). A point of interrogation grips the neck of the black-hooded woman. The face is completely covered, and our primary clue to an understanding of the masked character is immediately linked to markers of sexual difference, in this instance, the woman's eyes—long, dark eyelashes, thin eyebrows with a wide-eyed, trancelike gaze.

While on one level the sequence of questions is consistent with the genres of detective fiction and the *roman-feuilleton,* it also places the investigation within the journalistic context of the *faits divers,* or tabloid news story. Moreover, the newspapers of the era at times conflated the arenas of fiction and fact. Two examples from *Le Matin*—the newspaper that will carry a serialized version of *Les mystères de New York,*[7] the Pathé competitor to Gaumont's *Les vampires*—demonstrate this process. First, the same page of the November 8, 1915, issue featured *Le roi*

Uncertainty encircles the female body in *Les vampires*. Louis Feuillade. Poster for the film series. © Production Gaumont, 1915–16.

des cuistots, (a serialized novel) and a "factual" account of the activities of an organized gang ("Les exploits d'une bande organisée"). The news story recounts the adventures of a police commissioner and his associate as they trail a band of international jewel thieves. Moreover, the account shares the language and pace that we have seen in the *Fantômas* novels and films: "The trail of the individual [the suspect] was regained, and just as ["au moment où"] he was leaving from a bar at the rue Beaumarchais, the inspectors Pouce and Irmengaud apprehended him."[8]

A second example shows the crossover between the *faits divers* and fiction more clearly. The story, "La mystérieuse châtelaine" (The Mysterious Lady of the Manor), reads like a crime serial narrative, with its use of false identities, elaborate scams, and mild erotica (it even mimics the cliff-hanger structure of the *roman-feuilleton* with a conclusion that promises "to be continued" in the next day's edition). It recounts the arrest of a woman con artist who has been "living under the name" of Mme Duprez. But an exploration of Mme Duprez's past revealed numerous aliases and fictional family histories, which were utilized by the woman to reside in several luxurious locations without payment. In one instance, she explained her unescorted status as a product of the war—her husband, an officer in the army, was staying with his family in order to recover from his battle wounds. Perhaps more scandalously, in her "husband's" absence she had installed another young officer in her household, falsely introducing the man as her cousin. As if this information were not sordid enough, we also learn that the "cousin" was the son of an "honorable" magistrate and that, moreover, Duprez was able to extort a sum of money from the young man before his departure.[9]

Both examples are indicative of the preoccupation of the era with identity specific to the war years. The construction of the individual noted in the last chapter is now overlaid with a specifically defined morality based on nationality, sexuality, ethnicity, and even religion. It is not inconsequential that in the first example the criminals are demarcated as "foreigners." Closer examination of the text reveals that the suspect arrested was not simply foreign but, more specifically, was a regular client of neighborhood establishments typically frequented by Polish Jews.[10] Certainly, the First World War created a climate of fear and distrust (the November 7 issue contains propaganda inserts warning the readers about spies overhearing valuable information),[11] but this example also resonates with the anti-Semitism of turn-of-the-century

France. It also points to a more general turn away from a burgeoning and institutionalized secular culture in France to a reinstitution of Church authority. Unspoken, but surely present in this account, is a distrust of ethnic and religious differences, one of the important factors contributing to the war. Many French conservatives saw World War I as a kind of "holy war" against German materialism and scientism with a strong link made by many between German *Kultur* and militarism.[12] For one religious writer, Léon Bloy, the stakes are clear:

> A nation arose in the nineteenth and twentieth centuries to undertake what has never been seen before since the dawn of history: the extinction of souls. This is known as German culture.
>
> To degrade and debase souls was no longer enough for the Prince of Darkness. He had to annihilate them, and this he achieved. Prussianized Germany was no longer part of humanity. It became a great savage beast, and threatened the whole world. . . . God grant that this book may comfort . . . a few friends of God, a few rare and suffering bearers of that Christian Grandeur and Beauty which they wish to eliminate.[13]

Other religious thinkers had an even more radical assessment; the war was punishment from God to the French for their secular trends with the movement toward republicanism.[14]

The second example is a version of the *femme criminelle* with a war theme. In *La mystérieuse châtelaine,* Mme Duprez mocks not only matrimony but also, less explicitly, patriotism (e.g., her faux husband nursing his war wounds; one of her victims is an officer and judge's son). From all political perspectives during this era, the woman's body was territory to be disputed and claimed. Of particular importance was the significant change in women's education beginning in 1880 with the passage of the Carolyn See law, which proscribed not only more advanced education but provided state support as well.[15] As Debora L. Silverman argues, this development had an important dual impact. It opened up new and diverse professional opportunities for women and, perhaps more important, worked to undermine the Church's impact on the Third Republic, for the state-sponsored education was decidedly secular.[16]

Women working outside the home were already a significant part of France's economy prior to World War I, making up some 35 to 40 percent of the labor force, which was one of the highest percentages in Europe according to Jean Louis Robert. Moreover, the kinds of employment for women changed as well. Women moved into more nontraditional careers like transportation and manufacturing, and the numbers of females working in textiles and clothing faded. While the numbers in industry escalated as might be expected with the war, the trend of women's increased participation in these nonconventional sectors was already established *well before* World War I.[17] With the end of the war, there is a push toward more traditional roles for women and an aggressive pro-natalist policy,[18] but there were still a large number of women working outside the home, especially in the "white collar" and clerical professions.[19] The enhanced economic opportunities for women combined with the "modernized" divorce laws (1884) enabled women to instigate a divorce.[20] Certainly after World War I, the notion of marriage and family became central to the popular discourse surrounding female sexuality, but the excitement and fears over the *femme nouvelle* and even pro-natalist rhetoric had been well established by the 1890s.[21] Already by the turn of the century, the woman's role was a highly contested space: "The *femme nouvelle*, a middle class woman seeking independence and education rather than marriage and life at home, thus made her claims in a context where maternity and family were issues fraught with special political and national significance."[22]

Working-class women were especially held in suspicion, with the domestic servant being particularly singled out as someone unreliable at best and more likely, criminal.[23] It is Irma Vep's intrusion (in episode 3, *Le cryptogramme rouge*) into the Guérande's household under the guise of a replacement servant that represents the first disturbance of domestic space in the series. Philippe, his mother, and later his wife, will no longer be safe in their home. Moreover, while criminal acts were situated within a *private* space in the previous *Fantômas* series—for example, the attack on the artist, Dollon, in his study (episode 3, *Le mort qui tue*) and Lady Beltham's encounters with her lover, Fantômas, under a variety of intimate settings—the sense that the private, domestic space of the home, as the physical *site* of the bourgeois family, is more explicitly violated in *Les vampires*. The serials that follow *Les vampires* (*Judex*, *La nouvelle mission de Judex*, *Tih Minh*, and *Barrabas*) in turn narrativize the threat to domestic space with a shift to a melodramatic overarching structure, thereby following even more closely the narrative patterns discussed with respect to *Les mystères de Paris* and the *roman-feuilleton*.

But let us remember that the middle-class woman was the main "site" of the modern woman and thus her behavior is also under suspicion. Episode 7 of *Les vampires, Satanas*, links the two groups explicitly. A woman reporter (thereby registering a certain class "equality" with Philippe) from the *Femme Moderne* journal has come to interview George Baldwin, an American millionaire. The reporter is a member of the Vampire gang, and the interview is simply a ruse to gain Baldwin's signature. As she leaves, another woman enters the American's hotel room; it is Irma Vep "selling" phonograph equipment. She gets a record of his voice—a second essential component of an elaborate bank scam the bandits have planned. The scheme is then completed by Irma's entry into the workplace as a telephone operator; she relays Baldwin's recorded voice to the bank to ensure the fraudulent transaction. While this episode brings the middle-class woman into the suspicions surrounding the modern woman, perhaps equally troubling is Irma's mobility through a trajectory of roles across class lines (from journalist to clerical worker).

Thus, this representation of female criminality, too dangerous for the *Fantômas* series, shifts ground with the *Vampires* series. The unlawful woman must become recognizable, if not in the manner of Lady Beltham's melodramatic anguish, then with some other type of unambiguous sign. Moreover, the text moves to redefine the engine of disturbance and dislocation. That is to say, the representation of criminality as specifically *female* literally takes center stage with the introduction of the actress Musidora as Irma Vep in *Les vampires*. Irma's onstage performance is merely a front for the backstage plotting of the Vampire gang, just as her name, "Irma Vep," is a disguise, an anagram for "vampire." This initial presentation of the character is appropriate, as Irma goes through a variety of disguises/aliases in the series, and each of her criminal acts seems to necessitate a new role for Irma.

The use of the cabaret performance space in Irma's introduction runs curiously parallel to a scene in the previous episode. In *La bague qui tue* (episode 2), we are presented with Philippe's fiancée, Marfa (Stacia Napierkowsa), performing on stage in the Vampires' burglary costume—the black bodysuit. Like the first episode in the *Fantômas* series, the theatrical presentation of criminality suggests the public's fascination with these figures, and Marfa's performance points to the shift in presentation in the texts from a male to a female criminal. However, Marfa is the lead dancer for a ballet about the gang, and thus even beyond the bodysuit, her performance, unlike the theater, must be

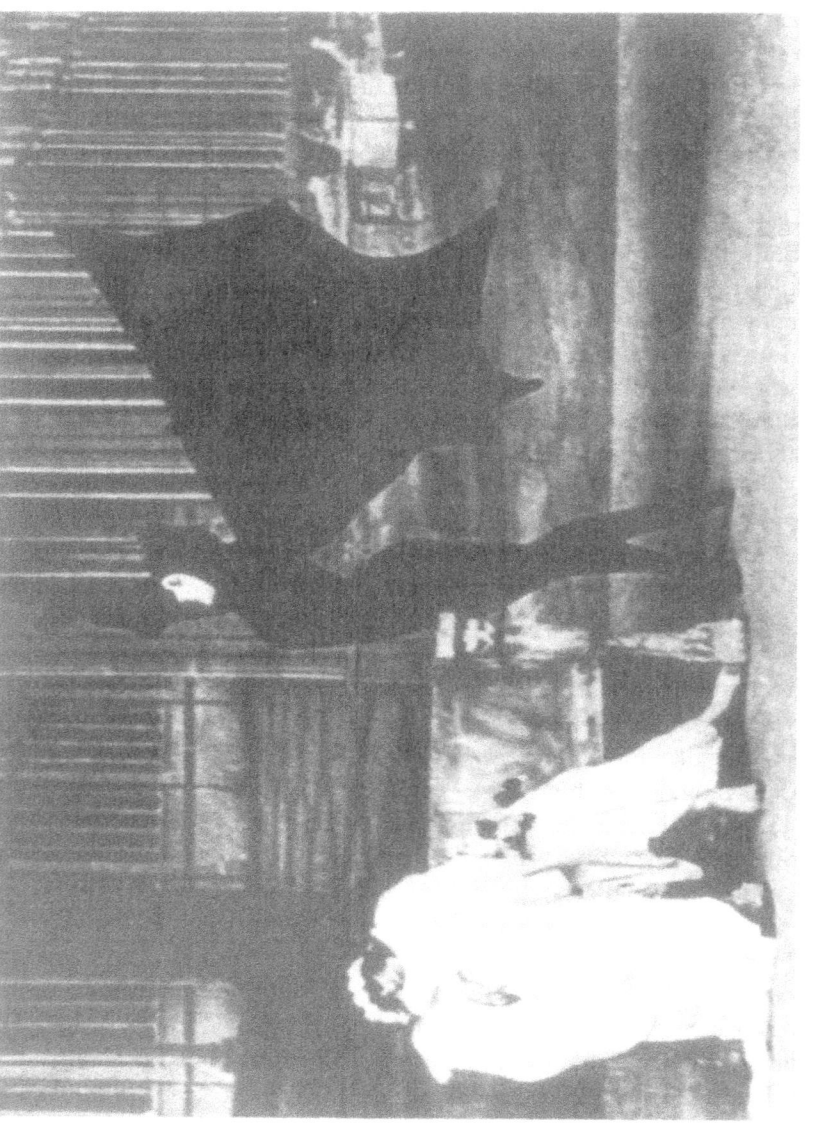

Philippe Guérande's fiancée, Marfa (Stacia Napierkowska), performs as the menacing female vampire and then dies onstage in *Le bague qui tue*, episode 2 of *Les vampires*. Louis Feuillade. © Production Gaumont, 1915.

solely driven by specific physical or external signs (i.e., the movement of her body rather than spoken language). The ballet suggests that signs of the woman's body—as figured in this black suit—are the signs of criminality. As we watch her performance in an extreme long shot, Marfa weakens in the middle of her dance (she has been poisoned by the Grand Vampire) and then collapses just as her character begins to envelope a sleeping *woman* with her cape. Marfa's "fictional" crime is denied a representation to the theater and film spectator. She thus dies "innocent," and Philippe's fiancée is rescued from any sexually ambivalent, or homoerotic, taint.

Irma's appearance in the next episode provides a point of contrast. Philippe's first encounter with the sinister criminal is through an *image* of her on a poster outside a cabaret, which announces her performance. It is here that Philippe sees that the name Irma Vep is in fact an anagram for vampire (the screen helpfully arranges the letters for us). Now the woman on stage, after a brief long shot introduction of the performer and cabaret setting, is seen in close-up.[24] Unlike the dancer's graceful and fluid movements, the focus is on Irma aggressively barking out a song to her cohorts. Her face pale, her eyes and lips darkened to exaggerate their size, Irma presents us with the clear signs of Shapiro's "vicious" and "uncontrollable" *femme criminelle*. However, more troubling perhaps is that this representation takes place *on stage*, thus warning of Irma's talent for performance. The mutability of Fantômas has now been transferred to a woman who can "act" any role.

As we take note of Musidora's star image through *Les vampires* and her next Feuillade serial, *Judex* (as Diana Monti), there will be a shift in emphasis with regard to her role; that is, as the films progress, Musidora/Irma/Diana will become the central figure of crime and evil. It is true that in *Les vampires* Irma is linked "romantically" with the various male leaders of the gang, and she does carry out their dictates with speed and pleasure. However, the frequent change of leadership and her ability to quickly realign her romantic attachments suggest that Irma's emotional investments in the leaders are primarily founded on expediency and self-interest. Thus, it is less out of "love" and more out of criminal *desire* (like Joséphine) that Irma participates in a variety of misdeeds/affairs. The disturbance of the heterosexual monogamous couple that Philippe's fiancée, Marfa, initiated is pursued relentlessly by Musidora through her multiple dalliances, murderous acts directed toward other couples (including her own lover), and, just for good measure, cross-dressing as her lover's son.

Irma Vep (Musidora) and Moréno (Fernand Hermann) in *Les yeux qui fascinent*, episode 6 of *Les vampires*. Louis Feuillade. © Production Gaumont, 1916

The one instance of a sexual/criminal liaison outside of her "control" is really the product of a ruse: she is chloroformed and then hypnotized by the thief Moréno (episode 6, *Les yeux qui fascinent*). Here, Irma's romantic interest and allegiance are dependent upon a male trick, not attraction. Moreover, if we take into consideration the extrafilmic materials surrounding *Les vampires*—the novelization of the series by Georges Meirs (with Feuillade receiving a coauthor credit, although he did not participate in the novelization)—then we will see that Moréno considers himself the hostage. His "capture" is tied to the fascinating quality of Irma's enormous black eyes; the one who hypnotizes has been, in effect, himself hypnotized: "He had believed only to have taken a hostage, and *voilà* it was he, in turn, who was prisoner. . . . Prisoner of beautiful large black eyes, of these eyes hypnotizing and disturbing that he had never encountered without excitement, even when a fierce hostility darkened the fascinating gaze."[25]

Moreover, Irma's response to Moréno after he confesses his love and asks her to stay with him is quite unsettling; she says simply, "why not" (*pourquoi pas*),[26] and she quickly agrees to kill her boss and lover, the Grand Vampire, in conjunction with her new romance and gang alliance. The ease with which Irma disposes of her prior criminal and sexual union is remarkable, as the novelization describes the Grand Vampire with rather Zeus-like powers: "Irma Vep! The name blazed before his eyes, this name that he [the Grand Vampire] had created, as he had created the woman."[27] Without much regard for sentiment, Irma dispatches what little there is of her "creation" or past (the Grand Vampire raised the foundling [*un enfant trouvée*])[28] and like Fantômas before her is now a complete emotional cipher, a shadowy figure, a blank character. This complicates our reading of the episode's title, *The Eyes which Hypnotize* (*Les yeux qui fascinent*), many times over. It is ambiguous precisely *whose* eyes the title is referencing even beyond Moréno's, and now an additional question must be posed: who is Irma?

Musidora is perhaps best known for her costume from *Les vampires*—a skintight black bodysuit—and almost every image or article about her features this attire. Of course, Irma Vep was not the first character in black tights on the early cinema screen (as we already know from *Fantômas*). But perhaps somewhat surprising, Musidora is not even the first actress to be costumed as such. Musidora's outfit was, in fact, preceded by one worn by Josette Andriot in the series *Protéa* (1913–19; directors of the series included Jasset, Faivre, Bourgeois, and Renaud).[29] Andriot was a rather large and unusually athletic woman, known primarily for her work in action/adventure films. Before her work in *Protéa*, she played the accomplice of the bandit Zigomar (another Jasset series mentioned previously). Her function in both cases, once again, was to represent the active and unfettered *femme nouvelle* of the modern world.

Andriot's representation of the new woman was not, however, identical to the one offered by the image of Musidora. One key difference might be found in the type of costume used by the two women. While both women wear black bodysuits/tights, Musidora herself has pointed out that Andriot's costume is made of cotton.[30] Cotton, being a flexible, practical material, emphasizes the athletic dimension of Andriot's activities. However, in the case of Musidora, her *maillot de soie* (silk bodysuit) is more suited to erotic adventures. As her biographer, Patrick Cazals, notes, Musidora's silk outfit presented "a figure more graceful and better accentuated."³¹ Although Musidora's use of the bodysuit was limited on film (supposedly only fifteen minutes of *Les vampires'* ten episodes features Musidora dressed in this fashion),³² it is this image that springs to mind when one hears the name Musidora.

The discourse surrounding the bodysuit often takes on rather fevered rhetorical flourishes. *Ciné-Mondial*'s introduction to Musidora's series of essays on her early film work includes the comment that the actress's all-black costume was a "beautiful transparent silk bodysuit."³³ Or as one critic explained more explicitly, "She had her nude body tightly gloved in black, which swayed in the nights of our adolescence as an enormous and delicate butterfly."³⁴ This commentary was echoed by yet another writer carried away by the "vision" of the actress, who noted that Musidora/Irma was a "catlike character, nude under her tights."³⁵

Musidora, as one might expect, was both amused and annoyed by the response to her outfit. She named one of her own stage plays *Le maillot noir*³⁶ but later decided to mock the obsession with the outfit by appearing in a flesh-colored version of the costume in a piece entitled *The Last Exploit of the Vampire.*³⁷

Paralleling this attention to the figure of the woman's body in *Les vampires* is an ongoing discourse about the eyes of Musidora. In one article Musidora wrote about her career, she recounts a gunpowder burn as a result of a neophyte actress firing a weapon at too close a range. She notes that she was fortunate that her eyes were not permanently damaged, as they were essentially her most important attribute on the screen. After reassuring her colleague she was all right, Musidora pointed out, "My eyes. . . . They're how I make my living now."³⁸ One early film journal, *Cinémagazine,* rhapsodizes over the star figure, again with a particular focus on Musidora's eyes: "Her voice sings and chants, her golden halo gives her a Madonna-like look, and her beautiful eyes, her large eyes, so intelligent are proof that one is in the presence of an intellectual, a young woman who, an artist to the tip of her fingers, can only use her grand talent to the constant progress of the cinematic art form, of which she was from the start, one of its most applauded stars."³⁹

The intense interest in Musidora's eyes is replicated at several textual levels in *Les vampires.* I have noted the attention given in the film poster, the character's introduction, and indeed, the episode title, *The Eyes which Hypnotize.* In addition, there are two extratextual sources, from the novelization of the series, that point to Philippe's recognition of Irma (in disguise) solely from her eyes (or by the look of her gaze).⁴⁰ In one instance in the volume *Le spectre,* the text describes the bandit: "There was no mistaking it. You know the admirable eyes of Irma; the eyes immense like lakes of light and of shadow at the same time, these disturbing eyes, enchanting, profound, which she uses with an incomparable mastery; oh yes, eyes like these, there are not two pairs in the whole world!"⁴¹

The focus on Musidora's body and eyes suggests a strategy to emphasize the difference in the body of the woman. But as has been noted, this difference can produce an uncanny effect in that, to the extent that the body of the woman might stand in for castration anxiety, this "representation" is, in essence, also trapped within the space of the "non-representable." Woman, rather than providing reassuring certitude, escalates and infinitely repeats the very uncertainty the female body is invoked to control, hence the ongoing need to fetishize the figure of the woman through the bodysuit and her "hypnotic" eyes. The absence of character and the black bodysuit traversing the frame like a moving reversal screen both point back to Irma's remarkable talent for performance. In the novelization, Philippe notes that by Irma masquerading as the new maid, Anne-Marie, she has not only taken on the disguise of a domestic servant but in effect has shed her own past (or other persona, we do not know). She was even able to

> exchange the atrocious suburban accent she had while singing at the *Chat Huant* for this other, which would make one swear she had never left her village of Brittany.
>
> What an act! And how this woman admirably filled the two roles so different in which I saw her.⁴²

A last textual clue from *Les vampires* perhaps reveals more concerning the fascination and fear associated with the star persona of Musidora. In a particularly "uncanny" turn, Irma, disguised as the newly arrived maid in the Guérande household, dusts the furniture in Philippe's room. Unenthusiastically carrying out her servant duties, she suddenly sees a photograph of Philippe's deceased fiancée, Marfa, on his desk. Irma regards the photo with a look of horror and shock. She appears to recognize the image, but significantly there is no textual reference for this response: that is, Irma and Marfa never encounter each other on-screen. It is not clear *how* she knows Marfa.

If we go to the extratextual materials subsequent to the film's release, we learn more about Marfa. In a conversation backstage with her dresser, Marfa discovers that she is reading the novel *Les mystèrieux drames de la maison du bourreau,* a book very much like *Les vampires.* The conversation between the two women goes as follows:

> [The dresser] "Oh, there are adventures there, and crimes, disappearances, and there is also love, and passion. Ah, that's good stuff there, mademoiselle."
> [Marfa] "Love, passion!" murmured the dancer sliding on a long divan which took up one side of the dressing room, "Yes, that must be sweet, very sweet."[43]

Shortly after Marfa's comments, she goes onstage to her performance and destiny—dying as she begins to embrace another woman's body. Perhaps this is what Irma later recognizes—the unspoken desire of woman and the punishment that must come with its performance. Marfa and Irma are doubled, a twin representation of the inability to contain, to define, woman's desire. The consequences of their desire invariably lead to another recursive chain of pursuit and death.

The use of fetish objects in *Les vampires* becomes one strategy in the effort to establish a *physical* place for anxiety. Once it is established as Irma, the text can then utilize a variety of mechanisms to ameliorate or, more typically, eliminate the threat. Another line of attack against the menace of anxiety is the text's creation of an alternative model or place for woman. Philippe's new fiancée, Jane (Louise Lagrange), appears from seemingly nowhere at the beginning of episode 9 (*L'homme des poisons*); her arrival holds out the promise of a more docile domestic space. Irma, returning from exile, immediately recognizes what is at stake and decides—with her new lover and Vampire chief, Venenos (Moriss)—to murder Philippe and Jane at their engagement party. Their plot fails, although they do manage to poison the concierge, with whose widow, Augustine, Mazamette will now be smitten.

Undeterred, the gang tries poison gas (a hypnotized Augustine has let Irma and Venenos into the Guerande home), an effort that fails but which is quickly followed by Jane and then Augustine's kidnapping by the Vampire gang. In hot pursuit, Philippe and the police close in on Irma and Venenos's hideout and lab for assembling assorted poisons. The Vampire leaders stage a spectacular escape, complete with an explosion and daring rope descents from their upper-floor lair. Afterward, Venenos and Irma decide that *they* should marry and throw a wedding celebration, which is the antithesis of middle-class reserve and respectability (complete with *apache* dances, quick-sketch artistry, and firearm tricks). The pure energy and unchained desire on display at Irma and Venenos's wedding party is quickly curtailed by a police raid (led by Philippe and Mazamette, naturally) that ends with the death or capture of all the Vampires . . . except Irma. The vengeful and resilent Irma decides to finish off Jane and Augustine, who are being held in a cell below the Vampire festivities. Irma pulls a gun on the two women but is shot by Philippe's new bride when she turns her back.

Only with Irma's death at the end of the series can a resolution of the narrative as domestic bliss take place. Earlier in the series, episode 5 closes with Philippe and Mazamette being outmaneuvered once again by the Vampire gang. Philippe turns to his discouraged cohort and quotes a fable by La Fontaine: "In all things one must consider the end." The Vampire fable ends not only with the defeat of female desire uncontained by heterosexual monogamy but, equally important, this desire is replaced by an alternative model of femininity based on marriage and the family. In a last act of repetition and gesture toward finality (if not certitude), the resolution is actually doubled—that is, Irma's death is followed by the formation of not one but two couples through marriage, as Mazamette and Augustine also wed.

Judex

> One can say that all the fundamentals of our world have been affected by the war, or more exactly, by the circumstances of the war; something deeper has been worn away than the renewable parts of the machine. You know how greatly the general economic situation has been disturbed, and the polity of the states, and the very life of the individual; you are familiar with the universal discomfort, hesitation, apprehension. But among all these injured things is the Mind. The Mind has indeed been cruelly wounded; its complaint is heard in the hearts of intellectual men; it passes a mournful judgment on itself. It doubts itself profoundly.[44]

Paul Valéry's comments on World War I are suggestive of the increased insecurity and uncertainty during and immediately following the war years. The profound cultural upheaval begun in the mid- to late nineteenth century is exacerbated by the trauma of the conflict. Already in *Les vampires* we can see direct traces of the war's effects, for example, in the often abrupt and brutal deaths of characters or in the implementation of new technology and weaponry (e.g., the repeated use of poison gas, the mobile and accurate cannon).

But the sheer numbers of wartime losses, coupled with the war against German *Kultur* noted earlier, produced a climate of increasing political conservatism in France that will be explicitly detailed and narrativized in Feuillade's next serial, *Judex,* shown in twelve weekly installments from January 19 to April 7, 1917.[45] Michelle Perrot argues that World War I provided a venue, through its invocation of traditional values (family, nation, patriarchy), to contain troubling shifts in gender boundaries.[46] Of particular importance was the role of the family to the *union sacrée,* and women were encouraged—even by parts of the feminist press—to reproduce for the glory of country. In 1915, *Le féminisme intégrale* pronounced the need for women to produce "children, lots of children to fill the gaps."[47]

Judex proposes a rather hybrid text for this context, blending elements from the mode of the fantastic and from melodrama. In effect, we are presented with the home-front "war" over femininity via the strategy of the double: a central character who personifies the *femme criminelle,* Diana Monti (Musidora), and her counterpart, the angelic and long-suffering widow, Jacqueline Favraux (Yvette Andreyor). Ostensibly the story is of Judex's revenge and punishment of the banker Favraux (Louis Leubas), a financial swindler whose destructive dealings ruin countless families. More particularly, Judex seeks to avenge the suicide of one Comte de Trémeuse (who is in fact, Judex's father, the justice figure's real name being Jacques de Trémeuse). However, this story of revenge serves as but a pretext for an examination of the film's *true* villain, Diana. In fact, Judex (René Cresté) has managed to have Favraux poisoned and locked up in the basement of his château in rather short order (soon after the prologue). For the rest of the film, whenever a crime is committed, we know that Diana has undoubtedly instigated the act. There is even now a reversal on the "crime of passion" scenario. At one point, the reluctant and temporarily reformed bandit Moralès (Jean Devalde) is presented by his father, Kerjean (Gaston Michel), to Judex with the following introduction: "Here's my son that a wicked woman [i.e., his cohort, Diana Monti] has pushed to the abyss."

With the focus of criminality shifted to the spectre of woman, the location of the crime series moves as well, from the urban space to the home and countryside. The provincial locale makes explicit the threat to the family and a past way of life. In turn, the hero, Judex, must negotiate a seemingly endless array of contradictions, between past and present, individual and family, city and country, modern and ancient. Judex exudes not only a clearly romantic notion of virtue but also champions contemporary justice within an aristocratic setting. He rides to the rescue of Jacqueline on horseback accompanied by his pack of trained dogs, and he imprisons Favraux in a remote château that features the latest panoptic devices of control. Judex employs a mobile mirror to follow the prisoner and allow for full-time surveillance from a distant lab. From this same lab, the figure of vengeance can also send out ominous messages of condemnation from a typewriter that "writes in fire," and these pronouncements magically appear in Favraux's cell.

Several story lines—Kerjean's discovery of his long-lost son, Judex's revenge of his father's personal and financial humiliation and suicide, Jacqueline's and Favraux's separation (not to mention the various kidnappings that separate Jacqueline and her son, Jean)—function to place one layer of the action within the domain of the family, thereby providing the narrative with a melodramatic overarching structure. But alongside this larger narrative trajectory, we still see elements of the fantastic. While it is true that there is less chaos and ellipsis in the *Judex* narrative form, the sheer number of repetitions (through the mechanism of the kidnapping) and the excessive attention to "minor" characters in the text (e.g., "*le môme* Réglisse's," Cocantin's, and Daisy Torp's stories) continue the pattern of temporal disruption and repetition discussed earlier. These seemingly superfluous stories are, in fact, a mechanism to prolong and even derail the narrative and to provide minor variations on the larger narrative form. That is, Cocantin's, Réglisse's, and Daisy's stories will finally intersect as they form a family unit, thereby paralleling and delaying (through the narration of this variation) the union of Jacques, Jacqueline, and Jean.

Running concurrent with the attention to the family—and again, consistent with the structure of melodrama—is the focus on issues of class. Kerjean, a respectable mill owner, is completely ruined by Favraux's machinations, a fate that Judex's/Jacques's family manages to avoid by the sudden appearance of a messenger with news of a gold strike in the family mine held in a foreign locale. Kerjean's plight serves as a reminder of the *potential* class decline brought on by the finance capitalist Favraux's dealings. After all, Jacques's family name is *de Trémeuse*, a title that implies hereditary wealth and property. The anxiety about class dislocation is displaced onto Kerjean, thus leaving Judex to seek his revenge above merely pecuniary interests.

But while the text foregrounds the anxiety of shifts in class status, it also proposes a strategy to ameliorate some of the disturbance. The series sets up a number of characters whose efforts at mobility are examined and evaluated for validity.[48] In the newspaper novelization of *Judex* (which ran concurrently with the film series), we are told that Jacqueline's second marriage (she is a young widow with a small child), like her first, was arranged by her father. In both cases, Favraux sought some social or financial advantage in the marriage.[49] Placed in the context of Favraux's other endeavors (for example, his financial and *physical* destruction of Kerjean—he runs the old man down with his automobile after refusing to speak to him), his efforts on Jacqueline's behalf appear ruthless and self-interested. However, while the banker's middle-class desire for aristocratic status and respectability is relentless, Jacqueline is untainted by Favraux's ambition. Learning of her father's crimes, Jacqueline performs a sort of familial penance by giving away all of her father's money and becoming self-supporting. Her new career (and new identity to hide the family dishonor) provides a respectable model for the *nouvelle femme*'s employment options; she gives music lessons to upper-class children. Moreover, in a great act of maternal sacrifice, she sends away her child to the countryside for boarding and care until she can support the two of them in a manner worthy of the child's past status. By the end of the serial, Jacqueline is able to enhance her monetary and social status through her marriage to Judex. But this upward mobility is legitimated by her love for Judex (and, of course, his innate virtue).

In contrast, Diana is also seeking to move up the social ladder; unfortunately, her planned marriage to Favraux (which he has secretly arranged upon Jacqueline's marriage) is scuttled by Judex's vengeance.[50] Again, like Irma Vep, this is a romantic attachment of convenience for Diana. After Favraux's apparent death (which is, in fact, a kidnapping by Judex), Diana immediately takes up with Moralès and later joins with the Vicomte de la Rochefontaine (Jacqueline's gold-digging ex-fiancée) in an explicit sexual and criminal union (at one point, Diana appears to maintain a relationship with Moralès and the Vicomte concurrently). Again, as in *Les vampires,* Diana's sexual and criminal alliances mock the monogamous heterosexual couple, and more disturbing, given the wartime obsession with children, she threatens the very foundation of the family unit. Diana begins the film as a faux nanny, surely a wartime sacrilege, but she compounds the crime by kidnapping Jean, Jacqueline's innocent and excruciatingly adorable son.

The long-suffering and virtuous widow Jacqueline Aubry (Yvette Andreyor) shares an all-too-brief idyllic moment with her son, *le petit* Jean (Olinda Mano) in *Judex*. Louis Feuillade. © Production Gaumont, 1917.

The dramatic split between Diana and Jacqueline as competing and fundamentally oppositional models of the *nouvelle femme* is consistent with the melodramatic tone prominent in *Judex*. The distinction between good (Jacqueline) and evil (Diana) points to the clear-cut moral universe in operation throughout the series. While *Fantômas* and *Les vampires* are driven by the problems of ambiguity around identity, *Judex* makes an all-out effort, like any good melodrama, to end such uncertainty. This is not to say that all characters are easily slotted into the "good" and "evil" categories; there are still questions of identity to be resolved or, perhaps more accurately, moral lessons to be learned in the course of the episodes. Almost all the characters make errors of moral judgment (with two important exceptions). Even the virtuous Judex is not immune from such a "fall," for the film opens with his condemnation of Favraux to death. Judex changes his "sentence" on the banker to a mere imprisonment upon seeing Jacqueline's suffering (after she believes her father is dead). The events point both to

Jacqueline's innate and impeccable virtue and to a repeated motif of sin and salvation throughout the film. Time and time again, characters face clear-cut options of good and evil, lawfulness or criminality. Quite often they choose the path of retribution, malice, or vice—only to be struck by an act of conscience and remorse. Upon seeing Jacqueline's and Jean's reunion (after one of many kidnappings), the Comtesse de Trémeuse decides to forgive the banker Favraux for her husband's death (and to agree to the sentence commuted by her similarly redeemed son). The greedy, social-climbing banker, Favraux, learns the error of his ways and ends the film giving money to the poor. Moralès makes a valiant effort to reform and tries to join the Foreign Legion, but he falls back into the "abyss" of Diana's control. Cocantin, after a brief criminal flirtation with Diana in her child-kidnapping scheme, is charmed by the precious Jean and joins forces with Judex.

The pattern of sin and salvation is consistent not only with melodrama but also the war years' larger trends toward conservatism and the established religious institution of Catholicism. The novelization of the series notes that *judex* is a Latin term for justice. And the wronged Kerjean underlines the moral authority behind the future dispensation of justice by telling Favraux, "God will punish you."[51] This series is very much concerned with the notion of not simply law but a *higher* law, and our past model of justice in *Les vampires*, the amateur detective (Philippe's role), is in *Judex* played for comic effect through the character of Cocantin (Marcel Levesque). The comic effect is heightened by Cocantin's pairing with the street urchin, and later adopted son, "*le môme* Réglisse," who is played by the child star René Poyen of the comic series *Bout de Zan*.

The name of "Judex" functions also as a marker of class. After Vallières points out the etymology of the term to Favraux, the banker observes that a threatening note signed by the vengeful Judex could not be from the wronged Kerjean but must be from someone of appropriate education (and by implication, class), for as he puts it: "this fellow [*garçon*] who hardly knows how to read or write [Kerjean] would not be able to choose this Latin pseudonym of Judex."[52] In the scenario for the film, the intersection between class, morality, and *acceptable* class mobility is evident in Kerjean's introduction to Favraux: "I am Pierre Kerjean. . . . I was an honest man, I was living happily with my wife and child. Seduced by the financial prospectus with which you flooded France, I entrusted my money to you. Not only did you ruin me, but you led me, in spite of myself, in dishonest speculations which ended in my sentencing to twenty years hard labor."[53]

Melodrama meets the fantastic in *Judex*. Louis Feuillade. Image from the newspaper novelization of the serial in *Le Petit Parisien*. Photo from the Musée Gaumont. © Production Gaumont, 1917.

The only characters exempt from the cycles of wrongdoing and reform are Jacqueline and Diana—our two fixed markers of good and evil. It is also important to note what events *trigger* the acts of conscience; they are typically familial reunions, mother and child, father and son, for example, or future family ties (Jacqueline's despair over the loss of her father in part kindles Jacques's/Judex's desire). Jacqueline's role as the perfect mother reinforces her righteousness, while Diana's complete lack of family ties (as in *Les vampires*) serves to guarantee her absence of conscience. Morality and indeed the heavens, the family, and the nation are all at stake during the war years, and the publicity materials for the series emphasize especially the homeland: one advertisement for the film and newspaper novelization in *Le Petit Parisien* notes that *Judex* is "the great novel of adventures, written by a French writer, created and filmed by a French [production] house and played by French artists."[54] Reading the *ciné-roman* and viewing the film almost appear to be one's civic duty during the wartime years of uncertainty.

With the death of Diana at the end of *Judex,* another reversal takes place. Of course, it is not surprising that the hero Judex has married the young widow Jacqueline Favraux, the daughter of the banker Favraux that Judex secretly imprisoned and the target for most of Diana's plots. But as noted earlier, the actress chosen to play Jacqueline is Yvette Andreyor— Joséphine from *Fantômas*. Andreyor was a major star in her own right during this period and had at one point formed her own production company (prior to *Judex*), and her status is acknowledged throughout the publicity for the film. She is featured prominently in a variety of publicity material and is the central figure on the cover of a *Le Petit Parisien* supplement that announces the forthcoming novelization and film series. In the image, Andreyor as Jacqueline holds her young son, while a faithful Judex protectively watches over them. Diana, wearing a tie, looks on the trio ominously.

Of course, as we have seen, casting reversals are not new to Feuillade's films and are in part brought about by the regular shifting of character types in early cinema troupes. But as with the Navarre shift from the detective to criminal figure (from Dervieux to Fantômas), this is nonetheless an interesting coincidence (and one that we will see again in Feuillade's last serial, *Barrabas*). It is almost as if the death of Irma/Diana has brought about the domestication of Joséphine or the domestication of the *nouvelle femme*.

Figuring the *Nouvelle Femme*

This is not all to be said about the modern woman of this era; there is more to our story than her threat to male identity and power and her demarcation as the ultimate evil, an evil that must then be resolutely dispatched. A useful point of contrast to Musidora's modern woman might be found in her competitor of the era—Pearl White. *Les vampires* was in fact launched as a type of defensive first-strike response to *Les mystères de New York;* Léon Gaumont heard about Pathé's film series and ordered Feuillade to produce a crime series *before Les mystères de New York*'s release in France. The advance knowledge of the Pathé series and Feuillade's own rapid pace production style[55] actually enabled one episode of *Les vampires* to open in France before the Pearl White series.[56] However, a variety of factors led to *Les mystères de New York*'s unquestioned box-office superiority over its rival. The White series was the beneficiary of an enormous publicity campaign and regular screenings with newspaper serialization that ran concurrently. In contrast, *Les vampires* screened its episodes irregularly and missed the marketing coup of a parallel print version of the series (a novel came out after the film was completed). It also was hindered by several war-related problems, most prominently a shortage of actors and materials.[57] Moreover, *Les vampires*, unlike *Les mystères de New York*, was subjected to censorship by the Paris police (an act that was reversed only after Musidora pleaded Gaumont's case to the head of the Paris police).[58]

At first glance, the juxtaposition of Pearl White and Musidora seems to be an oppositional gambit. White's characters function much like Jacqueline, as an alternative model for the new woman, which is much less threatening to gender boundaries. White is fashionable and adventurous but certainly not a deadly figure like Irma/Diana or even the Joséphine characters. As Ben Singer has noted in an article on the serial queen melodrama, early serials may be remarkable for their emphasis on female heroism, but this heroism had its price, leaving us with a text of often ambivalent impulses: "The genre is paradoxical ... in that its portrayal of female power is sometimes accompanied by the sadistic spectacle of women's victimization. The genre as a whole is thus animated by an oscillation between contradictory extremes of female prowess and distress, empowerment and imperilment."[59] At times, White is close to Jacqueline (and later Feuillade heroines) in that she is a passive object that is subject to innumerable kidnappings and seemingly in need of perpetual rescue. In one White serial, *The Perils of Pauline* (Gasnier and MacKenzie, 1914), Harry, the fiancé, is never far away and is always ready to provide aid to Pauline/Pearl. But there is something odd about Harry's rescues in that they are at times related more to coincidence and good fortune than skill or knowledge and, moreover, are dependent upon Pearl's own resourcefulness for success. An example of this can be found in episode 7, *The Tragic Plunge*. Pauline escapes from a sabotaged submarine; a detonation on board is sinking the vessel. She extracts herself from the submarine by crawling through a torpedo tube in the nose of the boat and swims to the surface of the water in an area where Harry happens to be cruising. Pauline is then "rescued" by Harry in the most minimal sense of the term. Pearl is thus clearly the star and focus of these series, and the hero/fiancé plays a rather ancillary role in each episode, at least in terms of the *action*. However, the role of Harry, while secondary, is not insignificant, for his presence ensures that Pauline's "adventures" will be framed within the boundaries of heterosexual romance.

While these women (including Musidora, White, Andreyor, Carl) provide us with a sense of the culture's ambivalence regarding the *nouvelle femme*, it is also important to note here that the new woman was not merely a category for understanding the shifting gender relations but also a representation of a more generalized shift in everyday life and thought. Take for example the surrealist homage to the film serial, *Le trésor des Jésuites* (The Treasure of the Jesuits [1928]). This was a play that was never performed but had been intended to benefit the widow of Réné Cresté (the lead actor in *Judex*). Supposedly, Musidora was to play the lead in the production.[60] In the prologue, Louis Aragon and André Breton link the White and Musidora texts: "One will soon understand that there was nothing more realist and more poetic at the same time as the *ciné-feuilleton*, which not long ago was the joy of 'les esprits forts.' It is in *Les mystères de New York*, it is in *Les vampires* that one will have to search for the great reality of the century. Beyond fashion, beyond taste. Come with me. I will show you how one writes history."[61] But White's persona in many ways defines the new woman as especially influenced by the American culture. In a Gaumont newsreel dated April 1921, Pearl White is shown as she arrives in Paris by plane, dressed in an aviator outfit.[62] The attire points toward her star image as the "Girl with Ninety-Nine Lives"[63] and her action status as a daredevil performer, a perpetual-motion instrument with a repertoire of countless death-defying stunts that were typically associated with American culture, especially the melodrama-inflected serials.[64] In contrast, Musidora's "stunts" are limited to criminal acts, cat burglary, shootings, and a few spectacular and shocking plunges out the window. White's unusual attire also points to an important consumer trend, the need for women's "sports" wear, with the emergence of outdoor cycling as an appropriate female activity.[65] But all these phenomona—like consumerism, the bicycle, the daredevil, and even the modern woman—were all seen in France as American imports, and they produced a range of ambivalent responses, from fascination and admiration to absolute horror.

But like Pearl White, Musidora is no stranger to this new world, and she underlines her shocking and inappropriate female behavior by driving an automobile while dressed as a young count. Moreover, like her counterpart Joséphine in *Fantômas,* she sets up an unsuspecting male victim for a criminal attack on the train—a space where *women,* not men, were warned to protect themselves. In both White's and Musidora's cases, one could argue that each national context puts in place its own narrative of containment, in the first case by marriage and the second by crime (and the ultimate punishment). Yet *is* woman contained by these narratives?

As we know from Stephen Kern's book *The Culture of Time and Space,* the era had a real fascination with speed, and the sense of accelerated speed through various technologies (e.g., the bicycle, train, auto, airplane) brought—much like the new woman—both pleasure and danger. Kern points to a warning in 1886 against "bicycle face," a condition caused by the cyclist moving too fast against the wind at high speeds.[66] But mobility of space is linked throughout the era to mobility of social and cultural boundaries, as can be noted in one cartoon of the era that featured the *nouvelle femme* journeying to a feminist congress on her bicycle.[67]

The alterations in space and time represent a kind of ethics, a new morality of pure action that the female body increasingly comes to convey. Louis Aragon notes that Pearl White was known in France as "Perle Vite," and he underlines the appeal to those ready for change: "It is without doubt that her [White's] unique subject is morality, the necessity for all action: our era can hardly be interested in this morality. In the cinema, speed appears in life, and Pearl White does not commit an act [agir] to obey her conscience, but by healthy reflex: she acts in order to act."[68]

Similar language is used by the filmmaker and critic Louis Delluc in a separate article to describe White's activities: "There is the moral power of Pearl White. Morally, the sight of Pearl White is a true cure. The spectacle of her exploits are better for the neurasthenic than the bitter genius of Charlot or even the sentimental and modest brilliance of Douglas Fairbanks. Pearl White is energy and brilliance, that's all. But what am I saying, it is good health on pure impulse."[69] Speed and energy as a countermorality are then attached to the *nouvelle femme,* a transgressive force not limited to the category of gender. In this instance, the transgression speaks to a fundamental upheaval of the old world and its lethargic pace of life. White's speed is given a particular Tayloresque twist in an article on the serial queen entitled "77 minutes avec Pearl White." The author repeatedly announces the amount of time remaining in the interview and has even calculated the cost per minute for the event. Throughout the article, White is in a state of perpetual motion, whether recounting her air travel to Paris or taking the journalist for a spin in her automobile.[70]

Thus despite their different screen personas and sometimes opposing narrative functions, one can see a process of circulation among particular kinds of women stars. A passage from "Le merle" (The Blackbird) by the surrealist poet Robert Desnos conveys a certain exchangeability of the figures:

> And then, one film chases the other, Musidora, followed Pearl White, Nazimova followed Musidora and others, others still emerged, whose charming names it is useless to repeat.
> This one was blonde. She disappeared, and the beautiful novel begun with her finished with the one who followed her, and who was brunette. They were dying only to be reborn.[71]

However, it is also clear from Desnos's language that the transgressions did not exclude questions of sexuality. Again, the language of the poet demonstrates the exchangeability of the stars and the conflation of social and sexual disturbance at work in these films (and their stars).

> Their life [the women stars above] was not ordinary, life was precious and they risked it. Squadrons of bandits and seducers developed around them, and twenty times ruined, one saw them twenty times rediscover fortune. One could have peopled entire cemeteries with those who died for them. . . . And love, love transfigured ensured its propaganda by them [the women]. Rid of vulgar laws, raised well above some ideas of tranquility, love defined itself equally in Destiny and Fortune.[72]

The paradoxical status or ambivalence surrounding the American serial queen's "heroic" exploits or the doubling of female characters through Feuillade's serials (Marfa/Irma, Irma/Jane, Diana/Jacqueline, and even Diana/Diasy Torp) demonstrates a variety of strategies to contain these movements through social and cultural space. While both White and Musidora were icons of the era and enjoyed popularity in France, the containment of the threat within the space of Musidora's body and the *memory* of the *maillot noir* speak to the particular historical context of the war years in France, the conservative movement against feminist gains in the culture, and one particular cinematic difference to the Hollywood classical model. Even with the hybrid of melodramatic and fantastic modes seen in *Judex*—and the next three serials—this is still a cinema displaying and displacing the cinema of uncertainty.

To a certain extent here, we need to backtrack to the questions posed by the poster for *Les vampires:* Who? What? When? Where? As I noted earlier, it is important to remember who asks these questions and how the questioner thereby shapes the very type of knowledge gained in the process of interrogation. The comments by Aragon, Delluc, and Desnos give a decidedly male cast to the questioning. We have seen the new woman as an extension of male anxiety of the epoch. There were a few fleeting moments of female pleasure as both Pearl White and Musidora (and even Andreyor's Joséphine) represented a certain type of autonomy for women (that was either defeated, punished, or reined in through the casting of the pleasure within a heterosexual romance). And last, we have also turned to several *male* critics, as they have appropriated this energy as their own, as a form of liberation from a static, traditional lifestyle.

At this point I would like to restart the questioning from a more explicitly female point of view. To return to the Cixous discussion of the "uncanny" once again, she argues that in Freud's essay, Olympia has become no more than an extension of Nathaniel's Oedipal struggles. Moreover, Cixous asks, what if woman could speak; if the woman in the poster for *Les vampires* could ask the series of questions, how might she frame the investigation?

Musidora's Signature

The history of Musidora in French cinema has largely been written as an erotic object and cultural sign of modernity as the result of her performance in *Les vampires* and *Judex*. And certainly even a cursory

Musidora self-portrait. Collection BiFi, D.R.

Musidora in *La vagabonde*, directed by Pérégo. Based on a novel by Colette. © ND Roger-Viollet.

glance at the two films demonstrates the validity of these claims. However, Musidora's presence in the Feuillade serials and in her own films and writings pose a further level of questioning, an interrogation beyond arenas of knowledge to the question of knowledge itself. The dilemma posed by the figure of Musidora circulates in the domain of the metacinematic and metaphysical: what do we know from the image (and how does that parallel or exceed human vision), and more fundamentally what can we know at all? But it is essential that we not stop the investigation of indeterminacy with Musidora's films with Feuillade but rather see her later work as part of the ongoing project of the mode of uncertainty.

If we look at Musidora's own life, we note that her name was one that she herself selected from a femme fatale character (who ultimately commits suicide over a love affair) in the Théophile Gautier novel *Fortunio*. She begins to use this name during her stage career, which starts in Paris around 1910. Her work in the theater and music hall also brings her in contact with the writer Colette and initiates a lifelong personal, professional, and rumored romantic relationship between the two women.[73] As an acknowledgement of Colette's centrality to her life, Musidora names the writer her *marraine* (godmother).[74] Colette and Musidora collaborated on at least three films together, and it is obvious from Musidora's own remarks on the topic that this was a close friendship. Musidora states in a lecture on Colette that their meeting in the music hall was, in fact, preceded by her fan letter to Colette in 1901. She goes on to say: "I am not ashamed to confess that it was a great love that I had for Colette. A very great and chaste love."[75]

Thus, we see Musidora not only naming herself (her original name being Jeanne Roques) but extending the domain of her heritage and family to Colette. And later, during World War I, she consciously adopts the title of *marraine* in her role as an ongoing pen pal (during the period 1915–19) with the French troops.[76] While the term *marraine* was common for the soldier's correspondent in wartime, the ambiguity of the term might also suggest Musidora now taking on Colette's prior role as godmother in her own life. Looking at a collection of these letters of correspondence, we can see Musidora's mythic status intact. One pilot notes that he received a picture of Musidora in response to his request for an autograph, which she had designated as a "good luck charm" (*un talisman*).[77] The pilot is convinced that the charm works, and he credits it with saving his life on numerous occasions. Another soldier requests a treasured and magical object of another kind: "Would you please present to me a *fétiche*—something of yours you have worn? A stocking, or better yet one of your *petits pantalons* . . . no matter what, finally, something you have touched, very closely, and that I could embrace, when I have a fancy for it."[78] It is quite clear from her popular writings (in film magazines) that in choosing her name and her roles as goddaughter and perhaps godmother, Musidora understands the importance of these acts. Many of her writings in popular film journals trace the background of her name and the significance of this selection, and she pointedly remarks on her careful understanding and protection of the act of naming.

In a salary dispute with his actors, Léon Gaumont decided to eliminate onscreen credits from his films. The studio founder and owner was a figure of great intimidation, and Gaumont's decisions were rarely questioned. Musidora, however, was determined to approach the owner directly. "This decision made me very angry. For me, the choice of my name was linked to my future."[79] She is quite clear on the genesis of her courage in this effort:

> Authority figures were never intimidating to me. Not because I took myself as a vampire, but simply because my mother had imparted to me her audacity. . . . M. Gaumont received me in his office, very astonished by such a gesture. Nobody, moreover, had ever dared to address him directly. I expressed my complaint. . . . I protect my publicity, that is to say, my future. If you don't use my name one will call me Irma Vep and later I will only be Irma Vep! I hold on essentially to Musidora. Théophile Gautier and Fortunio are the godfathers that I have chosen.[80]

But this is not to say that Irma Vep was a figure that Musidora tried to distance from her own public image. Many of her theater performances utilized the *maillot de soie* associated with the Irma Vep character, although she made ongoing efforts to ensure that Irma did not overshadow her own persona. Certainly the two extant films directed by Musidora do not utilize the costume, although *La tierra de los toros* (*La terre des taureaux* [1924]) does have an explicit display of a poster featuring Irma Vep in *Les vampires* during a backstage sequence in the film. And the star does know when to invoke the image as well. Later, as part of a series of correspondences to Louis Gaumont (Léon's son) in 1950 regarding the possibility of funding a new film project, she sends her own caricature of Irma with the inscription: "for Monsieur Louis Gaumont, Musidora/Irma Vep/*Les vampires*, still wearing the G

La tierra de los toros (*La terre des taureaux*) announces itself in the opening titles as part fiction, part autobiography. Here, the star, Musidora, arrives in Spain to find a performer for her upcoming film. Musidora, Films Musidora (1924). Collection BiFi, D.R.

of Gaumont."[81] It is interesting to note here that part of her "pitch" for the project (a short film, and she had just completed a ten-minute film for the Cinémathèque Française) was not simply this drawing and a script but a full reading/performance of her script for Louis Gaumont at a friend's home.[82]

Musidora's black silk costume circulates around almost every discussion and later filmic invocation of Musidora/Irma. In one of the most well-known sequences from *Les vampires*, the complexity, the excessiveness, and the incoherence of the narrative ensure that our attention is focused on the bodysuit. Irma, who has relinquished her cross-dressing costume as a young count for the maillot, is snooping about a luxury hotel looking for a map of buried treasure hidden by a separate group of thieves (the map is a Macguffin if ever there was one). She encounters in her exploits not the police nor the original thieves but the head of *another* criminal gang, Moréno. Moréno kid-

The jealous Juana (Musidora) in *Sol y sombra (Soleil et ombre)*. Musidora and Jacques Lasseyne, Films Musidora (1922). Collection BiFi, D.R.

naps her and replaces her with *another* black-clad woman (under hypnosis) who then *masquerades* as Irma as she returns the map to the head of the Vampires.

The sequence concisely sums up the appeal of Musidora/Irma. Intersecting with the eroticism of her costume is the narrative—and even visual—indeterminacy of Irma. And just as the woman under hypnosis slips on the mask and performs the role of Irma seamlessly, it is possible for us to do the same—cross-dressing, spinning out a window, exchanging lovers and allies, becoming another woman—all is possible in a heartbeat. If, as Judith Mayne has argued, the cinema screen functions as a kind of boundary or threshold space between numerous oppositions and subject positionings,[83] then it is possible to argue that the very presence of Musidora/Irma functions as a screen within a screen of cinema's possibilities and to our projection within the space of that screen. She becomes an embodied and mobile

Musidora as Juana, the spurned woman, in *Sol y sombra (Soleil et ombre)*. Musidora and Jacques Lasseyne, Films Musidora (1922). Collection BiFi, D.R.

Musidora as the nameless party girl, one of her dual roles in *Sol y sombra (Soleil et ombre)*. Musidora and Jacques Lasseyne, Films Musidora (1922). Collection BiFi, D.R.

metacinematic device floating through these films, which is perhaps one of the elements that the discourse on the "beautiful transparent silk bodysuit"[84] is pointing us toward.

Certainly a good part of her appeal is specifically erotic, and in no way do I want to diminish that aspect of her persona. What I do want to note is how she then controls and expands on this eroticism so that despite all the efforts of critics and historians, Musidora exceeds the limits of an objectified gaze. There have been numerous efforts by commentators from the surrealists to the contemporary critics to link these erotic qualities to the rebellious and revolutionary, but the discussion often places Musidora in the role of myth or muse, someone who can inspire, but not write, dreams. In Musidora's own films and writings, the emphasis is still on Musidora as a vibrant sexual being, but the framing of her sexual identity is marked by fluidity, play, and performance.

The two surviving films directed by (and starring) Musidora, *Sol y sombra* (*Soleil et ombre* [1922], co-directed Jacques Lasseyne) and *La tierra de los toros*, are set in Spain, with the world of bullfighting as an important backdrop for the action. Musidora's attention to bullfighting has been attributed to the influence of Feuillade (who began his writing career in Paris for a publication exclusively devoted to the sport). Her motivation was also described as partially self-interested, or rather, romantic, due to her attraction to Antonio Cañero, a well-known matador in Spain (who is the male lead in both of these films).[85] Certainly, her liaison with Cañero may well have played a part in the script and casting.

In *Sol y sombra*, Musidora plays two roles: Juana, the spurned fiancée (a dark-haired local woman), and the mysteriously nameless but obviously shallow party-girl (a blonde foreigner), who steals Cañero from Juana. A recent French critic, Jacques Durand, speculates that Musidora took the dual roles in part due to her passionate love for Cañero: "Perhaps one must search in Musidora's love for Cañero the reason for this doubling, of this dual role, at once the rejected fiancée and the femme fatale. She could have been too infatuated with him to share him with another, even on the screen. While giving herself two roles, she necessarily gives herself an excellent part and also encloses it within her desire."[86]

Whether pure passion or jealousy might be Musidora's motivation here it is difficult to say, but we do have some evidence from the films themselves that might point to another reading, a reading not

"Why can't life be as good as a novel?" Musidora addresses her audience in *La tierra de los toros (La terre des taureaux)*. Musidora, Films Musidora (1924). Collection BiFi, D.R.

unrelated to Feuillade's own interest in bullfighting. Although often framed in conservative rhetoric about the sport's virile and noble approach (in contrast to much of the era's affected and pretentious style), as Bernard Bastide points out, Feuillade's writings on the sport were particularly cinematic, with an attention to mise-en-scène and the correct gesture, whether it be highly ritualized or spontaneous.[87] Textual clues from Musidora's films point us in a similar direction.

La tierra de los toros follows her opening title question ("Why can't life be as good as a novel?") with a title card that states (and is "signed" by the filmmaker): "This film has been made in constant danger; but it must give you only the impression of the festivity of the sunlight and the splendor of the Art of gesture. Musidora."[88] Thus, the doubling of Musidora's character might not be an act of possessive love as much as a kind of performative turn.[89] That is to say, Musidora might not be gesturing toward any one definitive commentary on her public/private persona but rather might be demonstrating the multiple possibilities that could exist within any particular "identity." Or, more

"This film has been made in constant danger; but it must give you only the impression of the festivity of the sunlight and the splendor of the Art of gesture." *La tierra de los toros (La terre des taureaux).* Musidora, Films Musidora (1924). Collection BiFI, D.R.

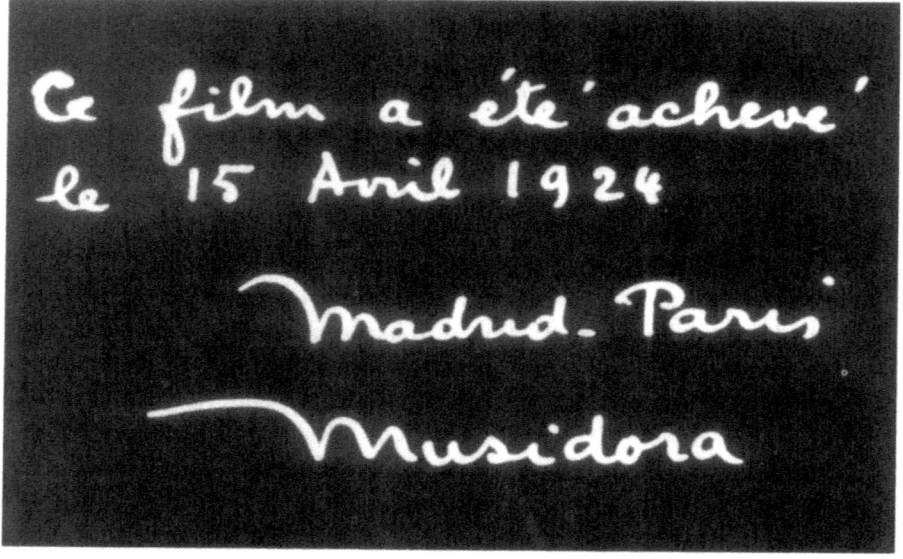

Musidora signs *La tierra de los toros (La terre des taureaux).* Musidora, Films Musidora (1924). Collection BiFi, D.R.

Juana is imprisoned after her murder of her rival, the blonde *étrangère*. *Sol y sombra* (*Soleil et ombre*). Musidora and Jacques Lasseyne, Films Musidora (1922). Collection BiFi, D.R.

important, Musidora might be pointing to the inability to limit or define identity itself, which would be consistent with the nondifferentiation that follows from recursive functions.

In part, we can see the recurrent motif of the bullfight (both films have long sequences devoted to Cañero's action in the ring) as supplementing her title card. In examining the art of bullfighting, one aspect we immediately notice is its quality of excess. It is a sport and skill, like other blood sports that transcend rationality and foreground the boundaries of life itself. Within the ring, and at any moment, your body might be crushed, your life ended. Success in the ring for both parties is dependent upon not so much reason as agility and speed. The bullfight places us in a state of pure emotion, one that transcends the rules and limits of language and concept. Passing beyond the world of narrow representation, where word and thing are equivalents, the gesture now stands for the excess of possibilities. The gesture, the performance, and the image, like Irma's presentation of a screen within a screen, are zones of indeterminacy.

However, this indeterminacy does not preclude activity in terms of identity, although it is important here to remember that identity cannot be reduced to a fixed entity or essence. "Playing" herself in *La tierra de los toros,* Musidora is convinced by her first glance upon Cañero in the ring that, as the title card notes: "I have found the performer for my film." Perhaps even more interesting, Cañero initially refuses her offer in the film. He then unaccountably places an ad for a performer in his own film, which Musidora, *disguised* as a pompous and ugly actress, accepts and then disappears (she returns to Paris). The couple is ultimately reunited through their ritual reenactment of the bullfighting gestures, and it is then, and only then, that Musidora leaves the life of the stage for love. However, as Cañero notes, just in case we think this is a normalizing or essentialist act, "it is still a theater set that I am offering you."[90] Musidora accepts a life "just as good as a novel" with this final performative turn and literally places her signature *yet again* on the closing credits, giving us simultaneously a materiality alongside this indeterminacy.

Despite her defeat in *Les vampires* and *Judex,* Musidora "returns" to the scene of the crime (although not literally on-screen) in a later extratextual reference. The scenario for the next serial, *La nouvelle mission de Judex* (1917), features a comment by Feuillade that his new female villain, the Baronne d'Apremont (Juana Borguese), is a worthy successor of Diana Monti.[91] Woman—this time Musidora—again haunts the text, refusing to stay silent or to remain in the margins of male anxiety.[92]

4 | Stigma and Stigmata
The Cries and Cure of the Fantastic Narrative

> Those wonderful hysterics, who subject Freud to so many voluptuous moments too shameful to mention, bombarding his mosaic statue/law of Moses with their carnal, passionate body-words, haunting him with their inaudible thundering denunciations, were more than just naked beneath their seven veils of modesty-they were dazzling. In a single word of the body they inscribed the endless vertigo of a history loosed like an arrow from all of men's history, from biblicocapitalist society. Following these yesterday's victims of torture, who anticipate the new women, no intersubjective relationship will ever be the same. It is you, Dora, you who cannot be tamed, the poetic body, the true "mistress" of the Signifier. Before tomorrow your effectiveness will be seen to work—when your words will no longer be retracted, pointed against your own breast, but will write themselves against the other and against men's grammar. Men must not have that place for their own any more than they have us for their own.
>
> Hélène Cixous, "Sorties: Out and Out: Attacks/New Ways/Forays"

> For man has evaded, at an early point, a confrontation with his own shadow. The black shade spreading out over the earth at his feet. Coming out toward the east, the shadow is in some way hidden. Still behind. It is under the cover of the shadows of others-men or things-that the man moves out into the sun.
>
> Luce Irigaray, *Speculum of the Other Woman*

Zone 3: Familial Space, Hysteria, and the Turn to Melodrama

With *Judex,* Feuillade's serials make a decided shift toward a more strongly pronounced melodramatic narrative structure. This movement is logical in that melodrama, like the mode of the fantastic, is preoccupied with questions of knowledge and visibility. As noted earlier, melodrama, like the fantastic, used a variety of excessive and sensationalistic strategies in the pursuit of knowledge. Indeed the two genres or modes overlap at times, and while they feature distinctive elements, they are never truly distant. However, melodrama specifically situates its investigations within the context of what Peter Brooks calls the "moral occult" or "spiritual values."[1] Melodrama typically structures the narrative around a "moral" center (an individual or institution, particularly the family) and the crises it must confront. But if melodrama is an ethical investigation that examines the demarcations between good and evil, the mode of the fantastic is an epistemological undertaking that questions if we can ever know or recognize such demarcations. Nonetheless, it may be useful to examine why Feuillade's later crime serials might take on this more dense melodramatic veneer (beyond the practical reasons noted in the last chapter) and how the resolution into a predominantly melodramatic mode functions ultimately to bring closure to the anxiety that has circulated throughout this series of texts.

It is important to reiterate that in both the fantastic and melodramatic modes, attention is directed to visible evidence, to the "signs" of a "data's" verification regardless of whether that data is physical (e.g., a criminal act or criminal physiognomy) or less tangible (e.g., a moral value such as "good" or "innocence"). In the case of these latter normative values, melodrama employs a particularly excessive presentation of information precisely as a type of compensation for these more amorphous or intangible qualities. And this rhetorical excess becomes primarily a mechanism for disposing uncertainty and ambiguity. As Brooks notes, in melodrama, "the play's outcome turns less on the triumph of virtue than on making the world morally legible, spelling out its ethical forces and imperatives in large and bold characters."[2]

Frequently, this exaggeration of expression is played out at the level of narrative, with some type of dualistic or Manichean universe, and then doubled within the arena of performance. As the narrative strives to clarify ethical or moral ambiguities, it often supplements or replaces language with broad physical gestures. Again, these gestures can be seen as an effort to present visual evidence of a moral or ethical concept and may be underlined by an absence of language. Brooks points out that the character of the mute is central to the mode: "The mute role is remarkably prevalent in melodrama. Mutes correspond first of all to a repeated use of extreme physical conditions to represent extreme moral and emotional conditions: as well as mutes, there are blind men, paralytics, invalids of various sorts whose very physical presence evokes the extremism and hyperbole of ethical conflict and manichaestic struggle."[3] The excess of the melodramatic narrative, and use of the body as a site to represent physically this excess, is suggestive of yet another term that had wide circulation in the discourse of the late nineteenth century—hysteria.[4]

Beyond the explicit representation of hysterical symptoms (e.g., amnesia and aphonia) within the later serials (from *Judex* to *Barrabas*), there are two qualities of hysterical illness that are particularly relevant to a discussion of the fantastic and Feuillade's films. The first is the ability of the symptom to shift meaning. As Freud notes, "We have already learnt that a single symptom corresponds quite regularly to several meanings *simultaneously*. We may now add that it can express several meanings *in succession*. In the course of years a symptom can change its meaning or its chief meaning, or the leading rôle can pass from one meaning to another."[5] Moreover, the very production of a hysterical symptom is a form of movement, a process of "conversion" or "translation" of a "purely psychical excitation into physical terms."[6] The mobility of the hysterical symptom functions as a process of substitution, much like the shifts in the zones of anxiety and the narrative pattern of repetition and transformation tracked throughout this book.

Second, with respect to the hysteric's description of his or her illness/history, Freud notes that the patient's account is nonlinear and elliptical, essentially due to gaps or inaccuracies in memory (of both the amnesiatic and paramnesiatic variety).[7] Of particular relevance to Feuillade's serials and the fantastic narrative is Freud's discussion of the end of treatment, or the "cure," of the hysterical illness. As Freud explains:

> In the further course of the treatment the patient supplies the facts which, though he had known them all along, had been kept back by him or had not occurred to his mind. The paramnesias prove untenable, and the gaps in his memory are filled in. It is only toward the end of the treatment that we have before us an intelligible, consistent, and unbroken case history. Whereas the practical aim of the treatment is to remove all possible symptoms and to replace them by unconscious thoughts, we may regard it as a second and theoretical aim to repair all the damages to the patient's memory. These two aims are coincident. When one is reached, so is the other; and the same path leads to them both.[8]

In other words, it is the closure of gaps in memory (through a "correct" retrieval of the past) followed by a reorganization of the narrative into a linear model that effects a "cure." But we should remember that this singular narrative trajectory concerns a process of "normalization" such that the "correct" retrieval is not so much "truthful" (or universal) as it is "appropriate" to a set of conventions, that is, the "norms" of heterosexuality. And of course this retrieval and reorganization is guided, or perhaps more accurately proscribed, by the (male) analyst.

The utility of an overarching melodramatic structure to the fantastic narrative in the Feuillade serials is now apparent. Central to both the *roman-populaire* and melodramatic narratives is a return to what Marc Angenot calls *la scène primitive,* some past event (usually a family secret or mystery) that clarifies an individual's status or history.[9] Thus, melodrama provides a format, the family "history," in which a particular crisis of identity can be narrativized and, consequently, reconfigured and controlled. And these reconstructed narratives are then sequential, linear, cohesive, and resoundingly within the paradigm of patriarchy.

At the same time, it is crucial to remember Samuel Weber's discussion concerning the double movement of the uncanny. Each iteration of uncertainty and dislocation is accompanied by a reciprocal pull, a defensive movement "against the crisis of perception and phenomenality."[10] Thus, the addition, or rather enhancement, of melodramatic qualities within the mode of the fantastic does not, in itself, signal the resolution of uncertainty. It may, in fact, serve as an indicator of yet another crisis or dislocation. In other words, the process of recursion continues.

LA NOUVELLE MISSION DE JUDEX

In *La nouvelle mission de Judex* (twelve weekly episodes),[11] the domestic perfection enjoyed by the romantic figure of vengeance, Jacques/Judex, and his long-suffering beloved, Jacqueline, is threatened by a criminal gang, "La Rafle aux Secrets" [the raiders of secrets], who steal plans of various new technologies for their resale value. Participants in the gang include two mysterious and dangerous women, Gaby (Cyprien Giles) and the Baronne d'Apremont (Juana Borguese), who wreck havoc in tandem while working for the shadowy figure known as the "One-Eyed Man" (N'a-qu'un-Châsse). Jacques and Jacqueline collide with this unpleasant group via their friendship with their neighbor, the inventor James Milton, and his daughter (by adoption), Primerose (Georgette de Nery). Primerose is the fiancée of Jacques's brother, Roger (Edouard Mathé). The plot thickens when it appears that Primerose has joined the criminal gang by stealing her father's plans and later kidnapping Jean, Jacqueline's son—and turning both over to Gaby and the Baronne. It is soon discovered that Primerose's crimes have been committed in a hypnotic state—a condition that in fact appears common among several of the female characters in the film. Primerose's "cure" is affected through the discovery of her "real" identity and the reconciliation of her "true" family, which in turn produces her "new" family, that is, her marriage to Roger.

In the previous Feuillade crime films—*Fantômas, Les vampires,* and *Judex*—the identifying marks of criminality were crucial to defining and isolating a character behind criminal behavior. The antagonist may be located in the suburbs, in the metro, in the home (especially among the servant class), or even within the figure of the woman (as a visible mark of difference), but in each instance there is the sense that the character enacts, or acts out, some type of criminal event. In the last three serials—*La nouvelle mission de Judex, Tih Minh,* and *Barrabas*—a different understanding of criminal behavior takes place. Now, the *act of criminality* is located *within* the body itself. To a certain extent, this is a logical progression of Irma's/Diana's supposed defeat. The repeated and resolute dispatch of the woman criminal initiates the trajectory of substitution—from the body of the woman to the body itself as a specific physical site, or rather symptom. That the female body is still, or will be for now, the text or screen onto which criminality has been located re-associates woman and body (both as essence and in opposition to the man/mind/rationality link) and locates her as the "abnormal" or dysfunctional unit within the family. To put it another way, in the first three series, the effort is to identify the body behind the disguise, to recognize a particular character. In the last three serials, the challenge is to locate the disguise within the body, for we recognize the individual characters, but we certainly are not clear on who they are. Disguise in the last films is aligned with performance, gesture, and the physical comportment of the body.

The textual substitution of bodily signs for the star figure of Musidora may also be seen as the product of the *failure* to defeat Irma/Diana/Musidora, as evidenced by the extratextual reference noted in the previous chapter and by an on-screen reference that appears in episode 10, *Les deux destinées*. The repression of Irma et al. *produces* the hysterical symptoms, which follow in her (on-screen) absence. Thus, Irma and company have not been vanquished so much as gone underground (that is, taken on a new form/symptom). This shift in "locale" is evident in *Les deux destinées* through an explicit visual reminder of Irma Vep, which immediately follows one of the many family reunions that will take place over the course of the next three serials. Here, Primerose (whose "real" name we learn is Maria), the long-lost and frequently amnesiatic daughter of the engineer M. Bianchini, is reunited with her father and sister inside the home of Jacques de Trémeuse (Judex). The coincidences mount exponentially, as Bianchini is the figure responsible for the restitution of the de Trémeuse fortune (after the father's death) in the first *Judex* series. Bianchini's family has endured a crisis of its own, and he relates in flashback the sequence of events (a dual kidnapping and a possible murder of his wife) that destroyed his home.

Bianchini's story not only coincides with the end of Primerose's criminal activities (which had been brought on by hypnotic trances) but also signifies the reformation of a *second* woman criminal, Gaby (who it turns out is actually Bianchini's *other* kidnapped daughter, Clara). However, Bianchini's reconstituted narrative receives the aid of a "false memory" supplied by Jacques/Judex. At one point, Primerose/Maria asserts that Gaby/Clara appears familiar to her. As Clara and Maria were separated at the ages of three and one respectively, Primerose's memory of her can only be through their joint criminal tasks (again, which Primerose performed under hypnosis). Jacques assures her this is not possible, and the family is then reunited through the effacement of one part of Primerose's and Gaby's history. Divine intervention is credited for the events leading to the wondrous and curative reunion when Bianchini states: "and thanks to God we are reunited here." This spiritual invocation by association legitimates and authorizes Judex's acts (as in the first *Judex*) and is consistent with the religious undertone set out in the first serial.

But this reunion is set immediately beside another story, for the film cuts from the space of the completed family unit to an exterior shot of the de Trémeuse home. A figure in a black bodysuit runs across the screen. It is not Irma, of course, but the Baroness d'Apremont, whose criminal "heritage" Feuillade addressed in his extratextual remarks. The event and costume are essentially unmotivated, occurring only once, as a type of flashback to counter the flashback offered by Bianchini. That is, beside the two sisters' history of reformed criminality (which is constructed by two men, Bianchini and Judex) is a second account of the *femme criminelle*—one whose story cannot be reconfigured into a coherent narrative, in other words, one who cannot be cured.

The use of the body as a *site* of action is particularly relevant given the text's emphasis on hysteria (an element that is central to the next two Feuillade serials as well). Our first introduction to hysterical illness in *La nouvelle mission de Judex* is comic. The nervous twitches of the family friend, Cocantin, whom we met in the last *Judex* film, have been diagnosed as "hypersensitivity" and "hysteria."[12] This incidence of male hysteria is played for broad comedy, with the diligent Cocantin following the doctor's prescription of "walking (or dancing) barefoot on wet grass in the moonlight."

As Elaine Showalter has discussed in *Sexual Anarchy: Gender and Culture at the Fin-de-Siècle,* male hysteria was a subject of great interest and debate within the scientific community in the late nineteenth century.[13] Although male hysteria was acknowledged as a phenomenon, the illness was generally seen during this period—as it had been historically—as a woman's disease; in men, the incidence was diagnosed typically within a lower- or working-class milieu.[14] The displacement of male hysteria at first on the working class is consistent with Cocantin's role. He is a fairly inept private detective whose lower-middle class and working-class status is established both by his financial position and by his family, which consists of an adopted street urchin and his wife, Daisy Torp, a circus performer (both traveling or living abroad in this series).

The possibility of the existence of such a condition in men was in addition an attack upon male sexual identity, or more specifically heterosexuality, for the male hysteric was often labeled as "effeminate."[15] And this is clear from Cocantin's comic turns as the hysteric. He must wear light, flowing clothing for his moonlit exercise, and at one point, his prone body (he has fallen in the course of the workout) is mistaken for the despondent Primerose's. Moreover, as part of his undercover detective work, Cocantin cross-dresses, a "performance" that in fact fools absolutely no one that he encounters. This is in marked contrast to Gaby's cross-dressing; her appearance in drag is in the main undetected (although it is obvious to the film viewers).

It is possible to argue that this anxiety regarding *male* hysteria, once comically dismissed, is then displaced onto the body of the woman. The displacement can play a dual role in this context. First, it allows for an investigation of the illness without "infecting" male identity; and second, it redefines female criminality within a medical discourse, where it can be contained and cured. The second factor is particularly useful given the troubling mobility and elusiveness of the *femme criminelle* throughout the course of the serials. However, we should be hesitant to read these symptoms as "only" a male projection of anxiety. Rather, simultaneous attention must be focused on what the repression of Irma, et al., represents.

The control of the woman criminal and her body is particularly important given the context for these crimes. The end of the first *Judex* serial featured the union of several nuclear and extended families (Favraux, Kerjean, Cocantin, and de Trémeuse); the death of Diana was to have meant harmony within the home setting. However, Roger de Trémeuse's pending marriage in the second *Judex* serial is threatened by the uncontrollable actions of his fiancée, Primerose. These actions are disturbing in that they are not explained through the crime of passion scenario (as Lady Beltham) or even by a fundamentally evil persona (as in Irma and Diana). While certainly the Baronne is a consistent criminal figure in the series, she does not provide the concentration or clarity of evil that Diana Monti represented. Criminality takes on much more diffuse, mobile, and amalgamated forms in *La nouvelle*, as in the case of Primerose, who functions as the junction of Jacqueline's and Diana's previous dualism.

Later the explanation is provided to us: Primerose has been under the spell of a hypnotic trance (a condition that Charcot claimed was a manifestation of a hysterical illness).[16] Not only does this information dispel notions concerning the guilt of Primerose—hysteria being an often cited criminal defense in fin-de-siècle France[17]—but it creates the conditions and a context under which she can be cured. At one point, Primerose disclaims knowledge of her actions over large segments of time: "Sometimes I have felt the sensation that life is abandoning me, then it seems to me that I am reborn, but I cannot recall what I did in the interval."[18]

As noted, these memory lapses are later completed by Judex and Bianchini, which effects the return of Primerose to her place within the family. At one point, Judex notes: "Primerose, you are at the mercy of an occult and formidable power.... But I will save you."[19]

The *placement* of this woman criminal back into the family unit thus attempts to fix a place for the hysterical body, something that the defeat of Irma/Diana/Musidora could not accomplish. As Janet Beizer has argued in *Ventriloquized Bodies: Narratives of Hysteria in Nineteenth-Century France*, the discourse of the era reveals a conflation of the psychic and social dimensions. It was generally suggested that the mobility of the hysterical body (whether through the underlying meaning or symptom) could be restored to health by its containment within rigidly prescribed gender roles (i.e., heterosexuality, marriage, and children).[20] This idea, though first presented in the late nineteenth century, may have gained particular sympathy during the war and postwar years, which as we have noted produced a much more conservative climate for women's rights.[21]

Nonetheless, this fixity of place serves as no guarantee for the woman criminal or the hysterical body in *La nouvelle mission de Judex*. Primerose is at one point restored to health only to have another case of hysteria recur in the de Trémeuse household. Jacqueline, who is also susceptible to hypnotic suggestion, takes a poisonous vial into her already ill child's bedroom (in an earlier trance she had attempted to exchange a note with the equally "possessed" Primerose). Clearly, any woman is at risk for such "attacks" if the virtuous Jacqueline can turn "criminal."

Jacqueline's action against her own child is the result of a hypnotic suggestion by Dr. Howey, who implanted the idea after following the distressed mother to her favored "sanctuary." The site is a park with a statue of the Virgin Mary, where Jacqueline and Jacques were married and where she has now come to pray for the recovery of her child. The turn to religion here is significant not only for the religiosity produced by the war era but also for the link between hysteria and religion made by psychiatrists during this time. That is to say, the explanation of religious passion, especially female religious excitation, or even spiritual "possession," was now defined as a form of hysterical attack.[22] Thus, the female body served as a site of contestation for yet another cultural struggle, this time between the competing definitions of France as a sacred or secular state. Hysteria became another discourse mobilized by the Third Republic to counter forces outside "rational" and "scientific" state control, which included religion, spiritualism, or any other "metaphysical" impulses (anti-positivist philosophy or ideology).[23]

The potential criminality of Jacqueline in *La nouvelle mission de Judex* is in striking contrast to her uncomplicated virtue in the first *Judex* serial and is paralleled by a markedly different activity level. She is conscious for most of the second film with the exception of a few trancelike states, but Jacqueline's "actions" are rare and are usually driven by hypnotic suggestion. Moreover, Andreyor's performance style as Jacqueline in *La nouvelle mission de Judex* invokes Renée Carl's movements as Lady Beltham in *Fantômas*. In large part immobile, with the main exceptions being the hypnotic states, Jacqueline is practically paralyzed by fear, despair, and grief. Her movements are restricted to principally facial expressions and hand gestures. These movements mirror an overall slowing of the pace within the second *Judex*—a feature that Lacassin scathingly isolates, along with melodrama, as contributing to the film's inferior quality.

> Except for two or three episodes, the adventure is reduced to the painful conflicts of melodrama; only a few dazzling images (Judex hidden behind a curtain, a skeleton's hand which bursts out from a desk) rise to the surface of a pool of tepid herbal tea. . . . The performances are without sparkle: Cresté is more and more placid, Mathé frozen in the expectations of his marriage, Yvette Andreyor in tears, Levesque vaudevillesque, Musidora absent and irreplaceable.
>
> The direction, very much open to criticism, abuses the depth of field in the exteriors which the characters cross in all its lengths slowing down the rhythm which it absolutely did not need. If the director would have had the heroic courage to suppress all scenes where the characters go up and down the stairs, all those where little Jean embraces the people passing his door, he would have ameliorated an unhappy film which deserved all the criticism it received.[24]

Despite melodramatic codes of slow pacing and broad gesture, it is important to underline that we are still in the mode of the fantastic. The structure of recursion is intact alongside this heightened family drama. There are repeated kidnappings, traps, captures, rescues (one by a very intelligent horse), and hypnotic possessions throughout the film, although, again, like *Les vampires* and *Judex*, the *reason* for these events in their criminal iteration is not particularly clear. The underlying motivation for the lawlessness is often left unexamined, obscured in financial shenanigans or, perhaps more accurately, simply opaque.

The invention developed by the father of Primerose, James Milton (she is, in fact, his adopted daughter), is stolen by the criminal gang (through Primerose's aid) in the second episode, but there is not the ongoing exchange of these design plans among the criminals and Judex, which one might then expect to occur. The supposed initiating event, the invention's theft from Milton, only infrequently returns to the narrative center and is reminiscent of the first *Judex* serial, where the crimes of Favraux are essentially dispensed with in the opening moments of the film. Moreover, in *La nouvelle mission de Judex*, the criminal gang suddenly decides that *they* are interested in the whereabouts of the banker Favraux (who is also Jacqueline's father, as we remember from the first *Judex*), but this particular objective has absolutely no narrative motivation. Thus, even a red herring can be repeated within Feuillade narrative.

It also should be noted that with the shift of action to the space of the body itself, particularly through the device of hypnosis and the attendant mobility that is therein attached, the central criminal protagonist is amorphous and diffuse. At one point in the film, Jacqueline is confused over the identity of the real villains; she believes Primerose should be banished from the de Trémeuse home. In addition, it is not entirely clear from the story precisely *who* holds the hypnotic power: the seeming mastermind, Dr. Howey, or the Baroness d'Apremont (Primerose manages to be hypnotized by both of the criminals with equal ease).

The issue of hypnotic control is complicated by the language used to describe the eyes of the Baroness. One character refers to a mysterious woman (the Baroness) staying in the village in terms remarkably familiar; the woman is described as having "two large black eyes which stare at everyone."[25] Thus, oblique references to Irma/Diana/Musidora circulate repeatedly throughout Feuillade's text.

There is even evidence that the Baroness herself may be a hysteric. At some points in the discourse on hysteria during the era there is an inversion, and the incoherent ramblings of the excessively expressive female body become poetic and prophetic; that is, the female body is able to envision and to speak more than conventional language[26]—a tendency that surely melodrama exploits. In episode 7, *La main morte*, the Baroness takes on the role of a psychic, Fatima, as part of a plot to trick Cocantin into giving information on Favraux's hiding place. Fatima is described as a woman who "knows all, sees all, says all" (*Elle sait tout, voit tout, dit tout*). Whether or not the skills of Fatima/Baroness are legitimate or simply part of a ruse is irrelevant. What is significant is the ease with which Cocantin is taken in by the performance, that is, his inability to recognize a "true hysteric." In other words, *all women* are borderline hysterics, as is evident by their heightened emotionalism, expressivity, and susceptibility to suggestion as is seen in the behavior of Primerose and Jacqueline. There is thus a kind of contagion at work, which is made more troubling by the fact that it cannot be as easily isolated by class distinctions. Jacqueline and Primerose are clearly established from the opening of the film as members of the respectable middle class (although Primerose's adopted status does inject some uncertainty). In the case of Gaby and the Baroness it is much more difficult to detect their class status. They both perform multiple roles. Gaby is a "message boy" and then later a servant to the Baroness, but these are both obvious *performances,* and it is not clear what Gaby's history and status might be (until it is fixed by the flashback). But Gaby, in particular, has all the signs of being one of those troubling *nouvelles femmes:* she smokes (and lights the Baroness's cigarette, no less), dresses in masculine clothes, and takes on less than feminine poses (by straddling a chair or taking an aggressive hands-on-hips stance). The Baroness offers a similar uncertainty. There is no flashback to clear up her "true" history, nor are her performances obviously marked for us. Perhaps the biggest tip-off to her status is her *location:* she works her criminal activity out of the city space, her Paris apartment (which is then in sharp contrast to Jacques's and Jacqueline's countryside home and Judex's remote prison known as the Château Rouge). Possibly most troubling of all, the Baroness's sexuality is equally "suspicious." Her work with Dr. Howey seems exclusively a business arrangement, and her closest "colleague" appears to be Gaby. The Baronness's "femme" moments with Gaby raise the lesbian specter that has been present since Marfa's interrupted stage performance and Irma's appropriation of Marfa's costume, figuratively speaking, in subsequent episodes of *Les vampires.* Moreover, the Baroness's psychic powers, whether as ruse or reality, speak to a woman without boundaries, "too close" especially to other women—hence Gaby's, Primerose's, and Jacqueline's "seduction."[27]

This contagion across, and most troubling, blurring, class distinctions among women parallels a similar fear about the entertainment pleasures of women found in the *roman-feuilleton* (and their cinematic counterparts). We saw in the novelization for *Les vampires* that Marfa and her dresser both longed for the exciting, dangerous, and romantic life found in these stories, a phenomenon that troubled some parts of "respectable society." The popularity and dominance of crime and romance as organizing themes is seen repeatedly in the advertisements for some of the upcoming titles in *Le livre de poche* series (the publishers of *Les vampires*): *Victims of Love, The Woman Criminal, The Heroic Fiancée, The Devotion of Love, Crime and Mystery.*[28] The ongoing alternation of these topics makes one wonder if perhaps the crime is not love itself and *women's* conception of the term.

Respectable society succumbed as well to these crime stories, as *Les vampires* demonstrates when the very proper and very rich

American, Mrs. Simpson, absolutely delights (while simultaneously being horrified) in hearing Philippe recount the gory details of a recent murder. Later, she cannot sleep—not because of her beautiful surroundings but rather because of her excitation in response to the atrocities of the Vampire gang.[29] In a distinct lack of gratitude for Mrs. Simpson's appreciation of their activities, the young woman is in short order robbed and then murdered by the gang.

But, importantly, this fascination worked across class, as many of the publicity materials from Feuillade's serials demonstrate. A program for *Les vampires* at the Cinéma des Nouveautés Aubert-Palace features an "open letter" from a society woman thanking the cinema for providing a refined respite from the "Cité Géant" and for creating "a relaxing atmosphere that dispels by enchantment sad thoughts."[30] But many of the advertisements that accompany the *Le Petit Parisien*'s serialization of *Judex* are appeals for courses in clerical work across a variety of business contexts.[31] Like many of the ads that immediately follow after that day's particular installment (e.g., for various female tonics), one might expect that they were directed to women due to the large influx of women workers in this field during the World War I era (an increase that remained in place even after the war).[32]

Ann-Louise Shapiro notes that women often publicly read aloud the newspaper stories/serializations or made and shared with friends homemade books featuring the excerpts.[33] There were calls to censor both the *faits divers* and *romans-feuilletons* on the basis of their negative influence on those unable to resist their suggestion of crime.[34] The censors' targets, as Shapiro observes, were clear:

> The language while coded, is in fact transparent. Those individuals who succumbed irresistibly to criminal suggestion were not the ones who peopled the serene and severe halls of science, were not competent and capable (bourgeois, professional) men of probity and discernment. They were, rather, the worrisome groups—workers and especially women—who, according to standard, unquestioned presumptions of the period, were likely to lose control; to be erratic, overexcited; in whom instinctive responses predominated over intellectual ones; in whom the will had become feeble through faulty biology or moral lassitude or both; who were more likely to respond to "unhealthy incitements, antialtruistic and antisocial suggestions."[35]

One counterstrategy that the text offers to the contagion and uncontrollable mobility of the hysterical female body is technology. It is not insignificant that the treasured plans stolen in the opening sequences of the film deal with "rationalized" and "scientific" movement (e.g., the transmission of images and automatic propulsion). These inventions speak to the desire to "know all, see all, say all" in a highly contained and controlled, and one must add, male defined, environment. This environment is doubled in the prison/lab of Judex's Château Rouge. Here prisoners are watched, interrogated, and disciplined through a variety of mechanisms such as the one-way mirror and the typewriter that projects messages over separated and seemingly unconnected spaces with visible, firelike script that is suspended in the air ("*la machine à écrire électrique*"[36]). Such devices reinforce the mastery and ubiquity of the jailer-spectator.

It is made clear for us that this spectator is gender specific (i.e., male) during Gaby's and the Baroness's imprisonment (episode 8, *Les captives*). A lengthy sequence in this episode features Cocantin surveying the two prisoners, with the Baroness in particular receiving his undivided attention (especially as she undresses). The Baroness attempts suicide with some glass that she has broken in her cell, and Cocantin, who has been watching, rushes into the room to aid her. His rescue of the Baroness acts out a remark that Judex has just made to Gaby during his interrogation: "My child, I want to save you" (*Mon enfant, je veux vous sauver*).

However, some hysterics cannot be saved, and the Baroness uses the ensuing struggle to escape (and it thus appears even her "suicide" may have been a performance for the benefit of the spectator, as she knows that Cocantin is "viewing" her actions). In the absence of a cure, either through marriage (as Jacqueline and Primerose) or a reconfigured narrative (as Gaby and Primerose), the Baroness is left but one fate—death. Both she and Dr. Howey are killed in the explosion of a boat, an occasion accidentally triggered by Cocantin. The mark of narrative closure, the sign that the threat has been dispelled, is the sight of the dead woman's body in the water. A point-of-view shot from Judex identifies the body of the criminal as the Baroness—an event that is followed shortly thereafter by Jacques's pronouncement that the family nightmare is over and that Roger and Primerose may now marry.

Another interesting inversion occurs with this happy ending, one very much in line with the turn toward melodramatic "clarity" and "certainty." Cocantin's voyeuristic yet naive spectatorship in the Château Rouge—he has probably been "seduced" by the Baroness's performance

Judex pronounces sentence on the criminal banker Favraux with the *machine à écrire électrique* in *Judex*. Louis Feuillade. Image from the newspaper novelization of the serial in *Le Petit Parisien*. Photo from the Musée Gaumont. © Production Gaumont, 1917.

of suicide—returns us to the duplicity and uncertainty of the image, especially a cinematic one. In contrast, Judex *controls* both the prison and cinematic image by first projecting into the prison space the authoritative commands of the "*machine à écrire électrique*" (e.g., note the godlike dictum in the first *Judex* serial: "Banker Favraux, I condemned you to death, the gesture of your daughter saved your life, but I condemn you to perpetual imprisonment. Judex.").[37] Then, when Jacques decides to return to his role as *justicier* (self-appointed judge), the memory of his past exploits is projected into his home's fireplace as a type of miniature cinema image. Part of Judex's objective here might be seen as an effort to control the image by freezing and authenticating the photograph. Each of the family reunions (which are initiated by Judex) are accompanied, or rather completed, by a type of onscreen family portrait whereby all of the members assemble in a carefully composed and *posed* image, which fills the frame with a vision of harmony.

The falseness and incompleteness of the photographic image has now been "stabilized" and validated by a cinematic image, whose

Jacues d' Athys (René Cresté) finds that Delorès (Georgette Faraboni) is "a living enigma and an extraordinary clairvoyant" (*une énigme vivante et un médium extraordinaire*) in *Tih Minh*. Louis Feuillade. © Production Gaumont, 1919.

completeness and veracity derives from both a melodramatic, and crucial for our purposes, male narration.

Tih Minh

The clairvoyant woman returns, this time as a central part of the narrative, in *Tih Minh* (twelve weekly episodes beginning in February 1919).[38] Marquise Delorès (Georgette Faraboni) is one member of an international gang out to steal an important document/testament from the explorer Jacques d'Athys (René Cresté). The visionary talents of Delorès are neither a performance nor a trick in *Tih Minh* but are essential qualities of the character and, in turn, function as a crucial mechanism to transport information and action. As Jacques notes at one point, Delorès is "a living enigma and an extraordinary clairvoyant" (*une énigme vivante et un médium extraordinaire*).

Perhaps the most remarkable attribute of this medium is her permeability; not only is Delorès able to see another's past, read minds, and leave post hypnotic suggestions, but she is able to transmit the most classic of hysterical symptoms (e.g., paralysis and aphonia) seemingly at will. While the film periodically offers some "scientific" or "medical" explanation for these events, for example, "the potion of oblivion" or some other narcotic drug (a title card speculates that one drug may be opium), such information can hardly account for the trail of inert or hyperactive bodies that she leaves in her wake. The ability of Delorès to transmit and to transport people and data is thus the quintessential body in *movement.*

Although the Marquise is but one of three criminals that are identified as key members of the gang (Kistna and Dr. Gilson being the other two), Delorès serves—alongside Tih Minh (Mary Harald)—as the focal point of narrative movement in the text. It is possible to link these two women here in that while Tih Minh, Jacques d'Athys's fiancée, is clearly an object of desire and exchange that supplies the narrative drive, it is also evident that this process of exchange is frequently mediated and, moreover, *translated* by Delorès.

Tih Minh utilizes some melodramatic strategies, but it is much closer to the mode of the fantastic via the recursive repetitions that I have outlined previously. Again, this is a film where seemingly everything and nothing happens. While there is an abundance of action—and the pace here moves much more briskly than *La nouvelle mission de Judex*—there is rarely an advance, or a progression, of events. In some sense, the film does offer a more clearly defined objective than the Feuillade films previously discussed. The final testament of an expatriate English aristocrat contains information regarding great treasures and other data that is valuable to the criminal gang. (The gang has some rather undefined ties to the forces of Central Europe, i.e., Germany. In fact, later we learn that Gilson's real name is Marx.) Much of the narrative action then circulates around the attainment or retrieval of the testament (later renamed as "Document 29") by the criminal gang or Jacques and his colleagues.

Nonetheless, the trajectory of the testament or document is paralleled by a similar process of exchange between the two groups of Jacques's fiancée, Tih Minh. Moreover, the document, at one point, is handed over as a ransom to the criminal gang under the mistaken assumption by the servant Rosette that Tih Minh is still their captive (episode 4, *L'homme dans la malle*). Consequently, the various crises initiated by the multiple kidnappings of Tih Minh lead attention far from the "plot" concerning the document; it is often unclear *where* the document is located. Instead, the focus is on the exchange of the body of Tih Minh—in varying states of consciousness.

After the first capture of Tih Minh by the criminal gang (episode 1, *Le philtre d'oubli*), Delorès is called upon to utilize her skills. Delorès, in an explicit display of her (and Tih Minh's) permeable boundary, holds her head next to Tih Minh, reads her thoughts, and prophesies future events. She attempts to leave a hypnotic suggestion, but meeting some resistance from Tih Minh, Kistna decides to utilize as well a drug that erases memory. Returning home, Tih Minh has neither speech nor memory. Later, it will require the efforts of both Dr. Clauzel ("the celebrated English psychiatrist") through hypnosis and Delorès through clairvoyance to construct Tih Minh's story and effect a cure.

However, before the cure can be completed (through marriage to Jacques), the hysterical body of Tih Minh must endure all manner of transport. Throughout the course of the film, Tih Minh will be kidnapped three times; returned once (in a semiconscious state); rescued by the servant, Placide (holding out her pet dog as temptation and then comically leading Tih Minh back to safety over an enormous distance with this "bait"); and rescued off the side of a mountain (where the kidnappers have thrown the body). Tih Minh's precipitous descent down the mountain matches a similar fall over a wall later at the d'Athys home. She is rescued from this last trauma by Delorès, who happens at that moment to be returning to the estate—in her own semi-hypnotic state—to see the magnetic Dr. Clauzel (episodes 9 and 10: *La branche de salut* and *Mercredi*).

Delorès's intervention at the wall is a physical display of the imbricated paths of these two female hysterics. Moreover, Delorès's movements in the film, while not quite as excessive, are quite similar to Tih Minh's—she is also the objective of several kidnapping or capture schemes (by both sides). In both instances, but perhaps most clearly in the case of Tih Minh, this exchange of the female body can be seen as an effort to literalize or narrativize the mobility represented in the body of the hysteric. It is also another recursive strand within the text. Delorès is not so much Tih Minh's double in the sense of an oppositional force, for surely these two women are too close to be a duality, but rather they form a kind of shadow or reversal of each other. The reversal images of the two women testify to an inability to fix a permanent sign for female criminality (which was attempted in the representation of Irma's black bodysuit); their ultimate exchangeability is an ongoing symptom rather than an erasure of the Musidora icon.

The functional linkage of the two women with respect to narrative movement is overlaid at the level of the melodramatic story line as well. Delorès is enlisted, under Dr. Clauzel's hypnosis, to recount (episode 7, *L'evocation*) the events that led to the gang's pursuit of "Document 29." However, this history, told in flashback, is Tih Minh's story (which despite Clauzel's treatment she still cannot recall), for the document was originally stolen from Tih Minh's father (who was then murdered by Gilson/Marx). But the recitation of Tih Minh's past by Delorès speaks not just to the closeness of the two women but also to the "clairvoyant's" ability to *act out or perform multiple* roles—the mark of a true hysteric.[39] More troubling, from the perspective of patriarchal ideology, is that this multiple identification occurs across the supposed markers of sexual difference. That is to say, the hysteric acts out a sexual fantasy that is bisexual, taking on both "masculine" and "feminine" roles.[40] Female sexuality, yet again, "too close" spirals further and further into uncertainty. Irma's recognition of Marfa's desire, the ultimate uncertainty about one's role or placement in patriarchy, is once more center stage.

Is it any wonder that Delorès is not just a "foreigner" but also an outsider of *unknown* origin—her dark features leading to the rumor she is either Andalusian or Cuban. Nor should we be surprised that her recursive twin, Tih Minh, is likewise foreign, but perhaps more significant, the product of a mixed race family (Caucasian and Asian). Her Vietnamese background adds not just an international component but speaks to the era's orientalist fantasies. As we know from Edward Said's work, *orientalism* is both a diffuse and highly specific term. That is to say, the area labeled the "Orient" can and did extend from the Middle East to Asia but referenced something quite particular (ideologically speaking). The Orient designated for the West all things non-European, all the things Europe both wanted to access and contain but not necessarily to claim: the nonrational, the exotic, the childlike or immature. The definition of the Oriental as different and "other" both sets in place a corollary definition of Europe as "obviously" superior and legitimates the "necessity" of European imperialism.[41] Distilled then on the body of Tih Minh is national, racial, and sexual otherness. Thus the "mysterious Hindu document" and Tih Minh are logically aligned, not only as valued treasures stolen from Jacques's home but as

Eastern enigmas whose true meaning must be retrieved and decoded. Moreover this process of decoding or translating is, as we know from the document, vital to Europe's security (and all that it represents, given Tih Minh's mark of "otherness": patriarchy, heterosexuality, colonialism).

It is equally crucial that Delorès be the instrument of Tih Minh's "translation." For Delorès's shadowy presence is yet another threat to be contained. Significantly, her reconstruction of Tih Minh's past comes through the intercession of Dr. Clauzel. Thus, Delorès's hysterical recitation is not so much the speech of a silenced woman (and all the subversive qualities that might potentially entail) but rather an act that Janet Beizer would label as "ventriloquy." As Beizer notes, "the potential scandal of the speaking body is neutralized by virtue of its production by an external agent. In fact, the body does not speak; it is spoken, ventriloquized by the master text that makes it signify. The woman becomes a text, but she is a text within a text, a text *framed* as signifying source by another, mediating text."[42] The frame or mediation for Delorès's speech is not just Dr. Clauzel but also Jacques and his friend, Sir Francis Grey, who supply, in turn, the narrative sequence for the story by posing a series of questions concerning the document and Tih Minh. The grouping suggests that science, patriarchy, and imperialism all align forces to decode and *fix* the troublesome data presented to them.

But, equally noteworthy, the doctor represents medicine not only as a "scientific" enterprise but as bastion of rationality, whose "other" is both spiritual and female. Mesmerism (Delorès's gift) in particular was perceived as an incorrect and dangerous use of hypnosis and was often banned from live performances in order to protect the more vulnerable elements in society (again, the working classes and women).[43] A whole series of troublesome anxieties can be defeated if science can triumph over spiritualism (represented by Delorès's mesmerism). Moreover, like *La nouvelle mission de Judex*, *Tih Minh* speaks to both the circulation of religious fervor during the war years and its containment by a secular governing apparatus.

Jacques's "narration" of Delorès's/Tih Minh's story (with the aid of Dr. Clauzel and Sir Francis) is one of the few "actions" that can be assigned to the lead male character. While the pace of the film may have increased from the last serial, René Cresté, who plays both Judex and Jacques d'Athys, has slowed his movements to broad, melodramatic gestures (much like Jacqueline in *La nouvelle mission de Judex*). In fact, as Lacassin noted earlier, the second *Judex* serial features an increasingly inactive—or perhaps even phlegmatic—Judex ("*de plus en plus calme*").[44] Throughout *La nouvelle mission de Judex,* Judex does not so much act as *pose,* standing in a doorway after an explosion or organizing a type of family "portrait" after each reunion.

This *calme* is transformed into melodramatic excess in *Tih Minh.* Jacques's poses are now inflected with exaggerated gestures that signify emotional despair, primarily over Tih Minh's illness. Most of the physical action with respect to encounters with the criminal gang (rescues, brawls, etc.) in the first half of the film is restricted to the servants Placide and Rosette. It is only with the beginnings of Tih Minh's recovery (her renewed health is signaled to Jacques by her first words in weeks: "*Je t'aime*") that the hero begins to have a more direct physical engagement with the enemy (episode 6, *Oiseaux de nuit*). In other words, it is only the assurance of Tih Minh's *place* within Jacques's family, her cure, that can alleviate Jacques's own excessive, or hysterical, gestures. Moreover, this placement, or fixity, of the woman's body is underlined at the conclusion of the film by not one, or even two, but three weddings. Surely the specter of unstable sexuality has been defeated.

One of these weddings is of the two loyal servants, Placide and Rosette, who have, in fact, done most of the work in the film not only domestically speaking but as active agents in pursuit of the gang while Jacques was stricken with despair. Of course, their role is to ensure that there *is* decent and trustworthy help out there for the middle and upper classes (which is a repetition of the problem of the unfaithful servant seen in *Les vampires* and *Judex*). However, their marriage functions also to demonstrate the ideal aspiration for the working classes (within the logic of the text). Placide's and Rosette's goal is to become like Jacques and Tih Minh, and strange enough there is a sequence when these two servants watch and mime the upper-class couple's romantic behavior. Their conduct is then mirrored at the end of the serial with an important difference, as the two upper-class couples (Jacques and Tih Minh, Francis and Jeanne) *watch* the wedding of Placide and Rosette—but from the safety of another space and, indeed, frame. Yet another troublesome group, the working class, is now fixed and contained. Nonetheless, this is not a completely "happy ending," for the remaining hysteric, Delorès, disturbs the proceedings. Delorès has begged Dr. Clauzel to continue his treatment of her: "Oh! yes Doctor, deliver me from the influences that have made me the accomplice of so many crimes" (episode 11: *Le document*).⁴⁵ Science triumphs over mesmerism or spiritualism. While the reconstructed narrative that she completes with his aid appears to produce a cure, it is brief. The written confession of her life of crime is immediately followed by her suicide. In this case, the ventriloquized body has the last word; Delorès, like Diana Monti (Musidora), scripts her own ending.

Zone 4: The Male Body as Dermographic Tableau

Barrabas

With *Barrabas* (twelve weekly episodes starting in 1920),⁴⁶ Feuillade's last crime serial, the alternative cinema mode we have been examining makes an interesting shift away from the figure of the woman to the male body. Up to the serials of *Barrabas,* we have traced a figure of the woman circulating throughout the five previous serials as one who has emerged from the Paris Metro and walked the city's streets (Joséphine); one who has effectively led a criminal gang (Irma/Diana, Baronne); one who has refused to speak or to remember (Primerose, Jacqueline, and Tih Minh); and one who has written a counternarrative (Delorès). But the threat she represents remains. Thus we see the turn in *Barrabas* to the one area where closure and resolution may be possible—the male body. This is not to argue that these films are solely, or ultimately, concerned with male identity but rather that a narrative more clearly preoccupied with these issues poses an opportunity finally to fix the mode of the fantastic's mobility—particularly in light of the mobility's recurrent alignment with the body of the woman. Lacassin states that after *Barrabas,* Feuillade believed the crime serial format to be exhausted and thus framed his subsequent serials specifically within the genre of melodrama.⁴⁷ Feuillade's observation here is particularly perceptive since the "exhaustion" of the format might well be the product of the narrative thread pursued and resolved in *Barrabas.*

It is even possible to argue that despite the recurrent motif of the criminal gang, *Barrabas* is a film that has in many ways already slipped from the mode of the fantastic to melodrama. While there are still episodic interludes taken up with the usual adventures—kidnapping, murder, and assorted assaults—the melodramatic framework has been strengthened considerably. Now, rather than the diffuse threat to the family and home offered in the previous three serials, we have a specific agenda at stake: the integrity of the father's name.

Certainly, Feuillade may have made a judgment about the commercial viability of the crime serial after *Barrabas*, but this particular serial's fascination, indeed one might say obsession, with paternal identity and its attendant class privilege is consistent with not just conventions of melodrama but also the conservative social forces mobilized in France during the postwar era. Moreover, this serial cites explicitly its historical placement via the use of a prologue that invokes a much less complicated time than the story to follow.

The prologue situates us prior to the war, in 1914, at a train station, where a reunion between an orphaned brother and sister, Jacques (Fernand Hermann) and Françoise Varèse (Blanche Montel), is taking place. Accompanying Jacques to the station is his good friend, Raoul (Edouard Mathé). In short order, Jacques and Raoul are off to a party in Passy thrown by their friend, Laure. At the party we are introduced to Rudolf Strelitz (Gaston Michel), a Parisian financier, and Lewis Mortimer, a rich American and soon-to-be philanthropist to the trustworthy itinerant merchants, Biscotin and Biscotine (husband and wife), who rescued Mortimer from a vicious assault on his way to Laure's party. The epilogue ends with Mortimer's endowment of a dairy shop to the working couple and the American's request to be godfather to their firstborn child.

With the beginning of the first episode, now set in 1919, the world has considerably altered. As Feuillade's scenario notes, "Five years have passed. The war has shaken the world."[48] The war years quickly and skillfully elided, we are left to examine these changes in more prosaic but perhaps more revelatory manner. Biscotin (Biscot) and his wife (Jane Rollette) are featured at the opening of their new store; Raoul and Françoise are engaged; and Laure is concerned about her absent lover, Mortimer, from whom she has received only letters but has not seen over the last five years. As the shop owners bemoan the missing godfather (they now have a son), the film cuts to the story of Jacques Rougier.

Rougier's story picks up the missing "father" scenario, for Rougier has just been released from prison for the earlier attack on Mortimer. However, Rougier is but an alias to protect his family; his true name is Joseph d'Albane, the father of single mother and war widow, Simone Delpierre (Lugane). Rougier/d'Albane hides his criminal past from Simone, but *le stigmate*, a gang tattoo, is visible on the repentant father and serves as a trace of his vulnerability. Despite his best efforts, Rougier is drawn quickly back into the web of crime. The agent of his recidivism is no less than Strelitz, the Parisian financier introduced in the prologue, who we now learn runs the criminal gang. Strelitz, much like the banker Favraux when we first see him, puts little value on family ties beyond financial gain. Strelitz uses the family to blackmail Rougier and at one point announces that his superior strength can be attributed to the very lack of familial ties: "Strelitz is stronger than you, and he holds you, Strelitz does not have a family." To put this another way, Strelitz the banker is beyond shame and not susceptible to the morality of bourgeois family life. He then frames Rougier for the murder of Laure (whose questions on Mortimer's absence jeopardize another Strelitz plot). Captured and convicted, Rougier faces execution. Enter the orphan, Jacques Varèse, the attorney for Rougier's defense. Despite considerable circumstantial evidence, Varèse believes in his client's innocence. However, Rougier will not aid in his own defense due to his sense of family honor, and he dies without telling Simone of his arrest and conviction. Varèse, still believing in Rougier's innocence, continues the investigation into the convict's past with the aid of a coded testament left by Rougier.

However, Varèse awakens one morning to find the mark (the identifying tattoo) of the outlaw gang, Barrabas, sketched on his arm. When Varèse attempts to confront the leader of the gang, Strelitz, about these marks, the mastermind informs him that the mark signifies his true destiny, for Rougier was Varèse's *father*. Varèse's past, then, is "a heritage of blood, madness, and crime."[49] As Varèse had believed he was an orphan, the information is both shocking and plausible. The revelation thus frames the entire narrative. What had begun as an investigation into Rougier's past becomes a necessary clarification of Varèse's own history.

At one level, it is possible to see Varèse as continuing the previous serials' preoccupation with hysteria. The hysteria of Jacques d'Athys expressed in stasis and excessive physical gestures is now literally inscribed on the body. Thus, Varèse's body becomes a type of dermographic tableau[50] that speaks the anxiety that has heretofore circulated largely, but not exclusively, on the body of woman. In the dermographic tableau the doctor's traces remain on the (usually female) patient, marking not only her sensitivity/illness but also the doctor's words. The writing on the body of Varèse by Strelitz speaks to an illegitimate, or rather illicit (in the sense of criminal), paternity. For Varèse to be healed, he must retake control of the story that surrounds the "text" on his arm. What is particularly crucial to *Barrabas* is that the "cure" undertaken in *La nouvelle mission de Judex* and *Tih Minh*—the reconstructed family history—is not presented as an episode or a flashback but rather as the central goal of the film. Thus, the mark of anxiety inscribed on Inspector Juve's arm in *Fantômas* has been narrativized in order that it can be finally healed in *Barrabas*. But it is the process of discovery, an assembly of clues from traces left by the father (photographs, wallet, watch, and boat ticket) rather than a single testimony, that reconstructs Jacques's history. To a certain extent, it is Jacques who structures and frames his own story. Nonetheless, the photographic image returns in this serial as a piece of evidence, but again a rather suspect one. At one point, Jacques turns to his friend Raoul and asks if an old portrait of his father bears any resemblance to him. If the photograph does provide this information it is not the kind that Varèse can readily see or read. The photograph in itself is incomplete and must be complemented by a full-scale narrative before the identifying marks can be read correctly.

The crisis of identity for Varèse is linked once again to several layers of anxiety within *Barrabas*. As Jacques pursues the criminal gang, he encounters a forlorn but essentially decent young woman, Noëlle Maupré, who has joined the gang as the result of Strelitz's framing of *her* father for embezzlement. Shamed into signing onto the criminal activity, Noëlle's desperate plight is further complicated (thanks to a Strelitz cohort) by her addiction to drugs and a life of wanton debauchery. The reference to drug addiction (opium and cocaine) and its attendant moral depravity circulates in the background of *Tih Minh* (episode 3, *The Mysteries of the Villa Circé*) and is exclusively linked to a problem besetting well-to-do women. But, of course in this instance, Noëlle's difficulties are initiated by the trauma induced on the father's name and obfuscate any class issues.

Beyond this concern with the personal and familial, the film foregrounds issues of social mobility as well. As in *Judex*, the rise of marginalized workers (and thieves) to members of the respectable middle class is featured in the film; in *Barrabas* we watch the rise of Biscotin and Raoul's wartime buddy, albeit prewar poacher, Laugier. Again mirroring *Judex*, the preoccupation with the rise of the servant or working class deflects the anxiety from Varèse's own potential class *descent*. Varèse is a lawyer, and unlike Jacques de Trémeuse (or d'Athys), his family has no title or independent wealth. Consequently, Varèse is even more vulnerable to the vagaries of the market or scandal.

The gang's (and Strelitz's) use of the title "Barrabas" is a biblical reference to an unpunished criminal (Barrabas escapes crucifixion with the substitution of Christ in his place). But Jacques's recovery of the past recontextualizes the mark and allows the rewriting of the dermographic tableau (and its attendant multilayered anxiety) from a stigma of crime to a stigmata of innocence and martyrdom. In fact, Varese's father was not Rougier, but a drowning victim whose stolen identity papers ultimately landed in Strelitz's hands. After learning the truth about his father, Varése tells Rougier's daughter, Simone, that they had all been framed (Simone had noted the marks on her father, Rougier, and Varése's friend, Noëlle Maupré). With Varése's story reassembled and his name cleared, his narrative, his past, becomes the point of reference for all of them, the abnegation of their criminal marks or guilt—this link between them is strengthened as they all share essentially the same class backgrounds. Jacques's story now frames these other past histories (Rougier's and Noëlle's were told as episodic flashbacks).

Nonetheless, even Jacques's reconstruction cannot serve as complete closure on this text. *Barrabas* ends with the requisite wedding; this time it is Françoise (Jacques's sister) and Raoul. But Jacques remains unmarried (although attracted to Noëlle) and an epilogue title card notes that while Varèse's extended "family" is now happy, the sadness of Rougier's daughter (Simone) casts a somber mood over the entire atmosphere. The woman's story can never be completely resolved or contained within Jacques's narrative or for that matter adequately narrativized.

The extratextual trajectory of Jacques Varèse is strikingly similar to the one of Joséphine (from *Fantômas*) to Jacqueline (in *Judex*) through the actress of Yvette Andreyor. That is to say, Varèse is portrayed by the actor Fernand Hermann—the "hypnotic" and "hypnotized" boyfriend of Irma Vep, Moréno, in *Les vampires*. However, while Joséphine's reformation is a textual slippage from one film to the next, Moréno gets an opportunity to erase the criminal stigma over the course of the film in *Barrabas*. This is precisely the narrative drive: the hysteric Moréno/Varèse is now cured, his true identity as the son of respectable father assured. And this cure has been the implementation of an Oedipal narrative. It is through this last shift in the zone of anxiety that the modality of the fantastic is exhausted in Feuillade's crime serials, leaving us with a film at the precipice of classical cinema form. But uncertainty is never far from cinematic narrative when we examine some other casting reversals in the serials. Strelitz, the incarnation of evil and the antithesis of family relations, is the long-suffering father, Kerjean (Gaston Michel), of *Judex*. Perhaps more important,

Strelitz's accomplice, Dr. Lucius, a somewhat minor character, is none other than Bréon, Inspector Juve of *Fantômas*. That Jacques's redemption is not ultimately completed and he is unable to end the Oedipal scenario successfully (through marriage) suggests that Juve's slippage from frame to frame, from character to character, from law to disorder, circulates endlessly in all our narratives.

Afterword
The Cinematic Legacy of Feuillade and Musidora and a Different Way of Knowing

> "She has no morals . . . is that a problem?"
> Comment by Maggie Cheung's "character" during the film *Irma Vep* on the persona of Irma Vep/Musidora

Olivier Assayas's invocation of Irma Vep in a 1996 film is but one of many repetitions of the Irma/Musidora character in cinema history. Indeed, the figure is one that haunts not just Feuillade's texts but marks a significant strain of French cinema and can even be seen in other national cinema contexts (e.g., Fritz Lang's *Spiders*, 1919). Perhaps more significant, Irma/Musidora can be understood as a type of visual shorthand for another mode of cinematic representation, another model for cinema history. If my focus on Musidora in a concluding discussion on Feuillade seems a bit tangential or digressive, let me take the opportunity to underline once again the centrality of the actress to the films and aesthetic mode in question. This is neither a feminist polemic nor a fan's plea for Musidora's recognition in cinema history (although perhaps a bit of both these elements are here) as much as an effort to foreground a key component of Feuillade's serials; what Musidora represents in her bodysuit is indeterminacy as a different mode of knowing.

To provide a bit of context for the 1996 variation on the figure of Irma/Musidora, let us look at the path that leads to Cheung's comments. Henri d'Ursel's surrealist short film *La perle* (1928), based on a poem by Georges Hugnet, operates much like one of Todorov's classic fantastic tales that feature an ongoing hesitation between the dream and waking states; the ambiguity in *La perle* is only resolved with the last shot of the film. The narrative finds a young man on the track of a pearl that has fallen from a necklace he has just purchased for his girlfriend. As he pursues the pearl, he murders one woman in a forest, but on waking afterward all trace of the crime has mysteriously vanished from his previously bloodied hands. The trail of the pearl then leads the man to a hotel, where a host of women, jewel thieves, can be found clad in the notorious black bodysuits. His sexual liaison with one of the women ends his romance with his original girlfriend, but as he chases his new love through the forest, she suddenly falls in the same place and in the same pose as the earlier murdered woman. Her body transforms into the image of his prior victim and suddenly the materiality of the crime and the pearl both appear all too clearly to the hero. The woman's death this time stops the narrative flow; there are no more transformations or chases, and we are left at the scene of the crime as the film ends.

This summary does little to convey the sense of repetition and the leaps of logic that drive *La perle* (just as any proper narrative reconstruction of a dream state must do to produce order). The pearl and its associative link with the female body—the man originally selects the pearl necklace gift from a woman's stocking—initiate a series of encounters with elusive and troublesome women (who operate as both crime victims and perpetrators). Perhaps the most troublesome aspects of these women are their exchangeability and mutability, and here again the necklace is telling. Such finery or ornamentation references not just the female consumer, who is so crucial to the period's sense of the *nouvelle femme*, but also to an understanding of the feminine as surface and construction. The film's homage to Musidora/Irma through the bodysuit is inspired by both the pleasure and danger behind this construction (and its implications for female and male identity).

Musidora is also central to the remake of *Judex* (1963) by Georges Franju. Franju continues the process of abstraction begun in Feuillade (and necessitated by a nonserialized version of the film), with some interesting alterations. First, the family melodrama is downplayed and the emphasis is on marvelous gadgets (the typewriter that writes "in fire"), secret passageways, and of course, Diana/Musidora. In an interview, Franju noted that he found Judex fairly passive and ineffective and that his sympathies were usually with the figures of criminality (like the character Fantômas).[1] In Franju's version, even more so than Feuillade's, Judex (Channing Pollock) is in the background, and random events rather than skill or logic seem to save the day. As in Feuillade's film, the center of gravity for the film is found in the figure of Diana/Musidora.

Also like Feuillade, Franju relies heavily on the reversal image and shock. Jacqueline (Edith Scob) and Diana (Francine Bergé) form one reversal (light and dark), and Daisy and Diana form another. In

Franju's *Judex*, it is clearly Daisy (Sylva Koscina) who defeats Diana, but this time their epic battle is played out on a rooftop in near silence with close-ups of their black and white legs (as both are in bodysuits), giving us again a reversal and ending with Diana's fall to her death.

But Diana also serves as a kind of visual shock. At one point, she dresses as a nun in order to kidnap Jacqueline. After the capture is complete, she whips out a small compact from the sleeve of her habit and ensures that not a hair is out of place. This gesture underlines the elements of performance to be sure, but also it is a violation of the image of the sacred through its representation of the vain nun (and later the nun who smokes, after she pulls a cigarette from the same sleeve). Moreover, the capture of Jacqueline produces another formal shock when the sound and image track seem to split, and Jacqueline's scream is replaced by a train whistle just as Diana plunges a sedative into her victim.

But if *Judex* is an explicit homage to Musidora and Feuillade, Franju's *Les yeux sans visage* (1959) is a prime example of the cinema of uncertainty and the preoccupations therein. The film deals with a plastic surgeon's efforts to graft a new face onto his daughter's damaged visage (which is a result of an automobile accident where her father was the driver). Perhaps the most astonishing scene in the film, and indeed one of the most startling and disturbing in all of cinema, occurs during the facial transplant. Here the film presents in graphic detail an operation whereby an entire face is traced, cut, and then lifted off intact for its new "owner." The surface quality of female identity is made quite literal for us in this impossible vision of surgical reconstruction.

Moreover, a bit of dialogue at the dinner table between the father (Pierre Brasseur) and his daughter, Christiane (Edith Scob) reminds us what is at stake in the domain of the uncertain. The surgeon pronounces his daughter "dead" and tells her that the new face is the opportunity for a new name and new identity. His declaration upsets the daughter since she wanted to regain her old life (and old love). Perhaps more distressing, the graft demonstrates the instability of all identity—no matter how carefully constructed—for it quickly deteriorates before our eyes. A sequence of still photographs documents the process of degradation over time. As Christiane's face returns to its earlier damaged state, the daughter is ordered to wear a mask, adding yet another level of explicit illusion to our already shaky sense of identity. The daughter is reluctant to don this disguise, perhaps in despair of her disfigurement but also in denial of her father's direct command. On one level the mask "covers" the crime of the doctor, but perhaps most significant, it also serves to ensure that it is the father's hand behind the mold of female identity. The mask therefore functions simultaneously as a sign of father's control and the arbitrary nature of that control.[2] The hollowness of the mask speaks to the ultimate ineffectiveness and capriciousness of both the father's naming and surgical talents.

The one thing that is stable or fixed in Christiane's face is her eyes. The transplant surgery carefully follows the tracing around this area and the daughter's mask is hollowed out at these spaces. Here one might speculate that the authentic self might be found, if it were not for the dilemma that all we see in the film is so visually suspect. Indeed, the film begins with the doctor's faithful assistant, Louise (Alida Valli), repeatedly wiping the windshield of her car in a effort to improve her vision, and then as we cut to her point of view shot, there are but two dimly lit circles formed by the headlights that fall off into complete darkness. But the visual uncertainty of the film resides at the level of logic or probability (could I, the viewer, have just seen this?), while its system of representation is highly realistic and invokes an almost documentary aesthetic.

Ultimately, Christiane revolts by murdering Louise and setting free the doctor's kennel of dogs, which attack and kill him. This vengeful turn against the father could be seen both as a rebellion against his effort to name Christiane (not just once, but twice) and the larger rational, medical practice that verifies the patriarchal order, enabling such naming. But this system of logic and order has been under assault throughout the film by its relentless pursuit of impossible vision.

Considerably less bleak, but equally engaged with the fluidity of identity, is Jacques Rivette's *Céline et Julie vont en bateau* (1974). At one point in the film the two lead characters, who are female, zip by on roller skates dressed in the tell-tale black bodysuits. Nonetheless, such visual markers are almost redundant, as the film is a perfect illustration of the recursion embodied in Musidora/Irma's suit. The two women, who seem to meet in the opening of the film by chance, are introduced with an accompanying title card that forewarns us that all is not as it seems: "Most of the time it started like this." Thus, a repetition is implied before the narrative even begins. This seriality is underlined as the two women go on together to participate in a narrative that they construct (with the help of some shared magical candy). Each woman inserts herself in the same role within the story line, but near the end

"She has no morals . . . is that a problem?" Maggie Cheung as *Irma Vep*. Olivier Assayas (1996), Zeitgeist Films.

of the film both women appear in the same role simultaneously. The somewhat suspect goal of the narrative is to save a young girl who is trapped in the "dangerous" story space, but clearly the pleasure and performance of Céline and Julie is the real story here. The recursion appears in the framing story as well, for the film ends as it began, with the two women's initial encounter repeated, but with their roles reversed. The last shot of the film breaks with what little diegetic unity might be remaining. A cat turns and looks directly at the camera, a distancing device (typical in early cinema) enhanced by the seemingly knowing glance of its nonhuman perpetrator.

More explicitly connected to Feuillade's *Les vampires*, Olivier Assayas's *Irma Vep* circulates around, or rather is obsessed with, the figure of Irma/Musidora/Maggie Cheung. Cheung, playing "herself" in the film, has been selected to star as Irma Vep in a remake of *Les vampires*. It is a project doomed from the start, and as usual Irma is at the center of the turmoil. While the film within a film's replacement director for the remake pronounces Irma/Musidora as fixed within a fin-de-siècle Parisian working-class context and decides that Cheung must be replaced, the original director, René Vidal (Jean-Pierre Léaud), understands the aptness of Cheung for the role. Of course, he is driven mad (or at least wildly neurotic) by the task.

On meeting Cheung, Vidal puts together a string of adjectives in the hopes of conveying to the actress the sense of Irma—"grace," "mysterious," "beautiful," "magical," "strong," "modern"—the litany alone demonstrating the ultimately futile desire to name and thereby limit Irma. However, Vidal then tries a much more productive strategy—he plays a clip from the Feuillade serial with Irma in her bodysuit and, most important, with the sound turned off. Now our reversal screen is free to move about without the restraints of narrative (a clip without introduction), language, or sound. The clip is significant not only for the bodysuit but for the sequence involved—Irma's abduction by Moréno in the middle of her own criminal activity of robbery. Irma moves from public to private space (from hotel hallway to hotel room), from criminal to crime victim (her kidnapping), exchanges places with another woman, and is shockingly propelled out the window (with the trademark impossible fall). These movements are a series of transgressions that include a deviation from cinematic norm (the disturbing and disruptive move between spaces).

Vidal notes that he has chosen Cheung for the part on the basis of *The Heroic Trio* (Ching Siu Tung, Johnny To, 1993), a film where the action and ambiguity of the female characters are served in equally large doses. The women are clad in black bodysuits much like Irma, which preserves the fetish and fascination of the female body while strangely downplaying difference. The masks and buffed body shapes lend a certain sexual ambiguity, thereby carrying on the slippage from male to female begun with the move from *Fantômas* to *Les vampires*. Moreover, the clip Vidal shows from *Trio* features not one but two black-clad women in the midst of a pitched battle with each other. The reversals literally fly across our screen, thereby demonstrating an ongoing exchangeability.

Cheung's extension of Irma Vep's sexual indeterminacy is made explicit in the Assayas film. Paralleling Vidal's none-too-subtle attraction to Cheung is Zoé's interest. Zoé, a wardrobe worker, expresses her desire for the actress to the hostess at a dinner party where much of the crew has gathered. The hostess in turn poses a "helpful" and yet not completely disinterested series of questions to Cheung: "So do you like girls?" "Do you like sex with girls?" "Do you like her [Zoé]?" Cheung's cheerful reply, "I never thought about it," seems not so much disingenuous as consistent with her function within the film and the film within the film—to be the projection screen of every possible desire. Moreover, Cheung's answer is complicated by a sequence after the party—is it her dream?—when Cheung dressed as Irma Vep (or rather in the updated latex version of the suit) commits her own transgressions via a hotel robbery and a lengthy voyeuristic surveillance of a nude woman's private phone conversation. The bodysuit provides a screen for Cheung herself to try on a number of desires.

Cheung's ethnic difference has been read as evidence that *Irma Vep* is not so much metacinematic as a commentary about the effects of globalization on contemporary filmmaking.[3] While certainly this question is one the film directly engages, the centrality of Cheung/Irma/Musidora points back to the enigma that woman has represented in cinema and abstracted through an almost infinite process of recursion in the Feuillade serials. In this instance, Cheung's Asian identity overdetermines or extends exponentially the difference embodied in Irma's costume. Such extension is hardly new to Western culture or even Assayas's *Irma Vep*, as is evidenced by the intersection of orientalist and patriarchal fantasies in *Tih Minh*. Although Cheung notes that Irma/Musidora has "no morals," it is perhaps more accurate to state that her real crime is that Irma has no stake in the *Western* moral paradigm represented by a rational, legible, and certain universe. Thus, one might say that there is an ethic, if not a morality (in the sense of a fixed code), at work in Irma Vep.

I have proposed a reading of Feuillade's/Musidora's contributions to cinema based on the underlying and unrelenting principle of uncertainty at work in the crime serials. I am not arguing for either one's willful inscription of this principle as much as I am identifying a mode of cinema and a method of history produced by the conditions of the times and yet very much informing our own. At the heart of the mode and the method—and perhaps the cinema itself—is a thoroughgoing critique of the real and the limits of representation. Moreover, the "structure" of the mode is flux, and movement for the uncertainty is not so much a concept in itself (e.g., nihilism or relativism) as a type of ongoing dialogue and criticism of the real. Thus, as the "real" and "certitude" shift ground, albeit under the codes of naturalism, so does the cinema of uncertainty, but in this case the fluidity of movement is telegraphed at each step along the way through the various devices of dislocation we have noted. Like the cat in *Céline et Julie vont en bateau*, we can only look on in bemusement, bewilderment, and wonder at the many possibilities proposed by the cinema.

The ethical stance of indeterminacy drives all these iterations and yet its very existence so threatens the conventional representations of cinema and indeed knowledge itself that the cycle of repetition from indeterminacy to repression to chaos is seen time and time again. The very ending of *Irma Vep* skillfully stages this for us. As the camera centers and fetishizes the body of Irma Vep/Cheung, the film begins to break down; any narrative context drops out, and the very image itself seems to degrade and disintegrate. Briefly, a clear picture reasserts itself, but appropriately enough it is of Irma crossing the rooftops. We might see this as narrative's resiliency except that we know from prior information that this sequence is shot with Maggie Cheung's double, thus denying the very stability of character identification that narrative seeks so often to establish. If this recursive reminder were not enough, the sequence's one bit of written text, Irma's name, is scratched on the film backward, pointing toward the reversal or inversion that lurks behind the black bodysuit. At last, the film image tries repeatedly to fix on Irma's eyes (a standard tactic, as we have seen), but the visual meltdown continues till we are left with only a completely blank, all-white screen. The filmmaker or historian may try to stabilize and contain the possibilities of the screen within a screen via the implementation of more legible or certain narrative or authorial forms, but the woman's body/screen space remains as the site of resistance.

Notes

Introduction

1. These works have particularly challenged my way of conceptualizing film history, but this has been an incredibly rich and exciting area within feminist film studies over the last decade or more. Other scholars who have produced groundbreaking work in this area include Patrice Petro, *Joyless Streets;* Miriam Hansen, *Babel and Babylon;* Giuliana Bruno, *Streetwalking on a Ruined Map;* and Janet Staiger, *Bad Women.* Although most of these works examine early and classical cinema traditions, I would be remiss if I did not also mention B. Ruby Rich's *Chick Flicks,* a fascinating history and critical work on the development of feminist film studies and women's filmmaking practices.
2. Schlüpmann, "Cinema as Anti-Theatre."
3. Stamp, *Movie Struck Girls,* 103–25.
4. Ibid., 126.
5. Rabinovitz, *For the Love of Pleasure,* 181–82.
6. Moi, *Sexual/Textual Politics,* 123–26.
7. Cixous, "Sorties," 83.
8. Cixous and Calle-Gruber, *Rootprints,* 4–9.
9. I have elsewhere argued that this model of history has already been put in place by the filmmaker Jean-Luc Godard in his monumental video series *Histoire(s) du cinéma* (1988–98). See my essay, "The Evidence and Uncertainty of Silent Film in *Histoire(s) du cinéma.*" Although this may seem bizarre, or at best ironic, to some feminist critics, Godard's *Histoire(s)* has served as another influential text on the formulation of my feminist methodology.
10. All dates for the Feuillade films are taken from Francis Lacassin's *Maître des lions.*
11. See particularly Francis Lacassin's richly detailed and beautifully illustrated *Maître des lions* and the special edition of *1895* on Louis Feuillade, edited by Jacques Champreux and Alain Carou. This edition was compiled with support of the *Giornate del Cinema Muto* in conjunction with the Sacile silent film festival, which featured a retrospective of Feuillade's films.
12. Richard Abel's publishing on this topic is substantial, but especially crucial are two books on this era, *French Cinema: The First Wave* and *The Ciné Goes to Town.*
13. A forthcoming work on silent film promises another feminist reading of Musidora's work in Feuillade's films as well as a much more detailed discussion of Musidora's other film, theater, and literary works. Annette Förster's *Questions of Fame and Failure* will be an important addition to our knowledge of this artist's multifaceted career.

14. Trinh, "Film as Translation," 122.
15. Bordo, *Unbearable Weight*, 227.
16. Trinh, "Film as Translation," 116.
17. The Women Film Pioneers project began in 1995 as a collaborative effort to promote research on women filmmakers. The project is based at Duke University, where it is chaired with enormous energy and goodwill by Jane Gaines. The Women Make Cinema series is edited by Pam Cook and Ginette Vincendeau and is directed explicitly toward research that looks at a range of "hidden history" in the cinema at the level of both artists and audiences.
18. McMahan, *Alice Guy Blaché*.
19. Mayne, *Cinema and Spectatorship*.
20. De Lauretis, *Practice of Love*, 111–25.
21. Ibid., 261.
22. De Lauretis, *Technologies of Gender*, 10.
23. Kuntzel, "Filmic Apparatus," 266–67.
24. See David Bordwell's *"La Nouvelle Mission de Feuillade."*
25. There are some excellent histories of perception that examine the problem of vision and its relation to knowledge and truth, and especially the increasing crisis in visible evidence in modernity. See Jonathan Crary, *Techniques of the Observer;* Martin Jay, *Downcast Eyes;* and Donald Lowe, *Bourgeois Perception*.
26. For an exposition of "the cinema of attractions," see Tom Gunning, "Cinema of Attractions." For a discussion of gender and narrative in early film, see Judith Mayne, *Woman at the Keyhole*, and Linda Williams, "Film Body."
27. Gunning, "Cinema of Attractions," 56–62.
28. Hofstadter, *Gödel, Escher, Bach*, 127. Hofstadter uses M. C. Escher's work as the quintessential visualization of recursion in *Gödel, Escher, Bach*. Another extended and extremely useful description of recursion occurs in David Berlinski, *Advent of the Algorithm*, 122–45.
29. Hofstadter, *Gödel, Escher, Bach*, 255.
30. There appears sometimes a parallel universe of discussion. Jonathan Auerbach's "Chasing Film Narrative: Repetition, Recursion, and the Body in Early Cinema" also uses the term *recursion*, but in a very different way, essentially referencing the process of repetition in itself. I am more interested in the *unique form of repetition* that recursion offers as derived from mathematics: a process of *abstraction*, which leads to *nonduality*. As Auerbach himself notes (804), he wants to retain the notion of binary opposition within his model (distinct from Gilles Deleuze's understanding of repetition), whereas my understanding of recursion would make that impossible. I first make the argument about Feuillade's recursive texts in "Evidence and Uncertainty of Silent Film in *Histoire(s) du cinéma.*"
31. Bean, "Technologies of Early Stardom."
32. Crary, "Modernizing Vision," 32.
33. Deleuze, *Cinema Two*, 37.
34. Ibid., 40–41.
35. Ibid., 37.
36. Ibid., 41.

Chapter 1

1. I am borrowing the term *dislocation* from two separate articles: Annette Michelson's "Breton's Surrealism" and Samuel Weber's "The Sideshow."
2. See especially Thomas Elsaesser and Adam Barker, *Early Cinema;* Noël Burch, *Life to those Shadows;* Tom Gunning, *D. W. Griffith;* John Fell, *Film Before Griffith.* Also, with particular reference to French early film, see Richard Abel's *French Cinema: The First Wave* and *The Ciné Goes to Town.*
3. Terry Ramsaye's *A Million and One Nights* and Lewis Jacobs's *Rise of American Film* are two notorious examples of early cinema filtered through a type of hagiography of film "pioneers."
4. Although by no means the only perpetrator of such language or views, Lewis Jacobs's discussion in *Rise of American Film* of the "genius" of Edwin Porter is instructive of this historical project: "The scenario for *The Life of the American Fireman,* published in the Edison Catalogue of 1903, after the film was completed, reveals the dramatic arrangement of its scenes and the new born technique of editing. The advance of Melies' [*sic*] artificially arranged scenes is evident. Melies merely listed scenes and roughly described their content, but Porter specified for the first time not only a full description of the dramatic action, but details of location, camera position, and transition. Porter's script . . . is the primitive of the continuity form used to this day in Hollywood" (38).
5. Over the course of his numerous articles on the subject, Burch's periodization of "primitive cinema" is at times vague and variable, in part it should be noted, due to the specificity of national cinema during the silent era. Nonetheless, at one point in *Life to those Shadows* (page 186), he notes that the primitive mode began to be displaced by a more linear and centering cinematic mode in 1906.
6. Ibid., 2.
7. Ibid., 188.
8. Ibid., 208.
9. Ibid., 241.
10. Ibid., 206.
11. Burch, "How We Got into Pictures," 32.
12. Ibid., 32.
13. Gunning, "Cinema of Attractions," 56–57.
14. Ibid., 57.
15. Ibid., 56.
16. Gunning, *D. W. Griffith,* 58.
17. Gunning, "Cinema of Attractions," 58–59.
18. Ibid., 56.
19. Ibid., 59.
20. For two provocative perspectives on the gendered gaze in early cinema and the complications therein, see Judith Mayne, *Woman at the Keyhole,* 165–66, and Lauren Rabinovitz, *For the Love of Pleasure,* 81–97.
21. Gunning, "Non-Continuity, Continuity, Discontinuity," 86; Burch, *Life to those Shadows,* 198.
22. Abel, "The Blank Screen of Reception"; Meusy, "Palaces and Holes in the Wall"; Garçon, *Gaumont,* 19.

23. Gunning, "Unseen Energy Swallows Space," 356.
24. Ibid., 355.
25. Burch, *Life to those Shadows*, 74, 186.
26. Ibid., 187; Gunning, "Non-Continuity, Continuity, Discontinuity."
27. Abel, "Cinégraphie," 200.
28. Lacassin, *Maître des lions*, 75, 234. As Lacassin notes, only one of the cowriters of the serialized novels took part in the film scenarios, Arthur Bernède. But even here, Bernède submitted a scenario and Feuillade altered it considerably. See Lacassin, *Maître des lions*, 240–42.
29. Abel, *The Ciné Goes to Town*, 371.
30. Ibid., 104.
31. Ibid., 429.
32. Brewster, "Deep Staging," 45–55; Bordwell, *Film Style*.
33. Brewster, "Deep Staging," 49; Bordwell, *Film Style*, 197–98.
34. Bordwell, *Film Style*, 190–97.
35. Ibid., 197–98.
36. This is a particular kind of possibility that is perhaps best expressed in another context by Gilles Deleuze (in interrogating the linking of images, the use of "and," or conjunction, in the films of Jean-Luc Godard): "all our thought's modeled, rather, on the verb 'to be,' IS. Philosophy's weighted down with discussions of attributive judgments (the sky is blue) and existential judgments (God is) and the possibility or impossibility of reducing one to the other. When Godard says everything has two parts, that in a day there's morning *and* evening, he's not saying it's one or the other, or that one becomes the other, becomes two. Because multiplicity is never in the terms, however many, nor in all the terms together, the whole. Multiplicity is precisely in the 'and,' which is different in nature from elementary components and collections of them" (Deleuze, *Negotiations*, 44).
37. Bessière, *Le récit fantastique*; Jackson, *Fantasy*.
38. Jackson, *Fantasy*, 26.
39. Ibid., 41–42.
40. For examples, see Alain Resnais, "Il a porté mes rêves à l'écran," 153; Jacques Champreux, "Louis Feuillade poète de la réalité"; Richard Roud, "Louis Feuillade and the Serial"; José Baldizzone, "La destinée critique de Louis Feuillade." More specifically, the label of "fantastic realism" can be found in Francis Lacassin, *Louis Feuillade*, 49–50; Jacques Siclier, "Le chevalier du bien" (a review of the restored *Judex*).
41. "Le fantastique chez Feuillade possède une parenté évidente avec ma propre conception, puisque celle-ci est résolument réaliste et qu'elle tend à montrer, à travers et même au-delà du fantastique, qui est un moyen, une arme et non pas un but, ce qu'il a de poétique, de tendre et de violent, de dramatique, dans la réalité la plus proche, la plus familière." (Franju, "Il était le cinéma," 151. All translations in this book are my own unless otherwise noted.)
42. Todorov, *The Fantastic*.
43. Ibid., 25.
44. Jackson, *Fantasy*, 6. Another important resource for this project is José Monleón, *A Specter is Haunting Europe: Sociohistorical Approach to the Fantastic* (Princeton: Princeton University Press, 1990).

45. Todorov does make the point that the literature of the fantastic can be seen as a response to the development of positivism in the nineteenth century, but this is more to account for the genre's demise (166–68) rather than an effort to put his outlined formal structures in a larger cultural context.
46. Jackson, *Fantasy*, 61.
47. Todorov, *Littérature fantastique,* 50–52.
48. Jackson, *Fantasy*, 62.
49. Ibid., 32.
50. Ibid., 62–73.
51. Bessière, *Le récit fantastique*, 37.
52. "Il ne faut pas assimiler fantastique et irrationnel. De Cazotte à Lovecraft, le récit fantastique est celui de l'ordre, qui ne décrit point l'illégal pour récuser la norme, mais pour la confirmer. . . . Narration toujours double, le fantastique installe l'étrange pour mieux établir la censure" (Bessière, *Le récit fantastique*, 28).
53. Avni, "Fantastic Tales," 676.
54. Cazotte, *Le diable amoureux,* 20–21.
55. Ibid., 136.
56. Ibid., 173.
57. Ibid., 178.
58. Gautier, *La morte amoureuse,* 27–28.
59. Ibid., 94.
60. Ibid., 109–10.
61. Higashi, *Virgins, Vamps, and Flappers,* 61.
62. Ibid., 169–70.
63. Higashi, *Cecil B. DeMille,* 103–7.
64. Le Fanu, "Camilla," *Best Ghost Stories,* 292.
65. Ibid., 293.
66. Brooks, *Melodramatic Imagination,* 13–15.
67. Ibid., 5, 15.
68. Ibid., 20.
69. Jay, *Downcast Eyes,* 113.
70. Ibid., 128–36.
71. Lowe, *Bourgeois Perception,* 109–11.
72. Brooks, *Melodramatic Imagination,* 39.
73. Gerould, "Americanization of Melodrama," 9
74. Singer, *Melodrama and Modernity,* 66–89.
75. Ibid., 80–89.
76. Turim, "French Melodrama," 307–27.
77. Gordon, *Grand Guignol,* 7–8.
78. Ibid., 17–22.
79. Gunning, "The Horror of Opacity."
80. Ibid., 53.
81. Ibid., 53.
82. See for example the following by Francis Lacassin: *Louis Feuillade;* "Louis Feuillade" (1961); "Un Inconnu nommé Feuillade."
83. Lacassin, *Louis Feuillade,* 16–24, 54.
84. See for example M. Ballot, "Prenez l'avance"; Louis Delluc, "Amateurs de

cinéma"; Ado Kyrou, "L'inhumaine Lola"; André Thirifays, "Un faux grand homme."

85. "L'idée fixe de la bande policière a été fatale à M. Feuillade. Il a tout sacrifié aux Fantômas, Squelettus, Spectras, Vampiras qui nous rasent aujourd'hui. Il s'acharne à exploiter une mine épuisée et dont les produits ne seraient plus de vente" (Ballot, "Des têtes de types," 5).

86. Delluc, "Amateurs de cinéma"; Lacassin, *Louis Feuillade*, 81.

87. "La sagesse eut pourtant commandé de ne point s'aventurer au-delà d'un premier triomphe qui avait épuisé le sujet et le pouvoir émotif de la foule. La vision de *La Nouvelle Mission de Judex* est rendue fort pénible en raison d'une absence de sujet et d'une vacuité de l'action qu'aggrave une longueur redoutable. Ce second sérial portait à leur paroxysme les préoccupations morales qui déjà alourdissaient l'intrigue du premier" (Lacassin, *Louis Feuillade*, 81).

88. "Le second *Judex* était inférieur à toute la production française de l'époque" (Delluc, "Amateurs de cinéma," 124).

89. "Après la guerre de 1914–1918, deux tendances très distinctement délimitées se partageaient les faveurs du public et de la critique. D'une part, les ciné-romans, les mélodrames, les burlesques, les films directement issues de Méliès, et d'autre part, les films intellectuels, littéraires, les 'recherches techniques.' La majorité du public suivait les premiers, la majorité des critiques, les seconds. Ceci est la meilleure preuve de la supériorité du public sur les critiques" (Kyrou, "L'inhumaine Lola," 4).

90. On the populist side, Kyrou lists Méliès, Feuillade, Buñuel, Vigo, and Franju; he places L'Herbier and Ophuls in the conservative, "art cinema" camp.

91. Thirifays, "Un faux grand homme."

92. "Mais qu'un homme de talent, un artiste, comme le metteur en scène de la plupart des grands films qui ont été le succès et la gloire de Gaumont, se mettre à traiter encore ce genre malsain, désuet et condamné par tous les gens de goût, voilà ce qui reste pour moi un veritable problème" (Ballot, "Prenez l'avance," 6, 7).

93. See Teresa de Lauretis, *Practice of Love*; Lynne Kirby, *Parallel Tracks;* and Patricia White, *The unInvited*, as current examples of feminist theory explicitly utilizing (and interrogating) psychoanalysis. Kirby's and White's works are especially noteworthy for their efforts to integrate archival texts and feminist psychoanalytic readings.

94. De Lauretis, *Practice of Love*, 24.

95. While there are numerous works that can be cited here, I will point to the following: Sarah Kofman, *Enigma of Woman*; Hélène Cixous, "Fiction and Its Phantoms"; Luce Irigaray, *Speculum*.

96. Mayne, *Cinema and Spectatorship*, 69.

97. De Lauretis, *Practice of Love*, xiv. De Lauretis draws the phrase "passionate fiction" from Leo Bersani and Ulysse Dutoit's *The Forms of Violence: Narrative in Assyrian Art and Modern Culture* (New York: Schocken, 1985), vii. It is worth reciting the quotation from their book that de Lauretis uses as it is particularly useful in this context: "Freud's theories of desire perform a certain violence against the very order on which their exposition depends. And perhaps the only guarantees we have of their 'authenticity' are the agitations, and doctrinal uncer-

tainties and mobility by which they are irremediably exposed as passionate fictions" (De Lauretis, *Practice of Love*, 3).
98. Conversation with Glenn Myrent at the Musée du Cinéma Henri-Langlois, spring 1992. Richard Abel's *The Ciné Goes to Town* (370–71) points out that this poster was originally drawn from the first cover of the *Fantômas* series of novels. As Abel notes, the book illustration, unlike the poster, features Fantômas holding a knife in his hand. According to Myrent, the dagger was removed as a result of the censorship process.
99. For an excellent discussion of the popular media of the era's fascination with the crime figure, see Richard Abel, "The Thrills of *Grande Peur*," 3–9. This article is part of a special issue of *Velvet Light Trap* on Feuillade and the French serial.
100. The memoirs of Eugen Vidocq (*Memoirs of Vidocq*) and Pierre-François Lacenaire (*Mémoires de Lacenaire*) provide two of the more well-known accounts of criminal activities. Vidocq's memoirs are rather interesting in that they recount not only a variety of prison and underworld goings-on but also his personal transition from criminal to policeman. Lacenaire, executed in 1836, continues to be a figure of fascination in France. Francis Girod's article "Pierre-François Lacenaire ou 'M'aimez-vous?'" examines the interest in Lacenaire from the surrealists and Carné (he is portrayed in Carné's *Les enfants du paradis*, 1945) to the 1990 film biography *Lacenaire* by Francis Girod and Georges Conchon.
101. A number of historians and critics have discussed the philosophical, cultural, and political upheavals of the era. See for example Eugen Weber, *Fin-de-Siècle*; Debora L. Silverman, *Art Nouveau*; Margaret Higonnet, *Behind the Lines*; Stephen Kern, *Culture of Time and Space*; and José Monleón, *A Specter is Haunting Europe*.
102. Freud, "The Uncanny"; Hélène Cixous, "Fiction and Its Phantoms."
103. Freud, "The Uncanny," 241.
104. Ibid., 241.
105. Ibid., 241.
106. Cixous, "Fiction and Its Phantoms," 535.
107. Freud, "The Uncanny," 230–31.
108. Cixous, "Fiction and Its Phantoms," 536.
109. Ibid., 536.
110. S. Weber, "The Sideshow," 1112.
111. Ibid., 1113.
112. Ibid., 1112.
113. Ibid., 1132–33.
114. Doane, *Femmes Fatales*, 1–3.
115. Kuntzel, "Filmic Apparatus," 269.
116. S. Weber, "The Sideshow," 1132–33.
117. This argument is clearly indebted to Jacqueline Rose's introduction to *Feminine Sexuality*. In this introduction she argues, following Lacan, that it is impossible to access a moment prior to language and the law: "For Lacan, as we have seen, there is no pre-discursive reality ('How return, other than by means of a special discourse, to a pre-discursive reality?' SXX, p.33), no place prior to the law which is available and can be retrieved. And there is no feminine outside language. First, because the unconscious severs the subject from any unmediated

relation to the body as such 'there is nothing in the unconscious which accords with the body,' O, p.165), and secondly because the 'feminine' is constituted as a division in language, a division which produces the feminine as its negative term. If woman is defined as other it is because the definition produces her as an other, and not because she has another essence" (55–56).

118. S. Weber, "The Sideshow," 1132–33.
119. Walter Benjamin, "The Second Empire in Baudelaire," 19–20.
120. It is useful to note here that a translation of "la zone" denotes not only a designated area or sphere but also conveys a sense of a shanty town (*faubourgs misérables*), according to Harraps French-English Dictionary.
121. E. Weber, *Fin de Siècle*, 70.
122. "*La loi du progrès*" consisted of three separate vignettes in the January/February 1911 edition of *Actualités Gaumont*. The remaining episodes featured two more "improvements" in urban centers: a horse protection league and motorized street cleaning. While these last two utilize cross cuts to suggest an evolution in city life, neither segment has the dramatic development seen in the crime episode.
123. Monleón, *A Specter Is Haunting Europe*.
124. Freud, "The Uncanny," xvii, 220–21.
125. Ibid., 224–25.
126. Ibid., 220.
127. Ibid., 245.
128. For a sampling of this phenomenon, see Francis Lacassin, "Louis Feuillade" (1974); "Aux temps 'héroïques' du cinéma"; Emile Breton, "L'avenir de Jeanne," 20; Robert Desnos, "*Fantômas*," 154–55.
129. Cixous, "Fiction and Its Phantoms," 537.
130. Ibid., 533.
131. Ibid., 533.
132. Ibid., 534.
133. This article was first published in 1924. Freud, "Oedipus-Complex," 178.
134. Cixous, "Fiction and Its Phantoms," 538.
135. Ibid., 535.
136. "What lies on the other side of castration? 'No meaning' other than the fear (resistance) of castration. It is this *no-other-meaning* (*Keine andere Bedeutung*) which presents itself anew (despite our wish to underplay it) in the infinite game of substitutions, through which what constitutes the elusive moment of fear returns and eclipses itself again. It is this dodging from fear to fear, the unthinkable secret since it does not open on any *other* meaning: its "agitation" (Hoffmann would say '*Unruhe*') is its affirmation. Even here, isn't everything a repercussion, a discontinuous spreading of the echo, but of the echo as a displacement, and not in any way as a referent to some transcendental meaning? The effect of uncanniness reverberates (rather than emerges), for the word is a relational signifier. *Unheimliche* is in fact a composite that infiltrates the interstices of the narrative and points to gaps we need to explain" (Cixous, "Fiction and Its Phantoms," 536).
137. De Lauretis, *Practice of Love*, xiv.
138. Freud, "Oedipus Complex," 178.
139. S. Weber, "The Sideshow," 1112.
140. Williams, "Film Body," 27.

Chapter 2

1. Nietzsche, "Beyond Good and Evil," 213–14.
2. Deslandes, "Victorin-Hippolyte Jasset," 251. For more on French silent-era crime films and their literary precursors, see also Tom Gunning, "Attractions," 111–35; Richard Abel, "Thrills of *Grande Peur*," 3–9; Francis Lacassin, *Maître des lions*, 138–52; and Robin Walz, *Pulp Surrealism*.
3. Lacassin, *Maître des lions*, 139.
4. The five episodes in the series are *Fantômas* (May 9, 1913), *Juve contre Fantômas* (September 12, 1913), *Le mort qui tue* (November 28, 1913), *Fantômas contre Fantômas* (March 13, 1914), and *Le faux magistrat* (May 8, 1914). I have relied on the release dates noted in Francis Lacassin's *Maître des lions* as the final arbiter for all Feuillade titles mentioned in this book.
5. Abel, *The Ciné Goes to Town*, 355, 358.
6. These sequences can be found in the following episodes of the *Fantômas* series: *Fantômas* (episode 1, 1913), *Juve contre Fantômas* (episode 2, 1913) and *Fantômas contre Fantômas* (episode 4, 1914).
7. See *Le Courrier Cinématographique*. All of the publicity booklets and theater programs described are found at the Bibliothèque de l'Arsenal (Rondel file 8 RK 4207-8). Original scenarios for the *Fantômas* films can also be found at the Bibliothèque de l'Arsenal.
8. Lacassin, *Maître des lions*, 140.
9. Walz, *Pulp Surrealism*, 45–46.
10. Ibid., 48.
11. "Feuillade élagua les digressions, supprima les redites au profit de la terreur, conserva les scènes dans les égouts et les poursuites sur les toits au détriment des voyages à Londres ou en Afrique du Sud, et parmi les meurtres et blessures, il montra les plus spectaculaires. De chacun de ces épais volumes de quatre cents pages, il conserva l'essentiel, distillant ainsi une essence précieuse et subtile, faite d'étrange, de grisaille et de cruauté" (Lacassin, *Maître des lions*, 143).
12. See especially Ben Singer, *Melodrama and Modernity*; Vanessa Schwartz, *Spectacular Realities*; and Mel Gordon, *Grand Guignol*.
13. "Le film le plus sensationnel de l'année défie la concurrence et les imitations de la dernière heure" (*Le Courrier Cinématographie*).
14. Lacassin, *Maître des lions*, 140.
15. Ibid., 141.
    > FANTÔMAS!
    > VOUS DITES?
    > JE DIS ... FANTÔMAS!
    > CELA SIGNIFIE QUOI?
    > RIEN ET TOUT.
    > POURTANT, QU'EST-CE QUE C'EST?
    > PERSONNE. MAIS CEPENDANT QUELQU'UN.
    > ENFIN QUE FAIT-IL. CE QUELQU'UN?
    > il fait PEUR.
16. Gunning, "Attractions, Detection, Disguise," 119.
17. Gunning, "Two Prologues," 31–35.
18. Gunning, "Attractions, Detection, Disguise," 127.

19. Ibid., 127.
20. See Carlo Ginzburg, "Clues, Morelli, Freud, and Sherlock Holmes"; H. Ashton-Wolfe, "Identification of Criminals"; and Henry T. F. Rhodes, *Alphonse Bertillon*, 15, 102–9.
21. Gunning, "Individual Body."
22. Cited in Gunning's "Individual Body," 23.
23. Nye, *Modern France*, 141–48.
24. Ibid., 181.
25. Cahm, "Revolt, Conservatism, and Reaction."
26. E. Weber, *Fin de Siècle*, 117–18.
27. Abel, *The Ciné Goes to Town*, 351.
28. See Thierry Kuntzel's discussion of the film by Peter Foldes, *Appétit d'oiseau*, in "Le défilement"; for a related argument, see Jean-Louis Baudry, "Ideological Effects."
29. See chapter 4, "The Cinematographical Mechanism of Thought and the Mechanistic Illusion—A Glance at the History of Systems—Real Becoming and False Evolutionism," in Henri Bergson's *Creative Evolution*.
30. Ibid., 334–35.
31. According to Eugen Weber, both Bell's telephone and Edison's phonograph were demonstrated at the Paris Exposition of 1878. Marconi's wireless radio signal first premiered, between Brittany and Newfoundland, in 1901. *Fin de Siècle*, 70–71.
32. Ibid., 71.
33. See Eugen Weber, *Fin de Siècle*, 70–71, and Steven Kern, *Culture of Time and Space*.
34. For a discussion of the many conflicting definitions of time during this period and the effects of these temporal reconceptualizations on everyday life, see Stephen Kern, *Culture of Time and Space*, chapters 1–5. Also, see Debora Silverman, *Art Nouveau*, 82.
35. Thorne, *Black Holes and Time Warps*, 82–83.
36. Ibid., 79.
37. Lynne Kirby's book *Parallel Tracks: The Railroad and Silent Cinema* is an interesting examination of the relationship between this era's cultural upheaval and the destabilization of the subject/spectator in early cinema.
38. Only the first episode, *Fantômas*, contains a plot strand concerning a planned escape by the criminal, as we will see later in the chapter.
39. Eco, "Rhetoric and Ideology," 132. For additional discussion of Sue's novel, see Peter Brooks, "Mark of the Beast," and Marc Angenot, *Le roman populaire*.
40. Eco, 132–33.
41. Abel, "Thrills of *Grande Peur*," 8.
42. "[E]lle se trouve, au moment où elle va se mettre au lit, face à face avec un homme, en habit, qui courtois, mais implacable et la menace, non formulée par la bouche, mais l'attente dans les yeux, la somme de lui remettre l'argent qu'elle vient de retirer.
   La princesse doit se soumettre. Au moment où le voleur va sortir, elle se jette sur le téléphone pour donner l'alarme. Fantômas la repousse et l'enferme." (Original scenario for *Fantômas*, episode 1, Bibliothèque de l'Arsenal)

43. Scenario *Fantômas*, episode 1. Bibliothèque de l'Arsenal.
44. Due to the absence of the cliff-hanger ending and the general autonomy of each episode, *Fantômas* and *Les vampires* are more accurately labeled series films rather than serials.
45. Cixous, "Fiction and Its Phantoms," 545.
46. Todorov, *The Fantastic*, 89.
47. Allain and Souvestre, *Les amours d'un prince*, 463.
48. Shapiro, "Love Stories," 45.
49. Ibid., 60–61.
50. Perrot, "The New Eve and the Old Adam," 53.
51. Ibid., 55; D. Silverman, *Art Nouveau*, 63.
52. Schaffer, "Nothing but Foolscap and Ink."
53. D. Silverman, *Art Nouveau*, 63–65.
54. Tiersten, *Marianne in Market*, 17–18.
55. Ibid., 32–34.
56. McMillan, *Housewife or Harlot*, 72.
57. Shapiro, "Love Stories," 60.
58. Ibid., 51.
59. Ibid., 60.
60. Ibid., 55–56.
61. "Vous savez que votre vie est en mon pouvoir et il est de votre intérêt de vous soumettre à ma volonté" (Title card for *Le mort qui tue*, episode 3 of the *Fantômas* series).
62. "Elle se rendit au rendez-vous et retombe en la possession de l'homme qu'elle voulait fuir" (Scenario for episode 2, *Juve contre Fantômas*, Bibliothèque de l'Arsenal).
63. Although unclear in the film or scenario, the novels detail Lady Beltham and Gurn's romance and Gurn's murder of Lord Beltham. Walz, *Pulp Surrealism*, 54–56.
64. Tiersten, *Marianne in Market*, 17, 43.
65. "C'était bien Joséphine, mais ce n'était plus la pierreuse; élégamment vêtue, chapeautée, elle présentait depuis la pointe de ses bottines jusqu'à la plume de son chapeau, l'aspect d'une bonne petite bourgeoise" (Publicity booklet accompanying scenario for episode 2, *Juve contre Fantômas*, 14, Bibliothèque de l'Arsenal).
66. "Ce ne sont que fêtes et parties de plaisir" (Booklet accompanying the scenario for episode 2, *Juve contre Fantômas*, Bibliothèque de l'Arsenal).

Chapter 3

1. *Les vampires*, 10 episodes: *La tête coupée* (1), *La bague qui tue* (2), November 12, 1915; *Le cryptogramme rouge* (3), December 3, 1915; *Le spectre* (4), January 7, 1916; *L'evasion du mort* (5), January 28, 1916; *Les yeux qui fascinent* (6) March 24, 1916; *Satanas* (7), April 14, 1916; *Le maître de la foudre* (8) May 12, 1916; *L'homme des poisons* (9), June 2, 1916; *Les noces sanglantes* (10), June 30, 1916.
2. Michelson, "Breton's Surrealism," 75.
3. See Kuntzel, "Filmic Apparatus," 269–70; Baudry, "Cinematic Apparatus"; and Kuntzel, "Le défilement."

4. For an examination of narrative space in early cinema see chapter 5, "'Primitive' Narration," in Judith Mayne's *Woman at the Keyhole*, 157–83. Mayne's discussion of "threshold space" as the space between multiple oppositional entities (e.g., interior/exterior, public/private, subject/object) is a crucial parallel text to Cixous's and Freud's discussions of the space occupied by the uncanny.
5. Brewster, "Deep Staging," 45–55; Bordwell, *"La Nouvelle Mission de Feuillade,"* 10–29.
6. Brewster, "Deep Staging," 50.
7. *Les mystères de New York* (Mackenzie/Garnier) was a Pathé film series launched with great fanfare in France in 1915. The films, accompanied by newspaper serialization of the episodes, were not in the format of a true serial. Indeed, *Les mystères de New York* was really an amalgam of three films previously released in the U.S: *The Exploits of Elaine, New Exploits of Elaine,* and *The Romance of Elaine.* (Mitry, "Pearl White.") The film title is an obvious homage to the novel by Sue.
8. "La piste de l'individu fut retrouvée, et au moment où il sortait d'un bar de la rue Beaumarchais, les inspecteurs Pouce et Irmengaud l'appréhendèrent." ("Les exploits d'une bande organisée.")
9. "La mystérieuse châtelaine."
10. "L'inspecteur principal Pouce, du 7e district, ne tarda pas à apprendre qu'un individu, bien connu dans certains établissements de la rue du Faubourg-Saint-Antoine, où se réunissent d'ordinaire un grand nombre d'Israélites polonais." ("Les exploits d'une bande organisée.")
11. "Taisez-vous!"
12. Hanna, *Mobilization of Intellect*, 87.
13. Bloy, *Au seuil de l'apocalypse*, quoted in Becker, *War and Faith*, 10.
14. Becker, *War and Faith*, 29.
15. D. Silverman, *Art Nouveau*, 65–66.
16. D. Silverman, *Art Nouveau*, 66.
17. Robert, "Women and Work in France," 253–63.
18. Huss, "Pronatalism."
19. Robert, "Women and Work in France," 256–57, 264.
20. D. Silverman, *Art Nouveau*, 66.
21. Huss, "Pronatalism," 330.
22. D. Silverman, *Art Nouveau*, 67.
23. McMillan, *Housewife or Harlot*, 72.
24. The poster *in* the film contains Musidora's name in the corner—serving not only as an on-screen but also internarrative credit for the actress.
25. "Il avait cru ne prendre qu'un ôtage, et voilà que c'était lui qui, à son tour, était prisonnier...
Prisonnier des jolis grands yeux noirs, de ces yeux fascinateurs et troublants qu'il n'avait jamais rencontrés sans émoi, même quand une hostilité farouche assombrissait leur regard merveilleux." (Meirs and Feuillade, *Les yeux*, 168–69)
26. Ibid., 168.
27. Ibid., 140.
28. Ibid., 170.
29. Deslandes, "Victorin-Hippolyte Jasset," 296.
30. Lacassin, *Une contre-histoire*, 108.

31. "La silhouette plus gracieuse et mieux soulignée" (Cazals, *Musidora*, 38).
32. Jacques Champreux, the grandson of Feuillade, pointed out this detail to me in an interview in Paris during the spring of 1992.
33. "Un beau maillot de soie transparente." (Uncredited introduction to Musidora's article, "La vie d'une vamp.")
34. "Elle avait son corps nu étroitment gainé de noir qui se balançait dans les nuits de notre adolescence comme un énorme et délicat papillon." (Loiselet, "Les pionniers du cinéma.")
35. "Ce personnage félin, nu sous son collant" (Breton, "L'avenir de Jeanne," 20).
36. André Breton supposedly brought a bouquet of roses for the actress to the stage following an evening's performance of the play. See "Musidora—The Original Vamp."
37. Cazals, *Musidora*, 95.
38. "Mes yeux. . . . C'est mon gagne-pain à l'heure actuelle." (Musidora, "La vie d'une vamp." *Ciné-Mondial* 48)
39. "Sa voix chante et psalmodie, ses lourds bandeaux lui donnent l'aspect d'une Madone et ses beaux yeux, ses grands yeux si intelligents témoignent que l'on est en présence d'une jeune femme qui, artiste jusqu'au bout des doigts, ne peut qu'employer son grand talent aux constants progrès de l'art cinégraphique dont elle fut, dès ses débuts, une des étoiles les plus applaudies." (Guillaume-Danvers, "Musidora.")
40. Meirs and Feuillade, *La tête coupée* and *Le spectre*.
41. "Il n'y avait pas à s'y tromper. Tu connais les admirables yeux d'Irma; les yeux immenses commes de lacs de lumière et de ténèbres à la fois, ces yeux troublants, enchanteurs, profonds dont elle use avec une maëstria incomparable; eh bien, des yeux comme ceux-là, il n'y en a pas deux paires dans le monde!" (Meirs and Feuillade, *Le spectre*, 58).
42. "Comment est-elle parvenue à troquer l'accent atrocement faubourien qu'elle avait, en chatant au *Chat Huant*, pour cet autre qui ferait jurer qu'elle n'a jamais quitté son patelin de Bretagne

    Quelle comédie! Et combien cette femme remplit admirablement les deux rôles si différents dans lesquels je l'ai vue." (Meirs and Feuillade, *La tête coupée*, 162)
43. "—Ah! y en a des aventures là-dedans, et puis des crimes, et puis des disparitions, et puis y a aussi de l'amour, de la passion. Ah! c'est beau allez, mademoiselle!

    —De l'amour, de la passion! murmure la danseuse se laissant glisser sur un long divan qui occupe tout un côté de la petite loge, oui, ce doit être doux, très doux." (Meirs and Feuillade, *La tête coupée*, 56)
44. Paul Valéry, *Variety*, quoted in Hans Kohn, "Crisis in European Thought and Culture," 29.
45. *Judex* featured a prologue and 11 episodes; the prologue *L'ombre mystérieuse* (1) appeared on January 19, 1917. Subsequent episodes appeared each following week with *L'expiation* (2), January 27; *La meute fantastique* (3), February 3; *Le secret d'une tombe* (4), February 10; *Le moulin tragique* (5), February 17; *Le môme Réglisse* (6), February 24; *La femme en noir* (7), March 3; *Les souterrians du Château Rouge* (8), March 10, *Lorsque l'enfant parut* (9), March 17; *Le secret de*

Jacqueline (10), March 24; *Ondine . . . et sirène* (11), March 31; *Le pardon d'amour* (12), April 7.
46. Perrot, "The New Eve and the Old Adam," 60.
47. Huss, "Pronatalism," 330.
48. For a discussion of class mobility in Feuillade's films, see François de la Bretèque and Michael Cadé, "La petite bourgeosie dans les films de Louis Feuillade," *Cahiers de la Cinémathèque* 50 (1989): 17–26.
49. The newspaper serialization ran concurrently in *Le Petit Parisien*. It is possible to assume that some viewers came to *Judex* with prior knowledge or information about the text. The first issue of the serialization that I viewed was undated, as it was a special newspaper supplement (part of the collection of Musée Gaumont), but it does encourage the reader to attend the cinema version of the series—thus suggesting an approximate simultaneity of the written and cinema texts. Later installments of the series that are held at the Musée Gaumont are the regular edition of *Le Petit Parisien*.
This first installment contains the story of Jacqueline's arranged marriage and engagement. See Arthur Bernède and Louis Feuillade, "*Judex*."
50. Ibid., 2.
51. Ibid., 1.
52. Ibid., 3.
53. "Je suis Pierre Kerjean . . . j'étais un honnête homme, je vivais heureux entre ma femme et mon enfant. Séduit par les prospectus financiers dont vous inondiez la France, je vous ai confié mon argent. Non seulement vous m'avez ruiné, mais vous avez entrainé malgré moi dans ces spéculations malhonnêtes qui ont abouti à ma condamnation à vingt ans de travaux forcés" ("*L'ombre mystérieuse*," original scenario for episode 1, *Judex*, Bibliothèque de l'Arsenal, July 29, 1916).
54. Bernède and Feuillade, *Judex*, 4.
55. According to Lacassin, Feuillade's scenarios for *Les vampires* were merely outlines for the day's shooting; often the end of the episode was decided in the process of filming. Lacassin likens Feuillade's production process, particularly in the *Les vampires* and his earlier films, to a type of automatic writing. See Lacassin and Raymond Bellour's article "Musidora," 106.
56. Lacassin, *Louis Feuillade*, 65.
57. Ibid., 65–66.
58. Musidora, "La vie d'une vamp."
59. Singer, "Female Power," 93.
60. Lacassin, "Musidora," 490.
61. "On comprendra bientôt qu'il n'y eut rien de plus réaliste et de plus poétique à la fois que le ciné-feuilleton qui faisait naguère la joie des esprits forts. C'est dans *Les Mystères de New York*, c'est dans *Les Vampires* qu'il faudra chercher la grande réalité de ce siècle. Au-delà la mode, au delà du goût. Viens avec moi. Je montrerai comment on écrit l'histoire" (Cazals, *Musidora*, 164–65).
62. "Actualités Gaumont," April 1921 (event 32), screened at *Vidéothèque de Paris*.
63. Bean, "Technologies," 12.
64. Singer, *Melodrama and Modernity*, 90–91.
65. Garvey, *Adman in the Parlor*, 122–34.
66. Kern, *Culture of Space and Time*, 111.
67. D. Silverman, *Art Nouveau*, 67.

68. "C'est sans doute que sa matière unique est la morale, règle de toute action: notre époque ne peut guère s'intéresser à la morale. Au cinéma, la vitesse apparaît dans la vie, et Pearl White n'agit pas pour obéir à sa conscience, mais par sport, par hygiène: elle agit pour agir" (Aragon, "Anicet," 127).
69. "Il y a la puissance morale de Pearl White. Moralement, la vue de Pearl White est une vrai cure. Le spectacle de ses exploits est meilleur pour la neurasthénie que le génie amer de Charlot ou même que la verve sentimentale et pudique de Douglas Fairbanks. Pearl White, C'est de l'énergie et de la verve, c'est tout. Mais qu'est-ce que je dis, c'est de la santé sans arrière-pensée" (Louis Delluc is quoted in Jean Mitry's "Pearl White," 11).
70. Hervouin, "77 minutes avec Pearl White." A similar sense of speed and energy is conveyed via an article title on the star, Musidora, many years later, in Serge, "3 secondes avec Musidora."
71. "Et puis, un film chasse l'autre, Musidora succéda à Pearl White, Nazimova à Musidora et d'autres, d'autres encore surgirent dont il est inutile de redire les adorables noms.
    Celle-ci était blonde. Elle disparaissait et le beau roman commencé avec elle s'achevait avec celle qui la suivait et qui était brune. Elles ne mouraient que pour renaître." (Desnos, "Le merle," 131)
72. "Leur vie n'était pas médiocre, elle était précieuse et elles la risquaient. Des escadrons de bandits et de séducteurs évoluaient autour d'elles, et vingt fois ruinées, on les voyait vingt fois retrouver la fortune. On aurait peuplé des cimetières entiers avec ceux qui mouraient pour elles. . . . Et l'amour, l'amour transfiguré assurait par elles sa propagande. Débarrassé des lois vulgaires, élevé bien au-dessus des idées de tranquillité, il s'affirmait égal au Destin et à la Fortune" (Desnos, "Le merle," 131).
73. Francis and Gontier, *Creating Colette,* 16.
74. Cazals, *Musidora,* 108.
75. "Je n'ai pas honte d'avouer que c'était un bien grand amour que j'avais pour Colette. Très grand et chaste amour" (Cazals, *Musidora,* 184).
76. See "Lettres d'admirateurs à Musidora."
77. "Lettres d'admirateurs à Musidora" (letter of December 19, 1917).
78. "Alors voulez-vous bien me soumettre un fétiche—quelque chose de vous, que vous ayez porté? Un bas, ou encore mieux un de vos petits pantalons . . . ou n'importe quoi, enfin quelque chose qui vous ait touché de très près, et que je pourrai embrasser, lorsque j'en aurai envie" ("Lettres d'admirateurs à Musidora" [letter of May 17, 1918]).
79. "Cette decision me trouvait fort en colère. Pour moi, le choix de mon nom était lié à mon avenir." (Musidora, "La vie d'une vamp.")
80. "Les êtres autoritaires ne m'ont jamais intimidée. Non pas que je me prisse pour une vampire, mais simplement parce que ma mère m'avait communiqué son audace. . . . M. Gaumont me reçut dans son bureau, très étonné d'une telle dèmarche. Personne d'ailleurs n'avait jamais osé s'adresser à lui directement. J'exposai ma réclamation. . . . Je défends ma publicité, c'est à dire mon avenir. Si vous ne mettez pas mon nom, on m'appellera Irma Vep et, plus tard, je ne pourrai plus être que Irma Vep! Je tiens essentiellement à celui de Musidora. Théophile Gautier et Fortunio sont les parrains que j'ai choisis." (Musidora, "La vie d'une vamp.")

81. "Pour Monsieur Louis Gaumont . . . Musidora. Irma Vep. *Les Vampires* portant toujours le G de Gaumont" ("Musidora, Boîte 1" [letter of October 4, 1950, to Louis Gaumont]).
82. Ibid.
83. Mayne, *Woman at the Keyhole*, 31–32.
84. Uncredited introduction to Musidora's "La vie d'une vamp."
85. Durand, "*Soleil et ombre*," 62.
86. "Peut-être faut-il chercher dans l'amour de Musidora pour Cañero la raison de son dédoublement, de ce rôle à deux têtes, la même à la fois fiancée rejetée et femme fatale. Elle aurait été trop éprise de lui pour le partager avec une autre, même à l'écran. En se donnant les deux rôles, elle se donne forcément le beau rôle et l'encercle dans son désir" (Durand, "*Soleil et ombre*," 62).
87. Bastide, postface to *Louis Feuillade*, 163–69.
88. "Ce film a été tourné au milieu du danger constant; mais, il ne doit vous donner que l'impression de la fête du soleil et de la gloire de l'Art du geste. Musidora" (Title card, *La tierra de los toros*).
89. My use of the term *performative* here is influenced by J. L. Austin, "Performative Utterances," 233–52; John R. Searle, *Speech Acts*; and, of course, with regard to issues of gender, Judith Butler, *Bodies that Matter*.
90. "C'est encore un décor de théâtre que je vous offre" (Title card, *La tierra de los toros*).
91. See original scenario for *La nouvelle mission de Judex* (prologue) at the Bibliothèque de l'Arsenal.
92. After her filmmaking and music-hall career, Musidora pursued a number of literary and musical activities. According to Francis Lacassin, these works include four novels (two of which were published), numerous works for the stage—over twenty of these were publicly performed—several unpublished scenarios for film and television, a collection of children's stories (illustrated by her), about fifteen songs, and a collection of poetry. For details on her later career, see Lacassin, "Musidora," 492.

Chapter 4

1. Brooks, *Melodramatic Imagination*, 5.
2. Ibid., 42.
3. Ibid., 56.
4. Beizer, *Ventriloquized Bodies*, 16.
5. Freud, *Dora*, 70.
6. Ibid., 70–71.
7. Ibid., 30–31.
8. Ibid., 32.
9. Angenot, *Roman populaire*, 54. Peter Brooks describes a similar phenomenon within a specifically melodramatic context through the recurrent use of *coups de théâtre* to reveal some crucial piece of data from the past (e.g., the repetitive use of the phrase "I am the man"). See Brooks, *Melodramatic Imagination*, 39–40.
10. S. Weber, "The Sideshow," 1132–33.
11. *La nouvelle mission de Judex* was shown in twelve weekly episodes from January

25 to April 12, 1918, beginning with *Le mystère d'une nuit d'été* (1); *L'adieu du bonheur* (2), February 1; *L'ensorcelée* (3), February 8; *La chambre aux embûches* (4), February 15; *La forêt hantée* (5), February 22; *Un lueur dans les ténébres* (6), March 1; *La main morte* (7), March 8; *Les captives* (8), March 15; *Le papiers du Dr. Howey* (9), March 22; *Les deux destinées* (10), March 29; *Les crime involontaire* (11), April 5; *Châtiment* (12), April 12.
12. Title card reads: "Mon cher Cocantin, vous êtes atteint d'hypéresthésie-hystérotomatique" (Prologue and episode 1, *Le mystère d'une nuit d'été*).
13. Showalter, *Sexual Anarchy*, 105.
14. Beizer, *Ventriloquized Bodies*, 49–50.
15. Showalter, *Sexual Anarchy*, 106; Beizer, *Ventriloquized Bodies*, 50.
16. See Debora L. Silverman, *Art Nouveau*, 79–88, for a discussion of the Charcot/Bernheim debate on the ideal subjects for hypnosis.
17. Ibid., 88.
18. "J'ai éprouvé parfois la sensation que la vie m'abandonne, puis il me semble que je renais, mais je ne peux pas me rappeler ce que j'ai fait dans l'intervalle" (Episode 4, *La chambre aux embûches*).
19. "Primerose, vous êtes à la merci d'une puissance occulte et redoutable. . . . Mais je vous sauverai" (Episode 4, *La chambre aux embûches*).
20. Beizer, *Ventriloquized Bodies*, 48–49.
21. See Michelle Perrot, "The New Eve and the Old Adam," 60; Steven Hause, "More Minerva than Mars"; James McMillan, *Housewife or Harlot*, 189.
22. Goldstein, "Hysteria Diagnosis," 237.
23. Ibid., 230–33.
24. "Hormis deux ou trois épisodes, l'aventure se réduit aux conflits douloureux du mélodrama; seules quelques images éblouissantes (Judex caché derrière un rideau, la main d'un squelette qui jaillit d'un secrétaire) remontent à la surface d'un flot de tisane tiède. . . . L'interprétation est sans éclat: Cresté de plus en plus calme, Mathé figé dans l'attente de ses noces, Yvette Andreyor en larmes, Levesque vaudevillesque, Musidora absente et irremplaçable.
  La mise en scène, très critiquable, abuse de la profondeur du champ dans les extérieurs que les personnages traversent dans toute leur longueur ralentissant un rythme qui n'en avait nul besoin. Si le réalisateur avait eu l'héroïsme de supprimer toutes les scènes où les personnages montent et descendent des escaliers, toutes celles où le petit Jean embrasse les gens passant à sa portée, il aurait amélioré un malheureux film qui eut droit à tous les sarcasmes." (Lacassin, *Maître des lions*, 244–45)
25. "Deux grands yeux noirs qui dévisagent tout le monde" (Episode 11, *Le crime involontaire*).
26. Beizer, *Ventriloquized Bodies*, 53.
27. For an absolutely fascinating reading of Hollywood cinema and lesbian spectatorship, see Patricia White's *The unInivited*. My reading of the Baronne's extrasensory powers as suggestive of a lesbian subtext is very much indebted to teaching this wonderful book as part of a feminist film theory course (and the enthusiasm it provoked). The discussion of the gothic horror films and female psychics in chapter 3, "Female Spectator, Lesbian Specter," was especially evocative in this context.

28. Meirs and Feuillade, *La tête coupée,* back page advertisement for *Le livre de poche* series.
29. Ibid., 33.
30. "Une reposante ambiance qui s'y dissipent comme par enchantement" (*Les vampires* program, 1916, Rondel file 9768).
31. *Le Petit Parisien,* January 20, 1917, p. 4.
32. Robert, "Women and Work," 264.
33. Shapiro, *Breaking the Codes,* 30–31.
34. Ibid., 31.
35. Ibid., 32.
36. Francis Lacassin includes the correct "technical" term for the machine in his article on Judex; see *"Judex," Cinéma* 61, no. 57: 68.
37. "Banker Favraux, Je vous avais condamné à mort le geste de votre fille vous a sauvé la vie mais je vous condamne à la réclusion perpétuelle." See Lacassin, *Maître des lions,* 240, for an example of the magical typewriter's projected script.
38. *Tih Minh,* twelve weekly episodes beginning with *Le philtre d'oubli* (1), February 7, 1919; *Drames dans la nuit* (2), February 14; *Les mystères de la Villa Circé* (3), February 21; *L'homme dans la malle* (4), February 28; *Chez les Fous* (5), March 7; *Oiseaux de nuit* (6), March 14; *L'évocation* (7), March 21; *Sous le voile* (8), March 28; *La branche de salut* (9), April 4; *Mercredi* (10), April 11; *Le document* (11), April 18; *Justice* (12), April 25.
39. Freud, *Dora,* 134.
40. Ibid., 151.
41. Said, *Orientalism,* 40.
42. Beizer, *Ventriloquized Bodies,* 26.
43. Harris, *Murders and Madness,* 194.
44. Lacassin, *Maître des lions,* 83.
45. "Oh! oui Docteur, délivrez-moi des influences qui ont fait de moi la complice de tant de crimes" (Episode 11, *Le document*).
46. *Barrabas* was shown in twelve installments, beginning March 5, 1920 with *La maîtresse du Juif errant* (1); *La justice des hommes* (2), March 12; *La villa des glycines* (3), March 19; *Le stigmate* (4), March 26; *Noëlle Maupré* (5), April 2; *La fille du condamné* (6), April 9; *Les ailes de Satan* (7), April 16; *Le manoir mystérieux* (8), April 23; *L'otage* (9), April 30; *L'oubliette* (10), May 7; *Le revenant* (11), May 14; *Justice* (12), May 21.
47. Lacassin, *Maître des lions,* 253.
48. Original scenario for *Barrabas,* Bibliotheque de l'Arsenal, 3876, p. 1.
49. "Un héritage de sang, de folie, et de crime" (Episodes 6 and 7, *La fille du condamné* and *Les ailes de Satan*).
50. Beizer, *Ventriloquized Bodies,* 26.

Afterword

1. Franju, *Cahiers de la Cinémathèque,* 84.
2. I want to thank Patrick Gonder for our conversation on *Les yeux sans visage* and his thoughtful commentary on the transgressive role of the mask in the film.
3. Rosenbaum, "Film Intimidates Art."

Works Cited

Abel, Richard. *French Cinema: The First Wave, 1915–1929.* Princeton: Princeton University Press, 1984.
———. "Cinégraphie and the Search for Specificity." *French Film Theory and Criticism, 1907–1939.* 2 vols. Princeton: Princeton University Press, 1988.
———. "The 'Blank Screen of Reception' in Early French Cinema." *Iris* 11 (summer 1990): 28–34.
———. *The Ciné Goes to Town: French Cinema, 1896–1914.* Berkeley: University of California Press, 1994.
———. "The Thrills of *Grande Peur:* Crime Series and the Serials in the Belle Epoque." *Velvet Light Trap* 37 (spring 1996).
Allain, Marcel, and Pierre Souvestre. *Fantômas.* 4 vols. Paris: Robert Laffont, 1987.
Angenot, Marc. *Le roman populaire: Recherches en paralittérature.* Montreal: Les Presses de l'Université de Québec, 1975.
Aragon, Louis. "Anicet." In *Les surréalistes et le cinéma,* ed. Alain Virmaux and Odette Virmaux, 127–29. Paris: Seghers, 1976.
Ashton-Wolfe, H. "Identification of Criminals." In *The Forgotten Clue: Tales and Methods of the Sûreté.* London: Hurst and Blackett, 1929.
Auerbach, Jonathan. "Chasing Film Narrative: Repetition, Recursion, and the Body in Early Cinema." *Critical Inquiry* 26 (summer 2000): 798–820.
Austin, J. L. "Performative Utterances." *Philosophical Papers.* London: Oxford University Press, 1970.
"Aux temps 'héroïques' du cinéma." *Ce Matin—Le Pays* (March 1951), 3–4. Rondel File, Bibliothèque de l'Arsenal RK 402.
L'Avant-Scène du Cinéma (July 1981): 271–72. Special issue on *Fantômas* and Feuillade.
Avni, Ora. "Fantastic Tales." In *A New History of French Literature,* ed. Denis Hollier, 675–81. Cambridge: Harvard University Press, 1989.
Baldizzone, José. "La destinée critique de Louis Feuillade." *Cahiers de la Cinémathèque* 48 (November 1987): 11–18.
Ballot, M. "Des têtes de types: Louis Feuillade." *Hebdo-Film* 24 (1916): 6–7. Rondel File, Bibliothèque de l'Arsenal RK 1971.
———. "Prenez l'avance." *Hebdo-Film* 8 (1916): 6–7. Rondel File, Bibliothèque de l'Arsenal RK 19718.
Bastide, Bernard. Postface to *Louis Feuillade: Chroniques taurines, 1899–1907.* Nimes, France: Ciné-Sud, 1988, 163–69.
Baudry, Jean-Louis. "Ideological Effects of the Basic Cinematographic Apparatus." In *Narrative, Apparatus, Ideology,* ed. Philip Rosen, 286–98. New York: Columbia University Press, 1986.

Becker, Annette. *War and Faith: The Religious Imagination in France, 1914–1930*, trans. Helen McPhail. New York: Berg, 1998.
Bean, Jennifer. "Technologies of Early Stardom and the Extraordinary Body." *Camera Obscura* 48(2001): 9–58.
Beizer, Janet. *Ventriloquized Bodies: Narratives of Hysteria in Nineteenth-Century France*. Ithaca: Cornell University Press, 1993.
Benjamin, Walter. "The Paris of the Second Empire in Baudelaire." In *Charles Baudelaire: A Lyric Poet in the Era of High Capitalism*, trans. Harry Zohn, 9–106. London: Verso, 1985.
Bergson, Henri. "The Cinematographical Mechanism of Thought and the Mechanistic Illusion: A Glance at the History of Systems: Real Becoming and False Evolutionism." In *Creative Evolution*, trans. Arthur Mitchell, 296–402. Westport, Conn.: Greenwood Press, 1977.
Berlinski, David. *The Advent of the Algorithm: The Idea that Rules the World*. New York: Harcourt, 2000.
Bernède, Arthur, and Louis Feuillade. "Judex." *Le Petit Parisien*, updated supplement, p. 2. Musée Gaumont, 1917.
Bersani, Leo, and Ulysse Dutoit. *The Forms of Violence: Narrative in Assyrian Art and Modern Culture*. New York: Schocken, 1985.
Bessière, Irène. *Le récit fantastique: la poétique de l'incertain*. Paris: Librairie Larousee, 1974.
Bloy, Léon. *Au seuil de l'apocalypse*, quoted in Annette Becker, *War and Faith: The Religious Imagination in France 1914–1930*.
Bordo, Susan. *Unbearable Weight: Feminism, Western Culture, and the Body*. Berkeley: University of California Press, 1993.
Bordwell, David, Janet Staiger, and Kristin Thompson. *The Classical Hollywood Cinema: Film Style and Mode of Production to 1960*. New York: Columbia University Press, 1985.
Bordwell, David. "*La Nouvelle Mission de Feuillade*, or What was Mise en Scene," *Velvet Light Trap* 37 (spring 1996): 10–29.
———. *On the History of Film Style*. Cambridge: Harvard University Press, 1997.
Bordwell, David, and Kristin Thompson. "Linearity, Materialism, and the Study of Early American Cinema." *Wide Angle* 5.3 (1983): 11.
Breton, Emile. "L'avenir de Jeanne." In *Femmes d'Images*. Paris: Editions Messidor, 1984.
Brewster, Ben. "Deep Staging in French Films, 1900–1914." In *Early Cinema: Space, Frame, Narrative*, ed. Thomas Elsaesser and Adam Barker, 45–55. London: BFI, 1990.
Brooks, Peter. *The Melodramatic Imagination*. New York: Columbia University Press, 1984.
———. "The Mark of the Beast: Prostitution, Serialization, and Narrative." In *Reading for Plot: Design and Intention in Narrative*, 143–70. Cambridge: Cambridge University Press, 1992.
Bruno, Giuliana. *Streetwalking on a Ruined Map: Cultural Theory and the City Films of Elvira Notari*. Princeton: Princeton University Press, 1991.
Burch, Noël. "How We Got into Pictures: Notes Accompanying *Correction Please*." *Afterimage* (spring 1981): 32.

———. *Life to those Shadows*, trans. Ben Brewster. London: BFI, 1990.
Butler, Judith. *Bodies that Matter: On the Discursive Limits of "Sex."* New York: Routledge, 1993.
Cahm, Eric. "Revolt, Conservatism, and Reaction in Paris, 1905–1925." In *Modernism: A Guide to European Literature: 1890–1930*, ed. Malcolm Bradbury and James McFarland, 165–67. London: Penguin, 1991.
Callahan, Vicki. "The Evidence and Uncertainty of Silent Film in *Histoire(s) du Cinéma.*" In *The Cinema Alone: Essays on the Work of Jean-Luc Godard 1985–2000*, ed. Michael Temple and James Williams, 141–57. Amsterdam: Amsterdam University Press, 2000.
Cazals, Patrick. *Musidora: la dixième muse*. Paris: Henri Veyrier, 1978.
Cazotte, Jacques. *Le diable amoureux* (The Devil in Love). New York: C. S. Van Winkle, 1810.
Champreux, Jacques. "Louis Feuillade poète de la réalité." *L'Avant-Scène du Cinéma* 271–72 (July 1981): 14.
———. Interview by author. Spring 1992.
Champreux, Jacques, and Alain Carou. *1895* AFRHC (October 2000). Special issue on Louis Feuillade.
Ciné-Mondial 42 (June 12, 1942). Uncredited introduction to "La vie d'une vamp" by Musidora.
Cixous, Hélène. "Fiction and Its Phantoms: A Reading of Freud's *Das Unheimliche* (The Uncanny)." *New Literary History* 7:3 (1976): 527–48.
Cixous, Hélène, and Mireille Calle-Gruber. *Rootprints*, trans. Eric Prenowitz. London: Routledge, 1997.
Cixous, Hélène. "Sorties: Out and Out: Attacks/Ways Out/Forays." In *The Newly Born Woman*, ed. Hélène Cixous and Catherine Clément, 63–132. Minneapolis: University of Minnesota Press, 1996.
Colette. *Colette at the Movies*, ed. Alain Virmaux and Odette Virmaux, trans. Sarah W. R. Smith. New York: Frederick Ungar, 1975.
Le Courrier Cinématographie. April 16, 1913, p. 17.
Crary, Jonathan. "Modernizing Vision." In *Viewing Positions: Ways of Seeing Film*, ed. Linda Williams, 23–35. New Brunswick: Rutgers University Press, 1995.
———. *Techniques of the Observer: On Vision and Modernity in the Nineteenth Century*. Cambridge: Massachusetts Institute of Technology Press, 1992.
Deleuze, Gilles. *Cinema Two: The Time Image*, trans. Hugh Tomlinson. Minneapolis: University of Minnesota Press, 1989.
———. *Negotiations, 1972–1990*, trans. Martin Joughin. New York: Columbia University Press, 1990.
De la Breteque, François, and Michael Cadé. "La petite bourgeoisie dans les films de Louis Feuillade." *Cahiers de la Cinémathèque* 50 (1989): 17–26.
De Lauretis, Teresa. *Technologies of Gender: Essays on Theory, Film, and Fiction*. Bloomington: Indiana University Press, 1987.
———. *The Practice of Love: Lesbian Sexuality and Perverse Desire*. Bloomington: Indiana University Press, 1994.
Delluc, Louis. "Petit Guide pour les amateurs de cinéma." *Cinéma et Cie* Écrits Cinématographiques II, 124–25. Paris: Cinémathèque Française, 1986.
Deslandes, Jacques. "Victorin-Hippolyte Jasset." *Anthologie du Cinéma* Tome 9,

244–97. Paris: L'Avant-Scène du Cinéma, 1976.
Desnos, Robert. "*Fantômas, Les vampires, Les mystères de New York*" *Cinéma*. Paris: Gallimard, 1966.
———. "Le merle." In *Les surréalistes et le cinéma*, ed. Alain Virmaux and Odette Virmaux, 129–32. Paris: Seghers, 1976.
Doane, Mary Ann. *Femmes Fatales: Feminism, Film Theory, Psychoanalysis*. New York: Routledge, 1991.
Durand, Jacques. "Soleil et ombre." In *La persistance des images*, 62–63. Paris: Cinémathèque Française, 1996.
Eco, Umberto. "Rhetoric and Ideology in Sue's *Les Mystères de Paris*." In *The Role of the Reader: Explorations in the Semiotics of Texts*, 125–43. Bloomington: Indiana University Press, 1984.
Elsaesser, Thomas, and Adam Barker, ed. *Early Cinema: Space, Frame, Narrative*. London: BFI, 1990.
Fell, John, ed. *Film Before Griffith*. Berkeley: University of California Press, 1994.
Feuillade, Louis. *Barrabas*. Original Scenario. Bibliothèque de l'Arsenal, 1920.
———. *Fantômas*. Original Scenario. Bibliothèque de l'Arsenal, 1913.
———. *Judex*. Original Scenario. Bibliothèque de l'Arsenal, 1916–17.
———. *Juve contre Fantômas*. Original Scenario. Bibliothèque de l'Arsenal, 1913.
———. *La nouvelle mission de Judex*. Original Scenario. Bibliothèque de l'Arsenal, 1917.
———. *Le faux magistrat*. Original Scenario. Bibliothèque de l'Arsenal, 1914.
———. *Le mort qui tue*. Original Scenario. Bibliothèque de l'Arsenal, 1913.
———. *Le policier apache*. Original Scenario. Bibliothèque de l'Arsenal, 1913.
———. *Les films mystérieux—Les vampires*. Original Scenario. Bibliothèque de l'Arsenal, 1915–16.
———. *Tih Minh*. Original Scenario. Bibliothèque de l'Arsenal, 1919.
Förster, Annette. *Questions of Fame and Failure. Adrienne Solser, Musidora, Nell Shipman: Women Acting and Directing in the Cinema*. Forthcoming.
Francis, Claude, and Fernande Gontier. *Creating Colette*. Vol. 2. South Royalton: Steerforth Press, 1998.
Franju, Georges. "Il était le cinéma . . ." In *Louis Feuillade*, ed. Francis Lacassin, 148–52. Paris: Seghers, 1964.
———. *Cahiers de la Cinémathèque* 25 (1978): 84. Special issue on *film policier*.
Freud, Sigmund. *Dora: An Analysis of a Case of Hysteria*, ed. Philip Rieff. New York: Collier, 1963.
———. "The Passing of the Oedipus-Complex." In *Sexuality and the Psychology of Love*, trans. Joan Riviere, 176–82. New York: Collier, 1963.
———. *Beyond the Pleasure Principle*, trans. James Strachey. London: Norton, 1961.
———. "The Uncanny." *The Standard Edition*, ed. and trans. James Strachey, 219–55. London: Hogarth, 1953–74.
Garçon, François. *Gaumont: A Century of French Cinema*, trans. Bruce Alderman and Jonathan Dickinson. New York: Harry N. Abrams, 1994.
Garvey, Ellen Gruber. *The Adman in the Parlor: Magazines and Gendering in Consumer Culture, 1880s to 1910*. Oxford: Oxford University Press, 1996.
Gautier, Théophile. *La morte amoureuse*, trans. Paul Hookham. New York: Robert M. McBride, 1927.

---. *Fortunio.* Paris: Georges Briffaut, 1946.
Gerould, Daniel. "The Americanization of Melodrama." In *American Melodrama*, 7–29. New York: Performing Arts Journal, 1983.
Ginzburg, Carlo. "Clues, Morelli, Freud, and Sherlock Holmes." *The Sign of the Three*, ed. Eco and Sebeok, 81–118. Bloomington: Indiana University Press, 1988.
Girod, Francis. "Pierre-François Lacenaire ou 'M'aimez-vous?'" *Cahiers de la Cinémathèque* 58 (May 1993): 61–70.
Goldstein, Jan. "The Hysteria Diagnosis and the Politics of Anti-Clericalism in Late Nineteenth Century France." *Journal of Modern History* 54 (June 1982): 209–39.
Gordon, Mel. *The Grand Guignol: The Theatre of Fear and Terror.* New York: Amok, 1988.
Guillaume-Danvers, V. "Musidora." *Cinémagazine* 27 (1921): 5–8.
Gunning, Tom. "An Unseen Energy Swallows Space: The Space in Early Film and Its Relation to American Avant-Garde Film." In *Film Before Griffith*, ed. John Fell, 355–66. Berkeley: University of California Press, 1994.
---. "A Tale of Two Prologues: Actors and Roles, Detectives and Disguises in *Fantômas*, Film, and Novel." *Velvet Light Trap* 37 (1996): 30–36.
---. "Attractions, Detection, Disguise, Zigomar, Jasset, and the History of Film Genres." *Griffithiana* 47 (1993): 111–35.
---. *D. W. Griffith and the Origins of American Narrative Film: The Early Years at Biograph.* Urbana: University of Illinois Press, 1994.
---. "Non-Continuity, Continuity, Discontinuity: A Theory of Genres in Early Film." In *Early Cinema: Space, Frame, Narrative*, ed. Thomas Elsaesser and Adam Barker, 86–94. London: BFI, 1990.
---. "Now You See It, Now You Don't: The Temporality of the Cinema of Attractions." *Velvet Light Trap* 32 (fall 1993): 3–12.
---. "The Cinema of Attractions: Early Film, its Spectator and the Avant Garde." In *Early Cinema: Space, Frame, Narrative*, ed. Thomas Elsaesser and Adam Barker, 56–62. London: BFI, 1990.
---."The Horror of Opacity: The Melodrama of Sensation in the Plays of André de Lorde." In *Melodrama: Stage, Picture, Screen*, ed. Jacky Bratton, Jim Cook, Christine Gledhill, 50–61. London: BFI, 1994.
---. "Tracing the Individual Body: Photography, Detectives, and Early Cinema." In *Cinema and the Invention of Modern Life*, ed. Leo Charney and Vanessa Schwartz, 15–45. Berkeley: University of California Press, 1995.
Hanna, Martha. *The Mobilization of Intellect: French Scholars and Writers during the Great War.* Cambridge: Harvard University Press, 1996.
Hansen, Miriam. *Babel and Babylon: Spectatorship in American Silent Film.* Cambridge: Harvard University Press, 1991.
Harris, Ruth. *Murders and Madness: Medicine, Law, and Society in the Fin de Siècle.* Oxford: Oxford University Press, 1988.
Hause, Steven C. "More Minerva than Mars: The French Women's Rights." In *Behind the Lines: Gender and the Two World Wars*, ed. Margaret Higonnet, 99–113. New Haven: Yale University Press, 1987.
Hervouin, René. "77 minutes avec Pearl White." *Hebdo-Film*, May 7, 1921, p. 36–39.
Higashi, Sumiko. *Cecil B. DeMille and American Culture: The Silent Era.* Berkeley:

University of California Press, 1994.

———. *Virgins, Vamps, and Flappers.* Montreal: Eden Press, Women's Publications, 1978.

Higonnet, Margaret, ed. *Behind the Lines: Gender and the Two World Wars.* New Haven: Yale University Press, 1987.

Hofstadter, Douglas. *Gödel, Escher, Bach: An Eternal Golden Braid.* New York: Vintage, 1979.

Huss, Mary Monique. "Pronatalism and the Popular Ideology of the Child in Wartime France: The Evidence of the Picture Postcard." In *The Upheaval of War: Family, Work, and Welfare in Europe, 1914–1918,* ed. Richard Wall and Jay Winter, 329–67. Cambridge: Cambridge University Press, 1988.

Irigaray, Luce. *Speculum of the Other Woman.* Ithaca: Cornell University Press, 1985.

Jackson, Rosemary. *Fantasy: The Literature of Subversion.* London: Methuen, 1981.

Jacobs, Lewis. *The Rise of American Film.* New York: Harcourt, Brace, 1939.

Jay, Martin. *Downcast Eyes: The Denigration of Vision in Twentieth Century French Thought.* Berkeley: University of California Press, 1994.

Kern, Stephen. *The Culture of Time and Space, (1880–1918).* Cambridge: Harvard University Press, 1983.

Kirby, Lynne. "Male Hysteria and Early Cinema." *Camera Obscura* 17 (1988): 113–31.

———. *Parallel Tracks: The Railroad and the Silent Cinema.* Durham: Duke University Press, 1997.

Kofman, Sarah. *The Enigma of Woman: Woman in Freud's Writings,* trans. Catherine Porter. Ithaca: Cornell University Press, 1985.

Kuhn, Annette. *Family Secrets: Acts of Memory and Imagination.* London: Verso, 1995.

Kuntzel, Thierry. "A Note Upon the Filmic Apparatus." *Quarterly Review of Film Studies* 1.3 (1976): 266–71.

———. "Le Défilement: A View in Close-Up." *Camera Obscura* 2 (fall 1979): 51–65.

Kyrou, Ado. "L'histoire se répète ou L'inhumaine Lola." *Positif* 16 (May 1956): 3–10.

Lacassin, Francis. Preface to *Fantômas,* by Marcel Allain and Pierre Souvestre. Paris: Robert Laffont, 1987.

———. "Louis Feuillade." *Anthologie du Cinéma* Tome 2. Paris: L'Avant-Scène, 1961.

———. "Louis Feuillade." *Dossiers du Cinéma Cinéastes* 3 (1974): 86.

———. *Maître des lions et des vampires, Louis Feuillade.* Paris: Pierre Bordas, 1995.

———. "Musidora." *Anthologie du Cinéma* Tome 6, 442–501. Paris: L'Avant-Scène, 1971.

———. "Un inconnu nommé Feuillade." *Cinéma 61* 55 (April 1961): 78–88.

———, ed. *Louis Feuillade.* Paris: Seghers, 1964.

———, ed. *Pour une contre-histoire du cinéma.* Paris: Union Générale d'Editions, 1972.

Lacassin, Francis, and Raymond Bellour. "Musidora et les quarante voleurs." In *Pour une contre-histoire du cinéma,* ed. Francis Lacassin, 103–12. Paris: Union Générale d'Editions, 1972.

Lacenaire, Pierre-François. *Mémoires de Lacenaire avec ses poèmes et ses lettres.* New edition. Paris: A. Michel, 1968.

Le Fanu, J. C. "Carmilla." In *Best Ghost Stories of J. C. Le Fanu,* ed. E. F. Bleider, 274–339. New York: Dover, 1964.

"Les exploits d'une bande organisée." *Le Matin,* November 8, 1915, p. 2.

"Lettres d'admirateurs à Musidora, 1915–1919." Fonds Musidora 12, Bibliothèque du Film (BiFi).

Leprohon, Pierre. "La toge antique et la casquette à point." *Radio-Cinéma-TV* 445 (July 1958): 43–44.
Loiselet, Pierre. "Les pionniers du cinéma: Musidora." *Soir,* August 8, 1930, p. 7. Rondel File, Bibliothèque de l'Arsenal 8 RK 18999.
Lowe, Donald. *History of Bourgeois Perception.* University of Chicago Press, 1983.
Mayne, Judith. *Cinema and Spectatorship.* London: Routledge, 1993.
———. *Directed by Dorothy Arzner.* Bloomington: Indiana University Press, 1994.
———. *The Woman at the Keyhole: Feminism and Women's Cinema.* Bloomington: Indiana University Press, 1990.
McMahan, Alison. *Alice Guy Blaché: Lost Visionary of the Cinema.* Continuum: New York, 2002.
McMillan, James. *Housewife or Harlot: The Place of Woman in French Society, 1870–1940.* New York: St. Martin's, 1981.
Meirs, George, and Louis Feuillade. *Les vampires.* 4 vols. Paris: Jules Tallandier, 1916.
———. *La tête coupée.* Vol. 1 of *Les vampires.* Paris: Jules Tallandier, 1916.
———. *Le spectre.* Vol. 2 of *Les vampires.* Paris: Jules Tallandier, 1916.
———. *Les yeux qui fascinent.* Vol. 3 of *Les vampires.* Paris: Jules Tallandier, 1916.
Meusy, Jean Jacques. "Palaces and Holes in the Wall: Conditions of Exhibition in Paris on the Eve of World War I." *Velvet Light Trap* 37 (spring 1996): 81–98.
Michelson, Annette. "Breton's Surrealism: The Peripeties of a Metaphor or a Journey Through Impossibility." *Artforum* 1 (September 1966): 72–77.
Mitry, Jean. "Pearl White." *Anthologie du Cinéma* Tome 5, 2–48. Paris: L'Avant-Scène, 1969.
Moi, Toril. *Sexual/Textual Politics: Feminist Literary Theory.* London: Routledge, 1985.
Monleón, José. *A Specter is Haunting Europe: Sociohistorical Approach to the Fantastic.* Princeton: Princeton University Press, 1990.
Mulvey, Laura. "Visual Pleasure and Narrative Cinema." *Screen* 16, no. 3 (1975): 6–18.
"Musidora, Boîte 1." Bibliothèque du Film (BIFI).
"Musidora—The Original Vamp." *BFI News* 38 (May 1979): 3.
Musidora. "La vie d'une vamp." *Ciné-Mondial* 47 (July 17, 1942).
———. "La vie d'une vamp." *Ciné-Mondial* 48 (July 24, 1942).
"La mystérieuse châtelaine." *Le Matin* 9 (November 1915): 3.
Nietzsche, Friedrich. "Beyond Good and Evil." In *Basic Writings of Nietzsche,* ed. and trans. Walter Kaufmann, 179–435. New York: Modern Library, 1992.
Nye, Robert. *Crime, Madness, and Politics in Modern France.* Princeton: Princeton University Press, 1984.
Perrot, Michelle. "The New Eve and the Old Adam: Changes in the French Women's Condition at the Turn of the Century." In *Behind the Lines: Gender and the Two World Wars,* ed. Margaret Higonnet, 51–60. New Haven: Yale University Press, 1987.
Petro, Patrice. *Joyless Streets: Women and Melodramatic Representation in Weimar Cinema.* Princeton: Princeton University Press, 1989.
Le Petit Parisien, January 20, 1917, p. 4.
Rabinovitz, Lauren. *For the Love of Pleasure: Women, Movies, and Culture in Turn-of-the-Century Chicago.* New Brunswick: Rutgers University Press, 1998.
Ramsaye, Terry. *A Million and One Nights: A History of the Motion Pictures.* 2 vols. New York: Simon and Schuster, 1926.
Resnais, Alain. "Il a porté mes rêves à l'écran." In *Louis Feuillade,* ed. Francis Lacassin,

152–54. Paris: Seghers, 1964.
Rhodes, Henry T. F. *Alphonse Bertillon: Father of Scientific Detection.* New York: Abelard-Schuman, 1956.
Rich, B. Ruby. *Chick Flicks: Theories and Memories of the Feminist Film Movement.* Durham: Duke University Press, 1998.
Riley, Denise. *"Am I that Name?": Feminism and the Category of "Women" in History.* Minneapolis: University of Minnesota Press, 1988.
Robert, Jean Louis. "Women and Work in France during the First World War." In *The Upheaval of War: Family, Work, and Welfare in Europe, 1914–1918,* ed. Richard Wall and Jay Winter. Cambridge: Cambridge University Press, 1988.
Rose, Jacqueline. Introduction to *Feminine Sexuality: Jacques Lacan and the École Freudienne,* ed. Juliet Mitchell and Jaqueline Rose, 27–57. New York: Norton, 1982.
Rosenbaum, Jonathan. "Film Intimidates Art." Review of *Irma Vep, Chicago Reader,* June 13, 1997.
Roud, Richard. "Louis Feuillade and the Serial." In *Rediscovering French Film,* ed. Mary Lee Bandy, 45–51. New York: Museum of Modern Art, 1983.
Said, Edward. *Orientalism.* New York: Vintage, 1979.
Schaffer, Talia. "'Nothing but Foolscap and Ink': Inventing the New Woman." In *The New Woman in Fiction and in Fact,* ed. Angelique Richardson and Chris Willis, 49–52. Basingstone, England: Palgrave Press, 2001.
Schlüpmann, Heide. "Cinema as Anti-Theatre." In *Silent Film,* ed. Richard Abel, 125–41. New Brunswick: Rutgers University Press, 1996.
Schwartz, Vanessa. *Spectacular Realities: Early Mass Culture in Fin-de-Siècle Paris.* Berkeley: University of California Press, 1998.
Searle, John R. *Speech Acts: An Essay in the Philosophy of Language.* Cambridge: Cambridge University Press, 1969.
Serge. "3 secondes avec Musidora." *Le Matin—Le Pays,* November, 2, 1949, p. 8. Rondel File: Bibliothèque de l'Arsenal, 8 RK 18999.
Shapiro, Ann-Louise. "Love Stories: Female Crimes of Passion in Fin-de-Siècle Paris." *differences* 3.3 (1991): 45–68.
———. *Breaking the Codes: Female Criminality in Fin-de-Siècle Paris.* Stanford: Stanford University Press, 1996.
Showalter, Elaine. *Sexual Anarchy: Gender and Culture at the Fin de Siècle.* New York: Viking, 1990.
Siclier, Jacques. "Le chevalier du bien." *Le Monde,* October 4, 1991.
Silverman, Debora L. *Art Nouveau in Fin-de-Siècle France: Politics, Psychology, Style.* Berkeley: University of California Press, 1989.
Silverman, Kaja. *The Acoustic Mirror: The Female Voice in Psychoanalysis and Cinema.* Bloomington: Indiana University Press, 1988.
Singer, Ben. "Female Power in the Serial-Queen Melodrama: The Etiology of an Anomaly." *Camera Obscura* 22 (1990): 91–129.
———. *Melodrama and Modernity: Early Sensational Cinema and Its Contexts.* New York: Columbia University Press, 2001.
Staiger, Janet. *Bad Women: Regulating Sexuality in Early American Cinema.* Minneapolis: University of Minnesota Press, 1995.
Stamp, Shelley. *Movie Struck Girls.* Princeton: Princeton University Press, 2000.

"Taisez-vous! Méfiez-vous! Les oreilles ennemies vous écoutent!!!" *Le Matin*, November 7, 1915, p. 2.
Thirifays, André. "Un faux grand homme Louis Feuillade." *Le Soir*, May 1, 1964, p. 51. Rondel File, Bibliothèque de l'Arsenal, RK 402.
Thorne, Kip. *Black Holes and Time Warps: Einstein's Outrageous Legacy*. New York: Norton, 1994.
Tiersten, Lisa. *Marianne in Market: Envisioning Consumer Society in Fin-de-Siècle France*. Berkeley: University of California Press, 2001.
Todorov, Tzvetan. *Introduction à la littérature fantastique*. Paris: Éditions du Seuil, 1970.
———. *The Fantastic: A Structural Approach to a Literary Genre*, trans. Richard Howard. Ithaca: Cornell University Press, 1975.
Trinh T. Minh-Ha. "Film as Translation: A Net with No Fisherman." In *Framer Framed*, 111–33. London: Routledge, 1992.
———. *Woman, Native, Other*. Bloomington: Indiana University Press, 1989.
Turim, Maureen. "French Melodrama: Theory of a Specific History." *Theatre Journal* 39 (October 1987): 307–28.
Valéry, Paul. *Variety*, quoted in Hans Kohn, "Crisis in European Thought and Culture." In *WWI, a Turning Point in Modern History, Essays on the Significance of War*, ed. Jack J. Roth, 25–46. New York: Knopf, 1967. Originally published as *Variety*, trans. Malcolm Cowley, 27–28. New York: Harcourt Brace, 1927.
Vidocq, Eugen. *Memoirs of Vidocq*. Philadelphia: T. B. Peterson, 1859.
Virmaux, Alain, and Odette, eds. *Les surréalistes et le cinéma*. Paris: Seghers, 1976.
Walz, Robin. *Pulp Surrealism: Insolent Popular Culture in Early Twentieth-Century Paris*. Berkeley: University of California Press, 2000.
Weber, Eugen. *Fin-de-Siècle*. Cambridge: Cambridge University Press, 1986.
Weber, Samuel. "The Sideshow; or Remarks on a Canny Moment." *Modern Language Notes* 88.6 (1973): 1102–33.
White, Patricia. *The unInvited: Classical Hollywood Cinema and Lesbian Representability*. Bloomington: Indiana University Press, 1999.
Williams, Linda. "Film Body an Implantation of Perversion." *Ciné-Tracts* 3.4 (1981): 19–35.

Index

Page numbers of photographs are in italic

Abel, Richard, 5, 17, 18, 19, 46, 56
aesthetics, 28, 29
agency, 2, 3, 6, 10, 30
Allain, Marcel, 48, 61, 64
alterity, 8, 16, 19
amnesia, 119
Amours d'un prince, Les (Allain and Souvestre), 66
anarchism, 31, 54
Andreyor, Yvette, 70, *71, 92, 95,* 100, 103, 126; as major film star, 98; performance style, 125
Andriot, Josette, 87
Angenot, Marc, 120
anti-Semitism, 80–81
anxiety: gender and, 29–31, 116; male hysteria and, 140; melodrama and, 118; physical place as site of, 74, 90; zones of, 31–38, 78, 119, 142. *See also* castration anxiety
aphonia, 119, 133
apparatus, cinematic, 1, 8, 15, 57–59
Apremont, Baronne d' (character), 116, 120, 122, 127; death of, 130; as "Fatima," 127; hysteria and, 127, 128
Aragon, Louis, 100, 101, 103
"archive," 3
art cinema, 29
Assayas, Olivier, 145, 150, 151
Athys, Jacques d' (character), 77, 132, *132,* 136, 140, 141
attractions, cinema of, 8, 10, 15, 16, 17, 50; distancing of spectator and, 16; Feuillade serials as, 18
audience, 16, 51
Augustine (character), 90, 91
authorship, 6
autobiography, 3
avant-garde film, 15

ballet, cinema compared to, 15
bandit subgenre, 26
Bara, Theda, 23
Barrabas (Feuillade serial), 4, 5, 14, 31; criminality within the body, 121; dislocation in, 43; male body in, 138–43; zones of anxiety in, 42
Bastide, Bernard, 113
Bean, Jennifer, 11
Beizer, Janet, 124, 136
Beltham, Lady (character), 61, 63, 66, 72, 82; crime of passion and, 124; as female criminal, 68–69, *69;* movements of, 125
Benjamin, Walter, 35
Bergé, Francine, 146
Bergson, Henri, 57–58
Bertillon, Alphonse, 53, 55
Bessière, Irène, 19, 21–22, 34
"Beyond Good and Evil" (Nietzsche), 45–46
Bianchini, M. (character), 122, 124
Bibliothèque de l'Arsenal, 48
Blaché, Alice Guy, 6
Bloy, Léon, 81
bodysuit, black *(maillot de soie),* 11, 38, *39,* 40–41, 83; cinematic legacy and, 146, 148, *149,* 151; cotton versus silk, 87–88; displacement of certitude and, 12; eroticism of, 109, 112; female criminality and, 135; fetishism and, 89; first appearance in cinema, 87; in Musidora's theater performances, 107; as signature of Musidora, 108–9
Bonnot gang, 54
Bordo, Susan, 6
Bordwell, David, 8, 18
Borguese, Juana, 116, 120

181

182 | INDEX

Bourgeois, Gérard, 87
bourgeois society, 29, 67, 68, 70
Brasseur, Pierre, 147
Breton, André, 100, 165n. 36
Brewster, Ben, 18, 76
Brooks, Peter, 24, 25, 118
bullfighting, 112, 113, 115
Burch, Noël, 14, 15, 17
burlesques, 28

camera movements, 4
Cañero, Antonio, 112, 115, 116
Carl, Renée, 49, *69*, 100, 125
castration anxiety, 32–33, 34, 39–40, 89, 160n. 136. *See also* anxiety
Catholic Church, 24, 81, 96
Cazals, Patrick, 87–88
Cazotte, Jacques, 22
Cecil B. DeMille and American Culture (Higashi), 1
Céline et Julie vont en bateau (film, 1974), 148, 150, 152
censorship, 27, 31, 34, 56, 99, 129
centering, 6, 12
certainty/certitude, 10, 45–46, 47
Chaplin, Charles ("Charlot"), 102
Charcot, Jean-Martin, 124
chase, tri-leveled, 59–60, 73–74
Cheat, The (silent film, 1915), 23, 24
Cheung, Maggie, 145, *149*, 150–52
children, as audience, 16
Ching Siu Tung, 150
Ciné Goes to Town, The (Abel), 18
cinema: apparatus, 1, 8, 15, 57–59; classical period of, 16; cliff-hanger format, 2; contradictory forces in, 33; devices of, 8; early history of, 14–17; feminist history of, 1; instability of, 34; legacy of Irma/Musidora and, 145–52, *149*; silent, 2–3, 4, 13–17; time image of, 12; transformation of materiality and, 4; of uncertainty, 7, 8, 10, 19, 103, 147. *See also* apparatus, cinematic; attractions, cinema of
Cinémagazine, 88
Ciné-Mondial (journal), 88
ciné-romans, 28, 47, 98
circus, cinema compared to, 15

Cixous, Hélène, 1, 3–4, 13, 21, 30, 103; on castration anxiety, 32, 160n. 136; on Freud and the "uncanny," 32, 38, 40, 64, 73; on hysteria, 117
clairvoyance, 132–33, 135
classes, social: anxiety about class dislocation, 93–94; early cinema and, 15, 16; film criticism and, 29; film studies and, 6; hysteria and, 127–28; "new woman" and, 67; shifting boundaries of, 54; social mobility, 141; urban poor of Paris, 35; women and, 82–83. *See also* working class
Clauzel, Dr. (character), 134, 135, 136, 137
cliff-hanger device, 2, 4, 64, 80
close-up shots, 36, 40
Cocantin (character), 123, 127, 130–31
coherence, 10, 65
Colette, Sidonie-Gabrielle, 106
colonialism, 136
comfort, zone of, 36, 37
communication, technologies of, 58
conservatism, 28, 29, 81, 96, 113, 125
consumerism, 2, 23, 67, 101
continuity editing, 17–18
contradiction, 31, 33, 93
Courrier Cinématographique, Le (journal), 48, 49
Crary, Jonathan, 11
Creative Evolution (Bergson), 57
Cresté, René, 77, 92, 126, 132, *132;* melodramatic gestures of, 136; surrealists and, 100
crime genre, 4, 26, 29, 46
criminality, 24, 36, 159n. 100; crime as social phenomenon, 54; crime portraits, 53; female, 37–38, 42, 66, 68, 123, 135; foreigners as criminals, 80. *See also femme criminelle* (woman criminal); passion, crime of
critics, 103
cultural studies, 3
Culture of Time and Space, The (Kern), 101

Danidoff, Princess (character), 45, 62–63, 66
découpage, 8

deep space, 17, 76
De Lauretis, Teresa, 7, 30, 31, 158–59n. 97
Deleuze, Gilles, 12, 156n. 36
Delluc, Louis, 28, 101–2, 103
Delorès (character), 77–78, *132,* 132–33, 134, 137–38
Delpierre, Simone (character), 139, 140, 142
DeMille, Cecil B., 23
depth of field, 62
Derrida, Jacques, 13
Dervieux, Jean (character), 46, 47
desire, female, 7, 90, 91
Desnos, Robert, 102, 103
detective genre, 4, 19, 46
Devalde, Jean, 92
Diable amoureux, Le (Cazotte), 22
dialogue intertitles, 49
diegetic enclosure, 15–16, 150
difference, sexual, 6, 29–31, 36, 37; female body as sign of castration, 40; marked in film poster, 78, *79;* woman criminal and, 70
Directed by Dorothy Arzner (Mayne), 1
disguises, 47, 50, 51, 83; exchange of identities and, 66; performance and, 121; removal of, 52, 63; social class and, 89
dislocation, 19, 20, 83; defense mechanisms and, 34; female psyche and, 43; male castration anxiety and, 33; recursion and, 120; of social class, 93–94
dissolve, 8, 52, 53, 57, 61
divorce laws, 82
Doane, Mary Ann, 33
documentary aesthetic, 148
documentary news, 19
Dollon, Jacques (character), 55–56, 82
domesticity, 26, 120
dualism, 20, 118, 124
Durand, Jacques, 112

Eco, Umberto, 60
Edison, Thomas, 14
editing, 4, 17
education, for women, 81, 82

ego, 46
Einstein, Albert, 58–59
epistemology, crisis of, 24, 33
eroticism, 109, 112
Erreur tragique, L' (Feuillade film, 1913), 56–57
escapes, 62, 64, 77, 78
Escher, M. C., *9,* 154n. 28
essentialism, 3
exhibitionism, 10, 17
Exploits de Nick Carter (Jasset films), 46, 50, 51, 59
externality, of spectator, 14–15

Faber, Jane, 45, 49
Fairbanks, Douglas, 102
fairgrounds, cinema at, 14, 16
fairy tale, 29
faits divers, 19, 26, 29; calls for censorship of, 129; crossover with fiction, 78, 80; sensationalism and, 49
Faivre, Joseph, 87
fallen woman, 17
family crisis, 17, 68, 70, 82, 98; female criminality and, 121; melodrama and, 24, 118; reconstructed family history and, 141; *scène primitive* and, 120; World War I and, 92, 94
Family Secrets: Acts of Memory and Imagination (Kuhn), 1
Fandor (character), 60, 62, 65, 70, 72
fantastic mode, 19–22, 29, 45; exhaustion of, 142; family "history" and, 120; hysteria and, 119; melodrama and, 24, 92, 93, *97,* 103, 117, 120; positivism and, 157n. 45; recursion in, 126; structure of, 64–65. *See also* narrative
Fantasy: The Literature of Subversion (Jackson), 19–20
Fantômas (character), 5, 36; black suit of, 41; disguises of, 38, 49, 62; Franju's sympathy for, 146; as "Gurn," 63, 68, 69; identifying mark on arm, 42; lack of personal history, 61; limits of photographic evidence and, 55–56; as Loupart, 70–71; as master criminal of modern city, 46–47; mutability of,

Fantômas *(continued)*
85; narrative structure and, 59
Fantômas (Feuillade serial), 4–5, 14, 125; censors and, 27, 31; continuity editing style in, 17–18; crime in marginal urban space, 36; female criminality in, 38; Grand Guignol style in, 76; limits of photographic image in, 51–57; marks of criminality in, 121; mutable identity of, 50–51; narrative structure, 59–72; space in, 74; stills from, *53, 69;* time and cinematic apparatus in, 57–59; tri-leveled chase in, 73; urban *Unheimliche* (uncanny) in, 45–51
Fantômas novels (Allain and Souvestre), 48–49, 66, 80
Faraboni, Georgette, 77, 132, *132*
father's name, 138, 141
Favraux, Jacqueline (character), 92, 93, 94, *95;* contrast with Diana Monti, 95; *femme nouvelle* (new woman) and, 99; in Franju's remake of *Judex,* 146, 147; in *Judex* sequel, 120
Favraux the banker (character), 92, 93, 94, 95, 126, 127, 131
female body, 33, 37, 43, 146; castration anxiety and, 39–40; criminality and, 121; fetishistic use of, 41; hysteria and, 127, 129, 134; movement in space, 78; as site of cultural struggle, 81, 125; spatial dislocation and, 75; uncertainty surrounding, *79,* 89
femininity, 1, 34, 41, 91
feminism, 30, 67, 145; agency and, 6–7; alternative film form and, 2; conservative reaction against, 102; debate over psychoanalysis, 29–31; discussion of female criminality and, 66; gender ideology and, 7; poetic history and, 3; silent cinema and, 2–3
femme criminelle (criminal woman), 67–68, 85, 92, 122, 123–24
femme fatale, 33, 38, 106, 112
femme nouvelle (new woman), 66, 67, 82, 87, 146; employed outside the home, 94; figuring of, 99–103; flouting of gender roles by, 128; opposing models of, 95

fêtes foraines, 16
fetishes and fetishism, 42, 90, 152
Feuillade, Louis, 1, 4, 13, *27;* bullfighting and, 112, 113; cinematic devices and, 52–53; critical response to, 5, 12, 20, 27–29; detective genre and, 46; *Fantômas* novels and, 49; melodrama genre and, 138; mise-en-scène of, 8; "primitive" era of cinema and, 76; visual style, 18
Feuillade crime serials, 17–19, 24, 106; Freud's "uncanny" and, 32; melodrama and, 25–26; narrative structure, 126–27; recursion in, 151; turn to melodrama, 117–20; vision and crisis of perception in, 37. *See also* specific titles
feuilleton. See roman-feuilleton
"Fiction and Its Phantoms: A Reading of Freud's *Das Unheimliche*" (Cixous), 32, 73
film posters, 31, 78, *79,* 103
film stars, women as, 6, 11
Fool There Was, A (silent film, 1915), 23, 24
For the Love of Pleasure: Women, Movies, and Culture in Turn-of-the-Century Chicago (Rabinovitz), 2–3
Fortunio (Gautier novel), 106
France: anti-Semitism and anti-Germanism in, 80–81, 92; discourses about hysteria in, 124–25; early cinema in, 16, 17, 24; fascination with American culture, 100–101; women's rights in, 66–67, 81–83. *See also* Paris
Franju, Georges, 20, 146–48
Freud, Sigmund, 21, 31–32, 64, 103; on Hoffmann's "The Sandman," 38–39; on hysterical symptoms, 119; scientific detachment and, 30; theories of desire, 158–59n. 97; on the "uncanny," 37
frontality, 15

Gaby (character), 120, 122, 128, 130
Gaumont, Léon, 99, 107
Gaumont, Louis, 107, 108
Gaumont Company, 29, 48, 49, 50, 78; censorship constraints and, 56;

Gaumont Palace, 16; newsreels of, 35, 100
Gautier, Théophile, 22, 106, 107
gender: anxiety and, 29–31; boundaries of, 92; changing definitions of, 49, 54; early cinema and, 2; fantastic literary mode and, 22; subjectivity and, 21
genres, 19, 28
Germany, 133
Gerould, Daniel, 25
gesture, 115, 121, 126, 136
Gilbreth, Frank B., 58
Giles, Cyprian, 120
Gilson, Dr. (character), 133, 135
globalization, 151
Godard, Jean-Luc, 153n. 9, 156n. 36
Gordon, Mel, 26
Grandais, Suzanne, 56
Grand Guignol, 19, 26, 49
Griffith, D. W., 10, 14, 75
Guérande, Philippe (character), 42, 73, 82, 88, 90, 129; first encounter with Irma Vep, 85; social class and, 83
Gunning, Tom, 10, 14, 15, 16; on criminology and control of body, 53–54; on *Fantômas* prologues, 51; on Grand Guignol, 26; on Jasset crime serials, 50, 51–52; on transition from early to classical cinema, 16

Harald, Mary, 77, 133
Haussmann, Baron Georges-Eugène, 74
Hayakawa, Sessue, 23
Hebdo-Film (journal), 28
Hermann, Fernand, 75, *86,* 139, 142
Heroic Trio, The (film, 1993), 150–51
heterosexuality, 7, 22; crimes of passion and, 68, 70; "cure" of hysteria and, 120; disturbance of monogamous couple, 85, 94; heroine's adventures framed within, 100; male hysteria and, 123; monogamy and, 91; narrative of, 31; orientalism and, 136; prescribed gender roles and, 125; psychoanalysis and, 30
Higashi, Sumiko, 1, 23
Histoire(s) du cinéma (video series, 1988–98), 153n. 9
Hoffmann, E.T.A., 38

Hollywood, classical cinema of, 10, 14
homoeroticism, 85
homosexuality, 24, 40
horror tales, 19
Howard, Richard, 21
Howey, Dr. (character), 127, 128, 130
Hugnet, Georges, 145
hypnosis, 42, 77, 86, 121, 122, 125; action in space of body, 127; fantastic narrative and, 126; hysteria and, 134; mesmerism and, 136
hysteria, 42, 117, 118–19, 134; gender roles and, 124–25; in *Judex* sequel, 122–23, 124; male, 123, 140

identity, 7, 25, 50; crisis of, 70; cultural, 54; exchanges of, 66; founding moment of, 34; male sexual identity, 30, 138; marker of criminality and, 11; multiple possibilities within, 113, 115; mutability of, 50–51; paternal, 139, 140; randomness/chaos and, 23; spatial dislocation and, 74; surgical reconstruction of female identity, 147–48; uncertainty and, 95; vision of difference and, 33
ideology, dominant, 4, 7, 30
imperialism, 135, 136
improvisation, 17
individuality, 50, 54
industrialization, 49
information, revealing of, 64
"Institutional Mode of Production," 14
Irigaray, Luce, 30, 117
Irma Vep (film, 1996), *149,* 150–52

Jackson, Rosemary, 19–20, 21, 22
Jane (character), 90, 91
Jasset, Victorin, 46, 51–52, 87
Jay, Martin, 25
Jews, 80
Joséphine (character), 36, 66, 85; domestication of, 98; as female criminal, 69–72, *71;* transformation of, 142
Juana (character), *110,* 112, *115*
Judex (character), 92–93, 98, 122; errors of moral judgment and, 95; Franju's remake of *Judex* and, 146; prison and laboratory of, 128, 130

Judex (Feuillade serial), 4, 5, 14, 31, 91–98; *ciné-roman* format and, 47; defeat of Diana Monti, 42; disguise/transformation in, 52; Favraux's crimes, 126; female criminality in, 38; femme fatale in, 40; marks of criminality in, 121; melodramatic narrative in, 42–43; narrative repetitiveness in, 41; newspaper novelization of, *97;* space in, 75; stills from, *95;* turn to melodrama and, 117
Judex (film, 1963), 146–47
Juve (character), 36, 42, 47, 141, 143; disguises of, 65; Joséphine and, 71, 72; narrative structure and, 59, 63–64; obsession with capturing Fantômas, 50–51; "true" identity of, 51, 66

Kerjean, Pierre (character), 92, 93, 94, 96, 124, 142
Kern, Stephen, 101
Kirby, Lynne, 1
Kistna (character), 133
knowledge, 8, 21, 62, 106; crisis of, 36, 41; Freud's "uncanny" and, 32; improbable events, 76–77; limits of, 41; melodrama and, 117; Nietzsche on, 46; social markers of, 24
Kofman, Sarah, 30
Koscina, Sylvia, 147
Kuhn, Annette, 1
Kuntzel, Thierry, 8, 57
Kyrou, Ado, 28–29

Lacassin, Francis, 17, 27, 46, 126, 137; on Feuillade and *Fantômas* novels, 49; on *Judex* sequel, 28
Lacombe, Georges, 34–35, 36
Lagrange, Louise, 90
Lang, Fritz, 145
Lasseyne, Jacques, 112
Last Exploit of the Vampire, The, 88
Laure (character), 139
Léaud, Jean-Pierre, 150
Le Fanu, J. C., 23
legibility, of signs, 25
lesbian sexuality, 7, 169n. 27
Leubas, Louis, 92
Levesque, Marcel, 73, 96, 126

linearity, 10
Livre du poche, Le, 128
location shooting, 49, 62
logic, defeat of, 77
Loi du progrès, La: Passage à tabac (Gaumont newsreel, 1911), 35–36
Lonely Villa, The (film, 1909), 75
long takes, 14, 40, 49
Lovecraft, H. P., 33
"Love Stories: Female Crimes of Passion in Fin-de-Siècle Paris" (Shapiro), 66
Lowe, Donald, 25
Lupin, Arsène (character), 46

Mack, Max, 52, 55
Maillot noir, Le (Musidora stage play), 88
male body, 138–43
Marfa (character), 83, *84,* 85, 89–90, 128
marginality, 35
marriage, 2, 67, 90–91, 98
"marvelous," the, 20, 21, 22
masculinity, 1, 34
match cut, 75
materiality, 4, 12, 26
Mathé, Edouard, 73, 120, 139
Maupré, Noëlle, 141, 142
Mayne, Judith, 1, 7, 109
Mazamette (character), 73, 90, 91
McMahan, Alison, 6
Meirs, Georges, 86
Melchior, Georges, 65
Méliès, Georges, 28, 155n. 4
melodrama, 17, 19, 24–27, 92; acting codes of, 126; critics and, 28, 29; gesture and, 136–37; hysteria and, 117–20; sin-and-salvation theme, 96; threat to domestic space and, 82. *See also* fantastic mode
memory, gaps in, 119, 124
"Merle, Le" (Desnos poem), 102
mesmerism, 136, 138
metamorphosis, 22
Michel, Gaston, 92, 139, 142
Michelson, Annette, 74
middle class, 82, 83
Milton, James (character), 120, 126
mimesis, 21
mise-en-scène, 49, 62, 113
modernism, 2
modernity, 26, 37, 103

"modern woman," 2, 11
Monleón, José, 36
Montel, Blanche, 139
Monti, Diana (character), 40, 85, 92; death of, 42, 98, 124, 138; in Franju's remake of *Judex*, 146–47; as threat to family, 94. *See also* Musidora
Moralès (character), 92, 94
morality, 101, 151–52
Moréno, Juan-José (character), 75–76, *86*, 87, 108–9, 142; as hypnotist, 77, 86; in *Irma Vep* (1996 film), 150
Morte amoureuse, La (Gautier), 22–23
Mortimer, Lewis (character), 139
mother-daughter relation, 7
motion, stasis and, 33
movement, 19, 57, 75, 133, 136
Movie Struck Girls: Women and Motion Picture Culture after the Nickelodeon (Stamp), 2
Muller, Gallus, 54
Mulvey, Laura, 1–2, 30
muse, woman as, 112
Musidora, 5, 6, 8, 43, 83; black bodysuit and, *39*, 87–88, 108–9; critics on, 126; eyes of, 88–89, 127; *femme nouvelle* (new woman) and, 99–103; as fetish object, 40–41; as icon of French cinema, 38; invoked in cinematic legacy, 145–52; life and career of, 103–16, *104–5, 108–11, 114–15,* 168n. 92; problem of recognition and, 41–42; psychoanalysis and, 30; star persona of, 12, 85, 121; uncertainty and, 11. *See also* Juana (character); Monti, Diana (character); Vep, Irma (character)
Mystères de New York, Les (Pathé film series), 78, 99, 100, 164n. 7
Mystères de Paris, Les (Sue), 60–61, 164n. 7
"Mystérieuse châtelaine, La" (newspaper story), 80, 81
mystery subgenre, 26

Napierkowsa, Stacia, 83, *84*
narrative, 28, 59–72, 126–27; character identification and, 152; cinema of attractions and, 15; of "classical" cinema, 8, 10, 75; denial as defense mechanism and, 34; melodrama and, 118; multiple, 12; Oedipal, 142, 143; repetition in, 74; uncertainty and, 4
Navarre, René, 46, 47, 49, 56, *69*
Nery, Georgette de, 120
newspapers, 78, 80
Nick Carter films and novels, 48, 50, 51
nickelodeons, 14
Nietzsche, Friedrich, 45–46
"Non-Continuity, Continuity, Discontinuity in Early Cinema" (Gunning), 10
noncontinuity edit, 4
nonlinearity, 60
nostalgia, 26
Nouvelle mission de Judex, La (Feuillade serial), 4, 5, 14, 31, 116; critical response to, 28; dislocation in, 43; female criminality in, 42; hysteria and, 120–32; movement in, 136–37
Nye, Robert, 54

Oedipal narrative, 39–40, 142, 143
"One-Eyed Man" (character), 120
ontology, 33
orientalism, 135–36, 151
Parallel Tracks: The Railroad and Silent Cinema (Kirby), 1
Paris, 31, 65; as dangerous place, 74; Metro, 35, 36, 138; morgue of, 49; trash collectors *(chiffoniers)* of, 35; women's rights congresses in, 67. *See also* France
"Passing of the Oedipus Complex, The" (Freud), 39–40
passion, crime of, 68, 70, 92, 124
Pathé Company, 78, 99
patriarchy, 8, 12, 92, 136, 148
performance, 11, 115, 118, 121, 123, 147
Perils of Pauline, The (film series, 1914), 100
Perle, La (film, 1928), 145–46
Perrot, Michelle, 92
perspectivalism, Cartesian, 25
Petit Parisien, Le (newspaper), 129, *131*, 166n. 49
phallocentrism, 2, 13
photography, 8, 25, 53–55, 57, 131–32
poetic history/language, 3–4, 5–6
police work, science of, 53

policier apache, 29
Pollock, Channing, 146
populism, 29
Porter, Edwin S., 14, 155n. 4
portrait photographs, 53
possibility, uncertainty and, 18
Powell, Frank, 23
Poyen, René, 96
Practice of Love, The: Lesbian Sexuality and Perverse Desire (De Lauretis), 7
Primerose (character), 120–27, 130
"primitive mode," early cinema as, 14, 16, 17
Protéa (film series, 1913–19), 87
psychoanalysis, 2, 3, 6, 21, 29–31

Rabinovitz, Lauren, 2, 3
race, 6, 135
Raoul (character), 139, 142
rationality, 22
realism, 12, 19–20, 29, 62
reason, 21
reception studies, 3
recognition, problem of, 38, 41, 62, 83
recursion, 4, 8, 9, 120, 126, 151; displacement of certitude and, 12; in *Fantômas*, 11; identity and, 115; in *Les vampires*, 1, 73; in mathematics, 10, 154n. 30; as repetition and simplification, 10
religion, 80, 81, 125, 136
Renaud, Jean-Joseph, 87
repetition, 52, 93, 119, 148, 152
representation, 5, 89, 148; bullfighting and, 115; primitive mode of, 17; in silent era, 14, 15
Rivette, Jacques, 148
Robert, Jean Louis, 82
Rocambole (character), 46
Roi des cuistots, Le (serialized novel), 80
Rollette, Jane, 139
roman-feuilleton, 29, 47, 78, 82, 128; calls for censorship of, 129; cliff-hanger structure of, 80
Rootprints (Cixous), 13
Roques, Jeanne. *See* Musidora
Rougier, Jacques (character), 139–40, 142

Said, Edward, 135

"Sandman, The" (Hoffmann), 38–39, 40, 41
Schlüpmann, Heide, 2, 11
science, 58–59, 136, 138
"scientific films," 28
Scob, Edith, 146, 147
screen, cinema, 109
screenwriters, 6
secular culture, in France, 81, 136
self, 20, 25, 45
sensationalism, 49
serialization, cinematic, 4–5, 28
serialization, print, 5
Sexual Anarchy: Gender and Culture at the Fin-de-Siècle (Showalter), 123
sexuality, 1, 6, 102, 137
Shapiro, Ann-Louise, 66, 67–68, 70, 85, 129
shock, 8, 26–27, 49, 50, 77, 147
shoppers, female, 67, 70
Showalter, Elaine, 123
silent cinema, 2–3, 4, 13–17
Silverman, Debora L., 67, 81
Singer, Ben, 26, 99
Sol y sombra (Soleil et ombre) (film, 1922), *109–11*, 112
"Sorties: Out and Out: Attacks/Ways Out/Forays" (Cixous), 1, 13, 117
Souvestre, Pierre, 48, 61, 64
space, 74–76, 82
spectacle, 15
spectatorship, female, 1, 2, 3, 30
Specter Is Haunting Europe, A (Monleón), 36
Speculum of the Other Woman (Irigaray), 117
Spiders (film, 1919), 145
spiritualism, 125, 136, 138
staging in depth, 18
Stamp, Shelley, 2
Strelitz, Rudolf (character), 139, 140, 141, 142
studio system, Hollywood, 14
subjectivity, 5–6, 31; classical humanist, 11; crisis of, 25, 33; dislocation of, 14; infinite layers of, 45
Sue, Eugène, 60, 61
surrealists, 27, 100, 112, 145
suspense subgenre, 26

Taylor, Frederick W., 58
technique, 4
technologies, 2, 8, 41; control of female body and, 129–30; Paris Metro, 35; pleasure and danger associated with, 101; sensationalism and, 49; view of time and, 58
textual analysis, 1
theatricality, 11
Thirifays, André, 29
Tierra de los toros, La (Terre des taureaux, La) (film, 1924), 107, *108*, 112, 113, 116
Tiersten, Lisa, 67
Tih Minh (character), 77–78, 133, 134, 135–36
Tih Minh (Feuillade serial), 4, 5, 14, 31; body in space in, 77–78; criminality within the body, 121; dislocation in, 43; female criminality in, 42; hysteria in, 132–38; orientalism in, 151; still from, *132*
time, 57–59
title cards, 77, 115, 116, 133, 142
To, Johnny, 150
Todorov, Tzvetan, 20–21, 64, 145, 157n. 45
Torp, Daisy (character), 123, 146–47
transportation, technologies of, 58
Trémeuse, Jacques de (character), 92, 122, 125–26
Trémeuse, Roger de (character), 120, 121, 124, 130
Trésor des Jésuits, Le (play, 1928), 100
"trick film," 52
Trinh, Minh-Ha T., 5, 6, 45
Turim, Maureen, 26

"uncanny," the, 20, 21, 22, 32–33; Bergson's critique of cinema and, 57–58; double movement of, 120; lexical root of, 37; as narrative drive, 62
uncertainty, 4, 5, 26, 152; boundaries of, 45; castration anxiety and, 32; gendered subjectivity and, 21; in narrative structure, 65; photographic images and, 57; poetic sensibility and, 18–19; resolution of, 120; World War I and, 91–92

unconscious, the, 7
"Unheimliche, Das" (The Uncanny) (Freud), 31–33
unInvited, The: Classical Hollywood Cinema and Lesbian Representability (White), 1, 169n. 27
urban space, 2, 26, 31, 35, 36
Ursel, Henri d,' 145
utopian paradigm, 16

Vagabonde, La (film), *105*
Valéry, Paul, 91
Valgrand (character), 69
Valli, Alida, 148
vampires, female, 22–24
Vampires, Les (Feuillade serial), 4–5, 14, 31; censors and, 27; class and fascination with crime in, 128–29; crime in marginal urban space, 36; defeat of Irma Vep, 42; disguise in, 52; dislocation of the familiar in, 73–91; effects of World War I visible in, 91–92; female criminality in, 38; femme fatale in, 40; Gaumont rivalry with Pathé and, 99; invoked in cinematic legacy, *149*, 150–52; marks of criminality in, 121; narrative comprehension in, 65; narrative repetitiveness in, 41; publicity photo from, *39*; stills from, *84*, *86*
Varèse, Françoise (character), 139
Varèse, Jacques (character), 42, 139, 140–43
Venenos (character), 90–91
Ventriloquized Bodies: Narratives of Hysteria in Nineteenth-Century France (Beizer), 124
Vep, Irma (character), 5, 40, 77, *86*, 107; as "abnormal" female criminal, 69; black bodysuit and, 108–9; class mobility and, 83; death of, 42; disguises of, 83, 89; disruption of domestic space and, 82; female desire and, 85, 86–87; improbable escapes, 77, 78; invoked in cinematic legacy, 145–52, *149*; lack of personal history, 61; representation of space and, 76; significance of name, 83, 85; transformation of, 121. *See also* Musidora

violence, 26
visibility, 117, 118
vision, 25, 32, 33, 41, 76
"Visual Pleasure in Narrative Cinema" (Mulvey), 1–2
voyeurism, 10, 15, 16, 130, 151

Walz, Robin, 49
Ward, Fanny, 23
Weber, Eugen, 35, 54, 58
Weber, Samuel, 32–33, 41, 120
White, Patricia, 1, 169n. 27
White, Pearl, 99–103
Williams, Linda, 41–42
Wo ist Coletti? (German film, 1913), 52, 54–55
woman-identification, 7
woman in peril, 17
Woman Native Other (Minh-Ha), 45
women: crimes committed by, 66; French society after World War I and, 81–83; objectified by voyeurism, 16; public space of cinema and, 2; as shoppers, 67, 70; social class and, 82–83; woman as "epistemological trauma," 33; woman as unknowable and shifting identity, 22; women's rights in France, 66–67; as workers, 129. *See also* female body; *femme criminelle* (criminal woman); *femme nouvelle* (new woman)
Women Film Pioneers, 6, 154n. 17
Women Make Cinema series, 6, 154n. 17
working class, 49, 54, 67, 82, 123, 137. *See also* classes, social
World War I, 66, 80–81, 82, 91–92, 139; Musidora and, 106; women workers and, 129

Yeux sans visage, Les (film, 1959), 147–48

Zigomar contre Nick Carter (film, 1912), 51
Zigomar film series, 46, 50, 51, 87
Zone, La (film, 1928), 34–35

www.ingramcontent.com/pod-product-compliance
Lightning Source LLC
Chambersburg PA
CBHW071820230426
43670CB00013B/2511